A Practical Guide to
Business, Law
& the Internet

Peter Adediran

**KOGAN
PAGE**

ACKNOWLEDGEMENTS

As a trainee at Brough Skerrett in the City of London I did not have any idea that I would get so involved with the Internet. In fact it was not until after qualifying in April 1999 when Steven Salim, a friend of mine living in California, suggested to me that I advise him and some of his partners in a small fundraising venture for an entertainment Web site, that I got involved in the Internet. So my very special thanks to Steve Salim for introducing me to this exciting and challenging relatively new medium.

I would like to thank my good friend Martyn Berkin (Barrister), Crown Office Chambers, for reading the manuscript for the whole guide. My thanks also to Kogan Page and Curran Publishing Services for their contribution in getting this book published. A special thanks to my family for all their help and support.

Finally, I would like to thank God without whom nothing is possible.

Peter Adediran

INFORMATION AND THE LAW

Every effort has been made to ensure the accuracy of the information and guidance in this book. However, no legal responsibility can be accepted by the author or the publishers for the accuracy of that information and guidance. In the final analysis, it is for the courts and tribunals to give an authoritative interpretation of the law as laid down in Acts of Parliament and their attendant statutory instruments.

First published in 2002

Kogan Page Limited
120 Pentonville Road
London N1 9JN

© Peter Adediran, 2002

British Library Cataloguing in Publication Data

A CIP record for this book is available from the British Library.

ISBN 0 7494 3734 0

Typeset by Saxon Graphics Ltd, Derby
Printed and bound by Biddles Ltd, Guildford and King's Lynn
www.biddles.co.uk

Contents

Cases, Statutes, EU Directives, International Treaties and Commissions

CASES LISTED IN ALPHABETICAL ORDER

Algemeen Dagblad BV & Others v. *Eureka Internetdienstent* Case no 1399609/KGZA00–846 District Court of Rotterdam 22 August 2000

Apple Computers Inc v. *Formula International* [1983] 562 F Supp 575

Carlil v. *Carbolic Smoke Ball Co* [1893] 1 QB 256

CBS Songs Ltd v. *Amstrad Consumer Electronics plc* [1988] 2 AU ER 484

Deutsche Welle v. *DiamondeWare Ltd* (administrative panel decision case no: D2000–1200) 2001

Direct Line Group Ltd v. *Direct Line Estate Agency* [1997] FSR 374

Donoghue v. *Allied Newspapers Ltd* [1938] CH 106

Dunlop Pneumatic Tyre Co. Ltd v. *New Garage and Motor Co. Ltd* [1915] AC79 HL

Exxon Corporation v. *Exxon Insurance Consultants Intl Ltd* [1982] CH 119

Francis v. *Donoghue* v. *Allied Newspapers Ltd* [1938] CH 106

Francis Day and Hunter v. *20th Century Fox* 1940

Futuredontics Inc v. *Applied Anagramatics* [1998] 45 USPQ 2d (BNA) 2005

G A Modefine SA v. *A R Mani* WIPO no D2001–0537 July 2001

Green v. *Broadcasting Corporation of New Zealand* [1989] 3 NZLR 18

Halford v. *United Kingdom* [1997] IRLR 471

Hall-Brown v. *Little & Sons Ltd* [1928–35] MCC 88

Handmade Films v. *Express Newspapers* [1986] FSR 463

Harrods Ltd v. *Harrodian School Ltd* [1996] RPC 697

Harvey v. *Facey* [1893] AC 552

STATUTES LISTED IN ALPHABETICAL ORDER

UK legislation

Statutes

Betting and Gaming and Lotteries Act 1983
Betting and Gaming Duties Act 1981
Capital Allowances Act 1990
Companies Act 1985 as amended by the Companies Act 1989
Competition Act 1998
Consumer Credit Act 1974
Consumer Protection Act 1987
Contempt of Court Act 1981
Contracts (Rights of Third Parties) Act 1999
Copyright Designs and Patents Act 1988
Data Protection Act 1984
Data Protection Act 1998
Electronic Communications Act 2000
Finance Act 1991
Financial Services and Markets Act 2000
Gaming Act 1968
Human Rights Act 1998
Income and Corporation Taxes Act 1988
Inheritance Tax Act 1984
Interception of Communications Act 1985
Lotteries and Amusements Act 1976
Regulation of Investigatory Powers Act 2000
Taxation and Chargeable Gains Act 1992
Telecommunications Act 1984
Trade Descriptions Act 1968
Trade Mark Act 1994
Unfair Contract Terms Act 1977

Secondary legislation

Companies Act 1985 (Electronic Communications) Order 2000
Consumer Protection (Distance Selling) Regulations 2000
Control of Misleading Advertising Regulations 1988
Copyright and Rights in Databases Regulations (SI 1997 no 3032)
Financial Services and Markets Act (Financial Promotions (Exemptions))
    Order 2001
Lawful Business Practice Regulations (SI 2000 no 2699)
The Telecommunications (Lawful Business Practice) (Interception of
    Communications) Regulations 2000
Unfair Terms in Consumer Regulations 1999 (implementing Directive
    19/13)

Rules and guidelines

British Codes of Advertising and Sales Promotion 1999
British Standards Institution Code of Practice for Information Security
Management

EU Directives

Directive 1984/450/EEC Relating to the Approximation of the Laws,
Regulations and Administrative Provisions of the Member States
Concerning Misleading Advertising
Directive 1993/13/EC on Unfair Terms in Consumer Contracts
Directive 1998/27/EC on Injunctions and for the Protection of Consumers'
Interests
Directive 1999/93/EC on A Community Framework for Electronic
Signatures 13 December 1999
Directive 1997/55/EC on Comparative Advertising
Directive 1997/7/EC on the Protection of Consumers in Respect of Distance
Contracts
Directive 1997/66/EC Concerning the Processing of Personal Data and the
Protection of Privacy in the Telecommunications Sector
Directive 2000/31/EC on Electronic Commerce
Directive 2001/29/EC on the Harmonization of Certain Aspects of
Copyright and Related Rights in the Information Society 22 May 2001
Directive 1996/9/EC (OJ 1996 L77/20) on The Legal Protection of Databases
Draft Directive on Copyright in the Information Society 1997

Other legislation and treaties

Article 1316–4 of the French Civil Code on electronic signatures March
2001
Brazil Provisional Executive Act 2,200 (MP 2200/01), re-enacted on 29 June
2001 (MP 2200/01) regarding electronic documents
California Civil Code 1873
Dutch Copyright Act 1912
Guidelines on Vertical Restraints (OJ C291 13/10/2000)
US Federal Arbitration Act 1925
WTO Declaration on Global Electronic Commerce 1998

INTERNATIONAL TREATIES AND COMMISSIONS

Berne Convention for the Protection of Literary and Artistic Works 1971
Brussels Convention on Jurisdiction and the Enforcement of Judgement in Civil and Commercial Matters 1968
European Convention on Mutual Assistance in Criminal Matters (2000); OJ 1971/1, 12 July 2000
European Internet Engineering Task Force Policy 1999
National Commission on New Technology Uses of Copyright Work
Rome Convention on the Law applicable to Contractual Obligations of 1980
The TRIPS Agreement 1988
WIPO Copyright Treaty 20 December 1996
WIPO Performances and Phonograms Treaty 20 December 1996

Preface

We have seen the upside of the Internet hyped up by the media. This was a time when venture capitalists were investing in little more than concepts, even without credible revenue streams. Equally the so called 'dot.bum' or 'dot.bust' is a hyped up downside. The Internet is not dead. It was always more than just dot.coms. To terrestrial companies it is very useful as part of their business plan to reduce costs, improve quality of service and increase distribution. It has also left an indelible stamp on traditional business culture. If the rigid hierarchical structure of management was already being eroded then the dot.com era precipitated its eventual erosion. This was an environment where 18-year-olds were commanding the time of senior professionals and business people, and they were being funded. To my mind this encouragement of individual thinking, in a team environment, leads to more innovation and is better capitalism. Also be careful of the doom and gloom press. According to an article in *Fast Company* (November 2001), the latest published McKinsey & Co 'e-performance' survey of over 200 Internet businesses worldwide reveals that the e-tailers sector is not dead! In fact price.line.com, Google, Ebay, Travelocity.com and other companies all reported strong second-quarter earnings in 2001, an amazing feat considering that there has been a recent global economic slowdown.

This book tries to concentrate on the issues you might need to resolve in the day to day running of an Internet enterprise, including legal issues in a practical context.

Although the book considers international laws, it is primarily based on the domestic law of England and Wales. The law and business situation covered in the book is as at 31 October 2001, although it has proved possible to incorporate some more recent developments at the editorial stage.

I have designed this book to be a 'how to' book. I hope that its mixture of business ideas and technical legal information will make it easy to read and provide an optimistic view about this exciting and challenging new world of the Internet.

Part I

Getting Started

1

Domain names

1.1 INTRODUCTION

1.1.1

So you want to start up an Internet business. You may want initially to register a domain name and develop your Web site. However, the Internet is a medium that easily lends itself to abuse of intellectual property rights. This abuse ranges from content reproduction through unlicensed hypertext links, to brand corruption by pornsites using famous brand names in their meta tags, to fraud engineered by Web masters cheating their way to the top of search engine results and cybersquatters buying up hundreds of domain names and selling them to the trade mark owners. Such conduct was estimated to cost business £20 billion in 2001. In order to avoid innocently falling foul of intellectual property laws yourself, you need a good preliminary understanding of domain names and trade marks, content and copyright.

1.2 GETTING STARTED

1.2.1

Think of a catchy domain name that captures the imagination. After deciding on it you will need to consider protecting your domain name or names as a trade mark. Once you have registered your domain names and protected them as trade marks, you need to incorporate your company, complete your business plan, prepare a confidentiality agreement and start to seek seed funding from venture capitalists (please see Part II, Fundraising and Company Law).

1.3 WHAT A DOMAIN NAME IS

1.3.1
Every computer or service on the Internet such as a Web page or a file of information has its own address or Uniform Resource Locator (URL). A domain name is part of this address. An example of a domain name is 'yahoo.com'. Reading this from left to right 'yahoo' is the name of the service or host computer, and '.com' is the top level domain name and often describes the purpose of the organization.

1.4 HOW DOMAIN NAME GOVERNANCE WORKS

1.4.1
Only domain name registrars licensed by the Internet Corporation for Assigned Names and Numbers (ICANN[1] are authorized to register domain names. Nominet UK is the ICANN licensed UK registrar for all Internet domain names ending in '.uk'. It also operates the database for five general top level domain names: '.co.uk' for commercial enterprises, '.org.uk' for non-commercial organizations, '.net.uk' for the host machines of Internet service providers and '.ltd.uk' and '.plc.uk' for use by registered companies, with the same company name as the domain name only. Network Solutions Inc is the US counterpart of Nominet. It is licensed by ICANN to register the '.com', '.net' and '.org' general top level domain names. Verisign, a domain name registry, acquired Network Solutions in 1999. Neither Nominet UK nor Network Solutions Inc are regulatory bodies. They are non-profit organizations which maintain the domain name database for the Internet community. CentralNic also provides a wide range of alternative domain names. There are no local rules to qualify for a domain. The suffixes you may register include '.eu.com' for Europe, 'gb.com' for Great Britain, 'uk.com' for United Kingdom and 'us.com' for the United States. You can find the full list of available domains at www.centralnic.com. The range is constantly increasing. There are thousands of registrars or Internet service providers worldwide offering registration services such as Internet Advertising Corporation Limited, Netnames, BT, Register.Com and so on. However, each registrar will send your information to a central directory known as the 'registry' (a central

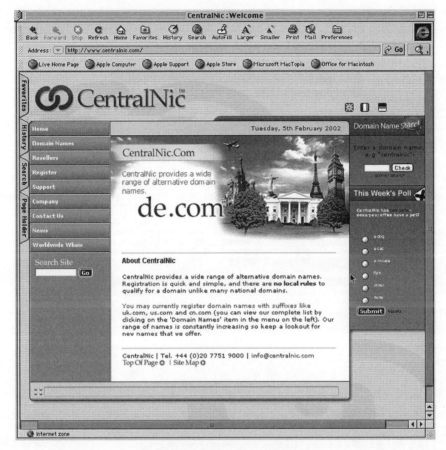

Figure 1.1   *CentralNic™ Web site*

computerized database). This registry provides other computers on the Internet with the information necessary to send you an e-mail or to find your Web site. Once your details have been sent to the 'registry' no other applicant will be allocated your domain name.

1.4.2
There is another step further than a domain name and that is a 'RealName'. RealNames are designed to make browsing easier and to do away with complicated URLs. Instead of entering say 'http://www. tomorrowslaw.com' in the address bar, all you would need to enter is your 'name', say, 'tomorrowslaw', and hey presto! you go directly to the tomor-rowslaw Web site. Similarly entering 'tomorrowslaw' into your search engine should give you the result of 'tomorrowslaw' at the top of the search. Currently RealNames are not used on the whole of the Web. This severely limits their usage. They are only supported in the following browsers:

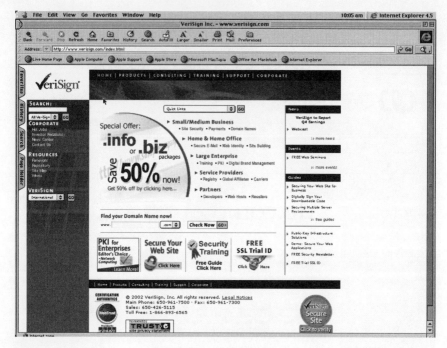

Figure 1.2   *Verisign Web site*

- IE5;
- Neoplanet.

They are also supported in the following search engines:

- AltaVista;
- Looksmart;
- Go;
- Inktomi;
- MSN;
- Fireball.

You can register any name that is available. However, it has to be unique to the organization (that is, you cannot register 'equity' as a key word, but you can register brand names and trade marks) and it must link to a live Web site. At the time of writing, each RealName registered costs $100 per year. You can only register trade marks that you have ownership of. This means that competitors cannot register 'tomorrowslaw' as a RealName for themselves. The only way you could lose out is if someone else owns your 'name' as a trade mark in their own country (for example, the United States).

1.5 DOMAIN NAME DISPUTES

1.5.1

Domain disputes are handled in different ways according to the type of domain in question. Country-specific domains such as '.co.uk' are dealt with by that country's network information centre (NIC). In the UK that is Nominet (www.nic.uk), which like most NICs has a dispute resolution service. It's worth remembering that Nominet can only resolve technical disputes; for trade mark disputes you need to go to the courts. Disputes over '.com', '.net' and '.org' domains are resolved under the Uniform Domain Dispute Resolution Policy (UDRP) by ICANN (www.icann.org). All ICANN-licensed registrars follow a uniform dispute resolution policy. Under that policy, disputes over entitlement to a domain name registration are ordinarily resolved by court litigation between the parties claiming rights to the registration. Once the court rules on who is entitled to the registration, the registrar will implement that ruling. These rulings are currently based on a cab rank principle (first come first served). [2]

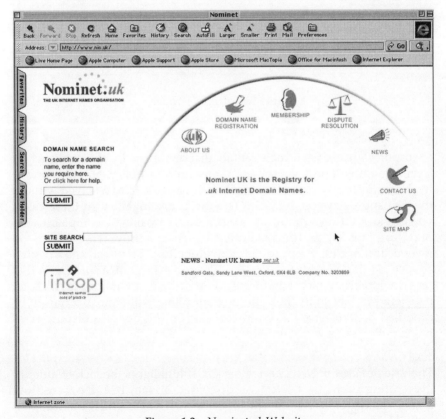

Figure 1.3   *Nominet.uk Web site*

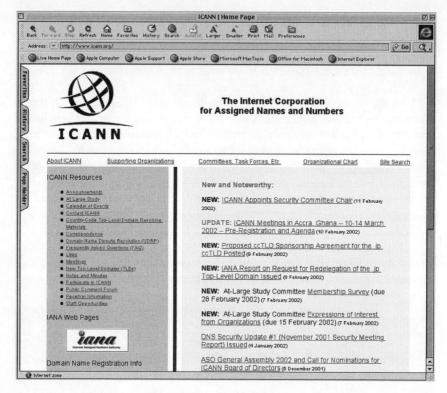

Figure 1.4   *ICANN Web site*

1.5.2
In disputes arising from registrations that are allegedly abusive (such as
'cybersquatting' and 'cyberpiracy'), the uniform policy provides a fast-
track administrative procedure to allow the dispute to be resolved without
the cost and delays often encountered in court litigation. In these cases,
you can kick off the administrative procedure by filing a complaint with
one of the dispute resolution service providers listed at
www.icann.org/urdp/approved-providers.htm. The best known such
service is the World Intellectual Property Organization or WIPO
(www.wipo.int), which adjudicates on the domain name. If it has been
registered in bad faith then the domain name will almost certainly be
cancelled or transferred. For more details on the uniform dispute resolution policy, see www.icann.org/urdp/urdp.htm.

1.5.3
The case of *Parisi* v. *Net Learning Inc* [2001] highlights the lack of a defin-
itive ruling with the UDRP. As discussed above, ICANN-accredited
domain name registrars must incorporate the UDRP, which was adopted
by ICANN to address disputes between trade mark owners and domain

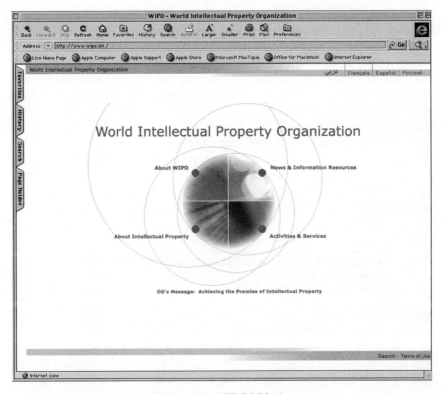

Figure 1.5   *WIPO Web site*

name registrants, into the domain name registration agreement with each of their customers. The UDRP is a contract-based dispute resolution mechanism which requires the domain name registrant to accept administrative proceedings before either a single or three member panel when a third party puts in a complaint alleging an abusive domain name registration. After Dan Parisi refused to sell netlearning.com to Net Learning Inc, the company began UDRP proceedings to challenge his registration of the domain name. In a two to one decision, a three member UDRP panel told Network Solutions Inc. to transfer the registration of the name from Parisi to Net Learning. Parisi then asked for a judgement declaring what was lawful use of the domain name and non-infringement under the relevant US statutes. Net Learning then attempted to dismiss Parisi's complaint, saying that it was improper not to comply with an arbitral award under the US Federal Arbitration Act ('FAA') 9 USC 1 et seq, which prescribes limited grounds and time limits for actions to set aside arbitral awards. Judge Leonie M Brinkemas found that 'mandatory administrative proceedings' under UDRP do not constitute an 'arbitration' subject to the FAA. Net Learning's attempt to dismiss Parisi's complaint was denied. Accordingly, the level of finality to be accorded to a UDRP decision by the courts is much less than can be expected when a party agrees to submit to arbitration and receives a final and binding arbitral award. While the UDRP requires a registrar to automatically implement a decision to transfer a domain name following the 10-day waiting period after a decision, if the losing party initiates litigation during this period, no transfer is to occur until the litigation is resolved. The UDRP itself is silent as to what effect, if any, a court should give in its considerations to a decision issued under the UDRP. You may well then conclude that there is little to be achieved from UDRP and that the courts are a more effective way to protect your domain names. This case demonstrates that a party facing an adverse decision under the UDRP retains the right to make its case before the courts. The paragraph below examines in more detail the effectiveness of ICANN as a regulatory body for domains.

1.6 THE EFFECTIVENESS OF DOMAIN GOVERNANCE

1.6.1

The neutrality of ICANN has been a controversial issue recently, mainly as a result of ICANN's relationship with the domain name registry Verisign. Indirect references to Verisign are invariably followed by the strap-line 'the world's largest domain name registry', which has the effect of highlighting a potential conflict of interest. It could be argued that ICANN is supporting an anti-competitive strategy by Verisign, as it currently owns the domain name registry business governing the technical process. Further, Verisign has expanded into multilingual domains in 70 languages. A new agreement between ICANN and Verisign was announced on 2 April 2001, allowing Verisign to continue with its dual function and retain control of '.com' until November 2007 (at which point it may renew for a four-year term). In return, its control over '.org' will expire on 31 December 2002, and similarly its control of '.net' will expire on 1 January 2006, after which it will be subject to a competitive renewal process. At the time of writing, the agreement has yet to be approved by the US Commerce department. Heads of the House Committee and the Commerce Committee's Telecommunications and Internet Subcommittee have already urged the Commerce Department to invoke its power to review the arrangement. ICANN has also already appeared several times before Congress this year to defend its domain name procedure with respect to the selection of seven new domains (see paragraph 1.7), which were to be implemented in 2001. This new domain procedure means that trade mark holders will have to register their names in the new domain or else face the disaster of the early 1990s, where the low qualifying criteria led to people owning domain addresses identical to a very famous mark without having any affiliation with that mark.

1.6.2
There is also a criticism that ICANN has no enforcement powers. In March 2001, New.Net purportedly offered 20 new unofficial top level domains, such as '.kids'. In reality, the domains are merely third level domains acting as top level domains. Accordingly, '.kids' would have two other domain levels attached that are hidden in the browser. Although there were hidden problems with the offer, such as the need for domain name registrars to update their browsers and a lack of proxy server support, ICANN could do very little about it.

1.7 HOW TO PROTECT YOUR INTELLECTUAL PROPERTY

1.7.1
Brand abuse takes a lot of forms. Brand diversion is one of them. This is where someone intends to go to your company's site but is diverted to a competitor's site, is confused and transacts business with your competitor thinking the site is associated with your brand. It is possible to point an Internet user somewhere other than their original destination through meta tags, hidden text and hidden links. Competing companies often use this technique to wrongly position themselves at the top of search engines.

1.7.2
Brand fraud and misrepresentation is another form of brand abuse. This is where either a competitor Web site uses your company logo without your permission or a person registers your domain name with no legitimate interest, so as to offer it to you for purchase at an extortionate price.

1.7.3
Brand corruption is another form of brand abuse. This is where a company in a dubious industry like pornography will take your well known brand and hide it on their Web site.

1.8 IDENTIFYING A BRAND ABUSER

1.8.1
It is not always clear-cut that a third party holder of a domain name identical or similar to a famous mark is a brand abuser. (The relationship between a domain name and a trade mark is examined in more detail below.) In many cases a third party may hold a domain name quite

innocently. EasyGroup, the organization behind Easyjet, Easyrentacar and Easyeverything, brought proceedings against Mr Richard Lowden. Mr Lowden was behind EasyCarhire. EasyCarhire had been trading online since 1998. EasyGroup launched Easyrentacar early in 2000. EasyGroup demanded that Mr Lowden change his company logo and the design of his Web site. Although, according to www.register.co.uk, the dispute was settled on 12 July 2001, EasyGroup failed to escape the beginning of a potential public relations disaster.

1.8.2

In a decision dated 20 July 2001 the WIPO Arbitration and Mediation Center held that although the registration of armani.com by Mr A R Mani is identical to the trade mark of the well known 'Armani' (of Mr Giorgio Armani), Mr Mani has a legitimate interest in the domain by virtue of the domain corresponding to his first two initials and his surname. Further, the complainant G A Modefine SA had failed to show that the domain was registered in bad faith or that it was subsequently used in bad faith. This case indicates that where there is no likelihood of confusion and there is no bad faith the court is unlikely to order the transfer or cancellation of the domain. The first come first served policy of the registrars will stand. In this case the WIPO commented on what it considered to be the abuse of the administrative procedure by the complainant. This included

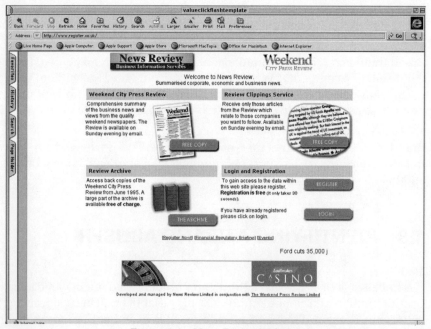

Figure 1.6   *News Review Web site*

Modefine's refusal of Mr Mani's offer to change his domain name in return for a payment of US$1,935. The court felt this was an 'entirely reasonable' sum as there was evidence that a legitimate business was in existence and there were incidental costs to changing domain for Mr Mani.

1.8.3
In summary, before you adopt an aggressive strategy against a third party who you perceive as a brand abuser, remember that they may be innocent. Make sure that there is real evidence of bad faith and that there is a likelihood of confusion, before commencing legal proceedings. Also make sure you register the domain in the first place and in certain circumstances be prepared to pay a reasonable sum if an offer is made to cede the domain name to you.

1.9 AVOIDING A DOMAIN DISPUTE

1.9.1
Alternatively you may be the defendant in a domain dispute. Think carefully about the domain name you wish to use. If you incorporate a well known trade mark into your Web site, make sure that your site differentiates itself and makes it so clear that it is not the official site related to that trade mark that no reasonable person would believe it to be so. Make sure that there are no issues of bad faith; it is unwise to try to register a domain name that someone might think you wish to use for the wrong reasons. You need to prepare your Web site before applying for name registration, so that as soon as the registration comes through you can get online, to avoid accusations of warehousing.

1.10 THE COST OF DOMAIN NAME REGISTRATION

1.10.1
Each registrar sets the price it charges for registering names, and prices vary significantly between different registrars. Some registrars offer a so-called 'free' registration service in connection with other offerings, such as Web hosting. Unless the Web host also hosts your Web site the domain name will have to be transferred, as in most circumstances you will want your domain name to point to your Web site. The catch is that they will charge a fee for allowing the transfer of the domain name from their server to another host server. As of the time of writing, if you are a member of Nominet UK then the charge to register your domain name for two years is £5 excluding VAT. Registration directly with Nominet requires the

provision of Internet protocol addresses of two name servers that are permanently connected to the Internet. You may pay by credit card or cheque. To locate the ISPs offering domain name registration, try the registrar directory at www.nic.org.

1.11 GETTING TOP LEVEL DOMAIN NAMES FOCUSED ON YOUR TYPE OF ORGANIZATION

1.11.1

ICANN were, at the time of writing, in the process of introducing seven further general top level domain names ('gTLDs'). These are due to be introduced in the near future, and in two cases the application process started in July 2001. The seven new gTLDs are as follows:

- ▪ .biz (businesses);
- ▪ .info (general);
- ▪ .name (individuals);
- ▪ .pro (qualified professionals);
- ▪ .aero (aviation);
- ▪ .coop (cooperatives);
- ▪ .museum (museums).

Due to user restrictions, it will not be possible for a trade mark owner to apply for all of the new gTLDs. Only members of the relevant profession or regulatory organization may apply for' .pro', '.aero' or '.museum'. These gTLDs are extremely narrow in scope and are unlikely to be relevant to most brand or trade mark owners. Demand for some of these gTLDs will be very high (since there are many trade mark owners applying for the same names), there is no guarantee, however, that applicants will obtain the name that they apply for, even if it represents their registered trade mark. To maximize your chances of obtaining these new domains you should complete multiple applications through registrars around the world. Further, you should use fully your relevant 'sunrise' periods, and be prepared to challenge registrations using either the uniform dispute resolution procedure (as outlined above) or trade mark laws. If you are a trade mark owner you may want to subscribe to such domain name watching services as are available, including registering for the .biz IP claim service. This should ensure that in the absence of obtaining blanket registrations you can keep aware of other parties interested in your brand name.

1.12 HOW TO APPLY

1.12.1
If you still have not applied then you have probably lost out on the most popular domain names for '.biz' gTLDs. There are different procedures for each of the new gTLDs. For the '.biz' gTLDs, registrations must be used or intended to be used primarily for bona fide businesses or commercial purposes. Where there are multiple applications for the same name the award is made on a random basis. Successful applicants' domain names were operational from 1st October 2001, subject to a 30 day hold on all domain names for which there was a match within the IP claim database. The .info registrations do not contain restrictions as to the type or class of registrant. '.name' registrations are names for individuals. '.pro' registrations are for qualified lawyers (including law firms), accountants and doctors. These are third level only: the second level will indicate the profession, such as '.law' for lawyers, '.acc' for accountants and '.med' for doctors. This gTLD is likely to be extended to other professions in due course, so watch this space.

1.13 WHAT TO CONSIDER WHEN DEVELOPING YOUR WEB SITE

1.13.1
Some of the issues you need to consider when building your Web site are as follows:

- Have a written contract with the Web site developer.
- Make sure you have ownership of the copyright and other rights in the completed Web site.
- State clearly who is responsible for the Web site design.
- Check whether the development is going to continue after you have gone 'live'.
- Make sure that you have protected yourself against any infringement of third party intellectual property or any other third party rights by the developer.
- Make sure you have access to the site to make changes yourself.

There is an example of a Web site development agreement in Appendix 2.

1.14 GENERAL CONTRACT TIPS

1.14.1
Here are some tips when dealing with contracts generally. These tips are by no means exhaustive. A detailed consideration of contract drafting requires another book.

1.14.1.1
A contract does not have to be in any particular form; however, there is a generally recognized format. A conventional contract is normally divided into five parts. The first part describes the parties to the contract. The second part, known generally as recitals or background clause, explains what the contract is about. This part should not contain any of the benefits or obligations under the contract. The third part is known as the operative provisions of the contract. This part addresses the commercial issues of the underlying transaction. Contained within this part is generally a definitions clause, followed by the benefits and obligations of the parties to the contract. The fourth part contains the boilerplate provisions. These provisions contain the less commercial provisions and focus on the legal aspects of the contract. An 'entire agreement' clause described in 1.14.1.2 is just one example of these provisions. Finally there is the execution clause to formally validate the contract. This clause is considered in more detail in 1.14.1.4.

1.14.1.2
You ignore the boilerplate provisions at the end of contracts at your peril. They may appear less important than other sections, but ignoring them may be commercially costly. Take for example the 'entire agreement' clause. This clause is used to stop parties trying to vary the agreed terms of the contract with some other document or contract, so make sure that any future variations you do make refer back to this clause. The courts have taken a robust attitude in enforcing this clause (*Inntrepreneur Pub Company Ltd* v. *East Crown Ltd* [2000], where an entire agreement clause invalidated a collateral warranty).

1.14.1.3
Watch out for ostensibly benign terms such as 'best endeavours' and 'reasonable endeavours'. In this case, reasonable endeavour is less of a burden than best endeavour (*UBH (Mechanical Services) Ltd* v. *Standard Life Assurance Co.* [1986]. If you have to be tied to fulfil an obligation to a certain standard, make it a reasonable standard.

1.14.1.4
Watch out for contracts that have not been validly executed by the other party. Sections 36 to 42 of the Companies Act 1985 as amended by the Companies Act 1989 cover the valid execution of contracts. Essentially, a

company may execute a contract either using its company seal or by the signature of any person acting under its authority, express or implied (so any director may sign). A document is executed either by company seal or by the signatures of a director and the secretary of a company, or by two directors of a company expressed as being executed by the company.[3]

1.15 UNDERSTANDING THE WORLD WIDE WEB ('THE WEB')

1.15.1
Before getting into a detailed discussion on content, I will summarize some of the technical issues underlying the legal issues on Internet content.

1.15.1.1
The Web operates on a text-based language called HTML. The text contained in triangular brackets (< and >) comprises the HTML directives that determine (in a manner that is similar to the embedded code used by word processing programs) how the text is to be formatted, and the points of insertion of graphics into text. HTML is much bigger than just the Web. A common misunderstanding is that the Web is the Internet. The Internet is based on three key technologies: first, packet switching, a means by which data is transmitted across the network is encapsulated in addressed packets or envelopes); second, client server technology, which allows a computer to access and use the services available on another computer; and third, a set of software protocols known as transmission control protocol (TCP) and Internet protocol (IP). Protocols are sets of specifications that allow computers to exchange information regardless of their make, type or operating system. Any computer that can recognize the TCP/IP set of protocols is known as 'Internet enabled'. One of the facilities available over the Internet is the Web. The Web is the most popular facility as it encompasses most of the IPs, such as file transfer protocol (FTP), GOPHER, news groups and e-mail. The effectiveness of HTML can be illustrated as follows:

<img src=http://MSNBC/news/Test1headline.jpg>

This statement contains a link to another computer system and directs the Web browser program on the user's computer in the following (or equivalent terms) as follows: 'This is a citation to an image source (img src). Use the hypertext transfer protocol (HTTP) to go to the computer site named 'MSNBC' and in the subdirectory 'news', retrieve the (jpg) file called Test1headline'. As this Web page is being displayed on the user's screen, its constituent parts are being retrieved from different computers. There is no limit imposed on the number of remote sites which can be used, nor on the physical locations of those sites.

1.15.1.2

Hyperlinking is, first, the means by which one Web page can refer a Web browser to another Web page. A Web page does not have to link to the default homepage of a particular site, it can link to any particular page. So a link may bypass any advertising text and images which may be present in a homepage. This was the background to the complaint in *Shetland Times* v. *Wills* (see below, page 20).

Second, a variation to linking is 'framing'. The remote user's Web browser display is subdivided into a set of rectangular windows or frames, each of which can be manipulated independently, or the text can be scrolled up or down. Framing is accomplished by using the provisions of HTML language. The first step is to define a 'frameset' which divides the screen into different sections (for example, see the MSNBC interactive homepage <http.//www.msnbc.com>).

Third, any site can prevent a link to its pages by including in its Web pages a small program written in Javascript (a net interpreted programming language developed by Sun Microsystems) that can detect that its page is being framed, and that the site performing the framing is a particular host site. The Web browser that detects the Javascript program

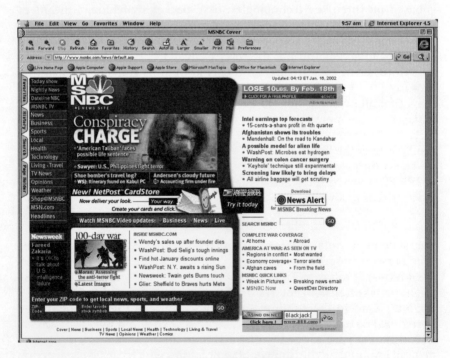

Figure 1.7   *MSNBC Web site*

also interprets each statement in the program when it is first encountered. It is also possible to include a common gateway interface (CGI) script on a Web page, which automatically directs a user to the advertising page, or to incorporate advertisements into a particular page as originally presented.

1.16 CONTENT

1.16.1
Content is dealt with in more detail in the section on copyright. It is worth mentioning briefly here that if your site includes scans of magazine pages, MP3 files from a personal CD collection, or text that you lifted from someone else's site without permission, then you are breaking the law. There are exceptions: you are usually fine if your site is a parody, or if you are using extracts for the purpose of criticism or review. If you discover that someone else is using your content without permission, then you can get in touch with the ISP or Web host for the site. The ISP or Web host will then get in touch with the offending Web site. Usually the ISP or Web host will ask for the offending material to be removed or modified within 24 hours, and then suspend the account until the content is removed. Other Web sites stealing your content can harm your profits and damage your reputation. There are companies that specialize in monitoring the Internet to find brand abusers, such as www.cyveillance.co.uk. According to cyveillance's research, typical large enterprises are incurring losses of between £2 million and £100 million a year through brand abuse (see paragraph 1.7).

1.16.2
In conclusion, linking and browsing are an integral part of the Internet. Linking to other Web sites not only assists users by pointing them to further information, it also drives traffic to the linked Web site. My thinking is that this competition (that is, both cooperation and competition) must be positive for all Web sites. However, you should appreciate the difference between linking to other Web sites (which is generally legitimate) and giving a false impression of your ownership of content on other Web sites, which would infringe on the exclusive rights of the rightful owners of that content. My opinion is that the risk involved in an unpermitted link to a home page or deep link which does not have any framing or implied distribution of third party content is a low risk. However, copying and distributing 'chunks' of content without a licence is clearly illegal. There has been no English case law on the legality of linking, and we are still waiting to see if the English courts will apply the law in favour of the aggrieved Web site owner. There are clear potential grounds for legal action if your site is the target of an unwanted link. These include passing off, copyright infringement and database infringement.

1.16.2.1

The claim of copyright infringement is illustrated by the case of *Shetland Times* v. *Wills* [1994]. A court decided on the issue of a Web site providing a link for its users to material on another Web site, which bypassed the home page. The court granted an interim injunction temporarily preventing the linking, primarily on the basis that a Web site was a cable programme under the Copyright Designs and Patents Act 1988 and such a hypertext link might constitute an infringement of copyright in a cable programme. It also decided that there was a potential loss of advertising revenue from the link bypassing the home page.

1.16.2.2

However, the courts do not always rule against the third party linker. In the Dutch case of *Algemeen Dagblad BV & Others* v. *Eureka Internetdienstent* [2000], the court ruled in favour of the third party linker on facts almost identical to those from the Shetland Times case. However, the key argument in *Shetland Times* (that a Web site is a cable programme service) was not used by the plaintiffs in this case. The plaintiffs were all newspapers and all operated Web sites that contained selections of news reports and articles from their papers. The home page of each Web site contained a complete list of news reports and articles available on the Web site. Eureka operated a Web site containing, among other pages, one entitled 'National newspapers'. This page contained a daily renewed list of the titles of the news reports and articles on the Web sites of the plaintiffs, headed by the names of the newspapers. The titles and the lists of titles were identical to those on the respective Web sites of the newspapers, and were deep links: to click on them took users directly to the plaintiffs' relevant Web page. The newspapers sought an interim injunction to protect their copyright and database rights. The court refused the injunction. Eureka argued that it was technically possible to prevent deep linking, and that the newspapers chose not to do so. This point was not contested by the newspapers. In addition the court rejected the argument by the newspapers of loss of advertising revenue from the deep link. The court decided that there was nothing to stop a user who had first accessed a Web site via a different page from visiting the home page, or to stop the newspapers spreading banner advertisements across different pages of their Web site, especially the most frequently visited pages. Further the Eureka Web site also had a promotional effect, drawing more visitors to the Web sites of the newspapers. On the issue of copyright the court stated that adding a link to a Web page did not constitute reproduction of those works. However, the complete adoption of the titles from the home page of the papers and its incorporation on Eureka's own site was a reproduction of those titles. Fortunately for Eureka, section 15 of the Dutch Copyright Act 1912 permits reproduction of a work by a press medium provided an indication of the source is given. The court then turned to the

Dutch Database Act, which grants protection to a collection that is systematically and methodologically arranged. The database in question was the list of titles of the reports and articles that appeared in the subsequent pages of the Web site. The court concluded that Eureka was not in conflict with the Database Act as the newspapers do not invest substantially in drafting the list of titles of their reports or articles.

1.16.2.3

In contrast to the Eureka case and in line with *Shetland Times* is *StepStone* v. *Ofir* [2000]. This case confirms that linking activities may constitute an infringement of what is known as the 'database right'. This case was one of the first to apply the EC Directive 96/9/EC (OJ 1996 L77/20) on the legal protection of databases, to control the activities of hypertext links over the Internet. StepStone operated an electronic recruitment business under the Internet address www.StepStone.de. Its homepage displayed advertising banners of third parties as well as various options for users to conduct a job search. Users entered the site through the home page and then, by clicking on one of the options listed on the homepage, were transferred to a page listing StepStone's total number of job vacancies, categorized into job types. By refining the search criteria users were presented with job vacancies in the relevant geographical and practice area, listed by date and so on. A user clicked on a particular vacancy to view the job advertisement and receive more information. Ofir also operated an Internet recruitment business. However, not all the jobs listed by Ofir had been canvassed by itself. Rather, Ofir's job advertisements comprised vacancies offered by other recruitment agencies including StepStone. To users of Ofir's site it was not clear until they had accessed the actual job advertisement that the job advertisement had been placed by another recruitment agency. In the case of StepStone, by taking the user straight to the relevant job advertisement rather than StepStone's home page, Ofir bypassed StepStone's banner advertisements. Despite a letter of warning from StepStone and a subsequent written request for an undertaking that it cease its actions, Ofir continued its activities. StepStone was granted an interim injunction on the basis that its rights of exclusivity in its database of job vacancies had been infringed by Ofir searching through its database and copying and distributing fundamental parts of it. StepStone also claimed that because the banner advertisements on its home page were bypassed if users accessed its job vacancies through Ofir's site, it was losing advertising revenue. StepStone successfully obtained a full injunction on the basis that its collection of job vacancies was a protected database under section 87a(1)(I) of the German Copyright Act. The exclusive right of StepStone to copy, distribute or reproduce the job vacancies was infringed by Ofir, since enabling users to access StepStone's job vacancies without going through the home page is distribution for the purposes of section 87(b)(1)(ii) of the German Act. By displaying the job vacancies on its Web site Ofir had also carried out repeated and systematic copying under section 87(b)(1)(ii) of the Act. Ofir's actions had further prejudiced the legitimate commercial interests of StepStone, as StepStone financed its activities, at least in part, by banner advertisements.

1.16.2.4

The European Directive on the legal protection of databases was implemented in the UK by the Copyright and Rights in Databases Regulations (SI 1997, No 3032) amending the Copyright, Designs and Patents Act 1988. Under these regulations a Web site constitutes a database provided that it is 'a collection of independent works, data or other materials which are arranged in a systematic or methodological way, and are individually accessible by electronic or other means'. Database protection therefore applies to a Web site if there has been a substantial investment in obtaining, verifying or presenting the contents of the database. This must be true of most Web sites. Your database right will be infringed if a third party linker, without your consent as site owner, extracts or reutilizes all, or a substantial part, of the contents of the database.

1.16.2.5

The US courts have also seen claims for breach of copyright, trade mark dilution and unfair competition as a result of unauthorized linking. Again a case is yet to go to full trial, leaving the matter in an uncertain state. In *TicketMaster* v. *Microsoft* [1997], TicketMaster asserted that a formal agreement was necessary before another company could offer a link to its site. TicketMaster sought such an agreement with Microsoft. When no agreement was reached in negotiations, Microsoft decided to create an unauthorized link. TicketMaster claimed that the unauthorized link affected the value of its sponsorship by diverting browsers away from its Web pages containing advertising and providing a deep link directly to its Web page entitled 'a Seattle event guide'. This matter was settled before it got to trial.

1.16.2.6

Another US claim *Futuredontics Inc* v. *Applied Anagramatics* [1998] resulted from framing technology (see 'implied affiliation' below, section 1.16.2.7). Futuredontics (whose online debt referral pages were referenced by the defendant's link within a frame) claimed breach of copyright and unfair competition. The preliminary hearing did not dismiss the case but did not grant an injunction, as the Scottish courts did in Shetland Times. However there is another view, that the Web site owner must ensure that the Web site is only accessed in the way it wants, using passwords or programming techniques.

1.16.2.7
Another difficulty with linking is that there may be an undesirable implied affiliation between Web sites. What happens regarding liability of one Web site for the content of another Web site to which a hyperlink is made? My view is that if an implied affiliation can be shown, then the site providing the link could be liable for that content. There are a few famous brand sites that use the frames technology. Their advertising banners, logo and URL remain at the top of the screen even when information from other Web sites is accessed. This means that information from other Web sites is encased within the frames of their Web site. This technique could be taken to increase the risk of liability. However if, when a link is selected, the screen is totally cleared of the first Web site and the new Web site is substituted in its place, then I do not see any implied affiliation with the new Web site or vice versa. This second issue was well illustrated in the case of the Washington Post where a Web site was built using the frames technology.

1.16.3
If you want to have reciprocal links to another Web site or to co-brand parts of your Web site or make third party video or music available on your Web site, then you will need express permission to do so. This issue is covered in more detail in Chapter 2.

1.16.4
So far I have been looking at third party linking where the links were undesirable and the site owner either successfully or unsuccessfully claimed for an infringement of its rights. However, the linker may also have rights to maintain a link on a Web site despite the lack of agreement by the Web site owner. In *(1) Internet Trading Clubs Ltd (2) Internet Trading Clubs (Isle of Man) Ltd; (3) UKNetclubs plc* v. *(1) Freeserve (Investments) Ltd (2) Freeserve plc* [2001], in the interim stage between the issuing of the suit and the judgment the court was willing to enjoin Freeserve to continue to maintain a link on their site.

1.17 SUMMARY

1.17.1
Generally, confidence in the Web is falling. People are losing confidence in the information they are being exposed to on the Web, are afraid of what will happen to their personal information and suspicious of payments online. These are all symptoms of weak brand management. If you want to build confidence in your users, then one of the ways of achieving this is by employing appropriate legal rules when managing your Web site.

Action checklist

- Your Web address will become your brand name, so select something catchy.
- Protect your Web address as a trade mark.

Approach domain disputes carefully; your reputation may be at stake.

- Have link management guidelines. Separate links into high and low risk. Put formal agreements in place for high risk links.

NOTES

1 ICANN is a non-profit organization. It has assumed responsibility from the IANA (Internet Assigned Numbers Authority) for coordinating certain Internet technical functions, including the management of domain name systems.

2 The UK Case of *Pitman Training Ltd and PTC Oxford Ltd* v. *Nominet UK Ltd and Pearson Professional Ltd* [1997] best illustrates the position. The dispute was over the name 'pitman.co.uk'. Both companies were entitled to use the trading name 'pitman'. Pearson could use it for its publishing business and Pitman could use it for its training and correspondence course business. Pearson originally obtained the domain name. Pitman later applied for the domain name and was negligently also allocated the name, depriving Pearson of it. The court upheld the Nominet decision, based on its first come first served principle, to return the domain name to Pearson.

3 If a contract is executed by a company as a deed then it takes effect as a deed. The circumstances in which a contract needs to be executed as a deed are: 1) where the nature of obligation or benefit is land related; 2) where there is no consideration for the contract like a deed of covenant; or 3) where there is some advantage in the 12 year limitation period for suing on a deed.

2

Content and copyright

2.1 INTRODUCTION

2.1.1
So you are concerned about your copyright. You may want to borrow content from other sites or make videos or music available for downloading from your Web site. In this chapter I cover the essential principles of copyright law.

2.2 WHAT COPYRIGHT IS

2.2.1
Copyright is basically the right to stop others copying your work without permission in the form of a licence or an assignment.

2.2.2
The Copyright Designs and Patents Act 1988 ('the 1988 Act') is the seminal statute governing UK copyright law.

2.3 WHAT WORK IS COPYRIGHTABLE

Your work for copyright purposes includes:

■   original literary, dramatic, musical or artistic property;
■   typographical arrangements of published editions.

2.4   HOW INTELLECTUAL PROPERTY IS PROTECTED BY COPYRIGHT

2.4.1

For original literary, dramatic, musical and artistic works, 'original' means an original expression of the idea; the idea itself is not copyrightable. Originality is indispensable to copyright protection. 'Literary' means any original work that is sung, written or spoken, recorded in writing, or otherwise expressed in words. 'Dramatic' means any acting, dancing or mime; 'musical' means any music, exclusive of words or performance; and 'artistic' refers to graphics, photographs, sculpture, buildings and models and the like. The general rules are that claims of copyright infringement of work that are seen as trivial will not be upheld, and that the work does not have to have any particular merit in order to receive copyright protection.[1]

2.4.2

Copyright in literary, dramatic and musical works lasts for 70 years from the end of the year in which the originator dies.

2.5   HOW FILMS, SOUND RECORDINGS AND CABLE PROGRAMMES ARE PROTECTED

2.5.1

Films, sound recordings and cable programmes may be derived from other copyright works. With derivative works there are often multiple rights to the same work. Take the recording of a song. The song itself is the underlying work. The song may now be performed as part of a film, and this performance also is capable of copyright.

2.5.2

There is no copyright in a sound recording or film that is a copy of an existing sound recording, or film. There is also no copyright in a cable programme that infringes copyright in an existing broadcast or cable programme.

2.5.3

Copyright in sound recordings, broadcasts and cable programmes lasts for 50 years and in films for 70 years.

2.6 OTHER WAYS IN WHICH OWNERS OF LITERARY, DRAMATIC, MUSICAL, ARTISTIC AND INTELLECTUAL PROPERTY AND THEIR DERIVATIVES ARE PROTECTED BY THE 1988 ACT

2.6.1

Moral rights: the Berne Convention for the Protection of Literary and Artistic Works 1986 distinguishes between economic rights and moral rights. Signatories to the Convention are known as the Berne Union and they include the UK, China and Russia. Member States must protect some of these moral rights, at least until the expiry of the copyright. The 1988 Act provides for the following rights:

- to be identified as author or director;
- to object to derogatory treatment;
- to correct false attribution; and
- to privacy of certain photographs and films.

If you consent to the waiver of your moral rights then there can be no infringement of any of these rights. Generally, a licensee (a person or organization to whom you license certain rights, ie your copyright work) will want you to waive your moral rights, and you will want to keep them.

2.6.2

Performer's rights: if you are a performer or a person with recording rights in relation to a performance, the 1988 Act requires your consent to the exploitation of that performance. 'Performer' means dramatic, musical, reading or recitation, or a variety act or any similar presentation, and 'recording' means a film or sound recording: 1) made from the live performance; 2) made from a broadcast of, or cable programme including, the performance; or 3) made directly or indirectly from another recording of the performance. Copyright in performer's rights lasts for 50 years.

2.7 HOW INTELLECTUAL PROPERTY CAN BE EXPLOITED TO GENERATE REVENUE WITH THE AUTHOR RETAINING ITS INTEGRITY AND OWNERSHIP

2.7.1

One method of exploiting your copyright is individually by licence of the copyright. The other way to exploit copyright is by bulk, through agencies like the Performing Rights Society or Phonographic Performance Limited.

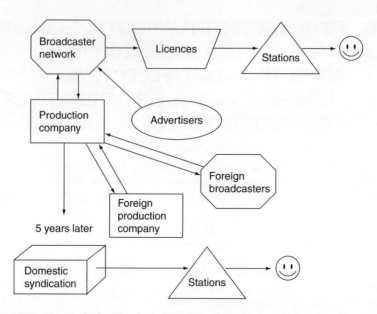

Figure 2.1 *A typical television food chain. The production company makes the series, finances it and packages it, for example to a major studio such as Warner Brothers, Fox, Paramount, Universal or Sony. These companies produce many prime time live shows, but independent companies such as Casey Warner, Gracie Films, Rysher Entertainment and Spelling Entertainment augment this work. The broadcaster network licenses the series for a specified number of episodes over a specified period, for a fee to the production company which represents about 80 per cent of the cost incurred by the production company to produce the series, and shows it on national television. The programme is broadcast to UK homes. The network also receives advertising revenue for the broadcast which is not shared with the production company. If the programme is successful more episodes are commissioned. It then becomes a candidate for syndication. This is when a programme is distributed to television stations around the country or/and cable networks. The production company may even distribute the programme to foreign broadcasters and the programme may be syndicated in the same way. So the production company recoups its losses and profits if it is successful on the licence fees paid by the broadcasters on syndication of the series*

2.8 HOW THE FORMAT OF A SERIES CAN BE EXPLOITED FOR FOREIGN JURISDICTIONS

2.8.1

TV format rights are licensed to enable international exploitation of television game shows and situation comedy. A contractual licence is entered into by the owner of the format to the third party producer or foreign broadcaster who wishes to use it.

2.9 A TYPICAL LICENCE FROM THE POINT OF VIEW OF THE LICENSOR AND THE LICENSEE FOR LITERARY, DRAMATIC, MUSICAL OR ARTISTIC INTELLECTUAL PROPERTY

2.9.1
From the licensor's viewpoint:

- Be careful to grant only those rights that you want to grant. (For example you might grant rights to use music but not lyrics.)
- State for how long and in what territories the rights are being granted.
- Ensure your moral rights are intact.
- Set out royalty payment schedules.
- Include termination provisions in the event of a breach, insolvency and so on. (Make sure the property is returned to you in the event of termination of the contract.)

2.9.2
From the licensee's viewpoint:

- Establish whether the right is capable of copyright protection. If so, set out the title of the licensor to the rights, and state what rights are covered by the agreement.
- Seek a right of first refusal to any future works.
- Consider restraint of trade. Contracts that restrain trade are void. The law protects an individual from negotiating away his or her livelihood, and a person should not be restricted in carrying out his lawful trade or business. (The seminal case is *Nordenfelt* v. *Maxim Nordenfelt Guns and Ammunition Co.*, 1849, which established that interference with an individual's liberty in trading is contrary to public policy and therefore void.) That is the rule; the exceptions include where the restraint is justified as reasonable, in reference to both the parties concerned and the interests of the public. A clause which effectively prevents the licensor from dealing with the intellectual property again may qualify as restraint of trade.
- Subject to the concerns about restraint of trade, seek exclusivity and consider excluding as many of the licensor's rights as possible.
- Seek warranties that the work is capable of copyright protection and that it is not defamatory or in breach of any third party rights. The Contracts (Rights of Third Parties) Act 1999 should be

considered. Prior to this Act, the *sine qua non* of contracts was that a contract could not confer a benefit on any person except the parties to it. *Tweddle* v. *Atkinson* [1861] and *Dunlop Pneumatic Tyre Co. Ltd* [1915] formed the paradigm as traditionally conceived. The recent law reform allows a third party in his or her own right to enforce a term of the contract, if the contract either expressly provides that he/she may benefit from that term, or on a proper construction of the contract it appears that the parties intended the term to be enforceable by the third party. To avoid the potential impact of this Act your contract should exclude all third party rights.

2.10 COPYRIGHT INFRINGEMENT

2.10.1
Certain acts are exclusive to the copyright owner. They include the rights to copy or issue copies to the public, to rent or lend works to the public, to perform the work in public, to broadcast or send a cable transmission, and to make adaptations of the work. For any of these acts to be done otherwise than by the owner or with the permission of the owner is an infringement of copyright. The consequences include damages being sought from the infringer or/and criminal charges.

2.11 DEFENCES AND PERMITTED ACTS

2.11.1
There is the defence of fair dealing with the intellectual property for private study. However, copies must be limited and not multiple. Also fair dealing for criticism, review and news reporting is permitted. However, copyright must be acknowledged. There is also the permitted incidental inclusion of work that might otherwise be copyright protected, such as buildings, advertising billboards, or music from cars or shops, for example as a backdrop to a documentary. There is no defence for the deliberate inclusion of protected work.

2.12 COPYRIGHT ONLINE

2.12.1
Mass copying and distribution can occur rapidly and surreptitiously from anywhere in the world through the Internet. Some of the most popular

Figure 2.2   *MP3 Web site*

online copyright material is music, which is downloaded, either legitimately or illegitimately, by individuals to CD ROM 'burners'. The year 2000 saw significant activity in the courts, particularly in the United States, where major record labels sought to quash what they perceived as unfair competition presented by music file sharing organizations like Napster and My.MP3.com, using the full force of copyright law. It has been said that online music plays will be worth an additional US$3.3 billion in sales to the music industry by 2005, so this strong action is little surprise.

2.12.1.1
The most famous US case is one in which A&M Records and 17 other companies filed a complaint for contributory and vicarious copyright infringement, violations of the California Civil Code Section 980 (a) (2) and unfair competition against Napster Inc. At the time of filing (6 December 1999) Napster was described as 'an Internet start-up that enables users to download MP3 music files without payment'. On 7 January 2000 Gerry Leiber, Mike Stoller and Frank Music Corporation also filed a complaint for vicarious and contributory copyright infringement on behalf of a putative class of similarly situated music publishers. In the summer of 2000 the District Court for the Northern District of California enjoined Napster 'from engaging in or facilitating others in copying, downloading,

uploading, transmitting or distributing Plaintiffs' copyrighted musical compositions and sound recordings... without the express permission of the rights owner'. The Appeal Court then stayed the injunction pending completion of the appeal process, and on 12 February 2001 the US Court of Appeals for the Ninth Circuit dissolved the stay and ordered the injunction to be reinstated. Before discussing the decision further, it is worth recapping Napster's activities.

2.12.1.2

An MP3 file is a compressed digital representation of a musical recording which filters out certain parts of the music, resulting in relatively minor loss of sound quality and resulting in significantly smaller files which require much less time to transfer and therefore are suited for transmission over the Internet. Napster provides a file swapping service for those who wish to collect MP3 music files. However, Napster does not maintain the recordings on its equipment. Instead the MP3 files reside on the hard drive of third parties, while Napster provides an index facility allowing one user to access the hard drive of another user. So if a user wanted an MP3 file for 'Still' by Dr Dre, he or she would contact the Napster Web site, be directed to an individual who maintained that file on a hard drive, and be able to copy the file. It is important to note that Napster does not itself reproduce 'Still', so while the copier might be liable for direct infringement, or the provider of the file might be liable for distributing a copy of 'Still', Napster could only be liable for vicarious or contributory liability, because its liability would depend on that of the copier and the file provider. One of the points, which does not appear to be in issue, is that Napster users infringe at least two of the rights which are exclusive to the copyright owners: the rights of distribution and reproduction of copyright works. Uploading files for others to copy would appear to violate distribution rights. Downloading files which contain copyright music would appear to violate the copyright owner's reproduction rights. Napster came up with two principal arguments against this. First, it claimed its users did not infringe copyright because sharing musical compositions or sound recordings using the Napster service is protected by the fair use doctrine. Second, it claimed that it should not be held responsible for its users' infringing conduct, since the Napster system is not capable of distinguishing between MP3 files which are copyright protected and those which are not, and it therefore had no knowledge of any infringement. Another argument relating to non-infringing use was mainly based on a very small number of new artists who deliberately used Napster as a way to distribute work for free to the public (and thus increase their public profile) without the work being filtered through major publishers. Copying those works was therefore not an infringement of copyright, since the copyright holder's permission had been given. However, the court decided that this use was too insignificant in amount to enable Napster to use the defence of non-infringing use.

2.12.1.3

Napster's fair dealing argument was based on what it alleged was 'personal use' (that is, individuals using Napster to make copies of CDs which they already owned, so they could then transfer the songs from, say, a home computer to a work computer), but the court again considered these issues to be too insignificant in the context of massive copying. The fair dealing argument was also based on what Napster referred to as 'space shifting', which it likened to the time shifting of a video recording (that is, recording television programmes on a video cassette for viewing at a later time). In this context it is worth looking back at *Sony Corporation* v. *Universal City Studios* [1984]. In that case the plaintiffs took action against the manufacturers of the Betamax video recorder in relation to contributory infringement, and it was decided by the Supreme Court in the US that time shifting was allowed under the fair dealing doctrine provided that it was done by private individuals for personal use. In a similar case *CBS Songs Ltd* v. *Amstrad Consumer Electronics plc* [1988], Amstrad was sued on the basis that, by offering a hi-fi for sale to the public which incorporated a facility for tape to tape recording, it was authorizing and inciting members of the public to infringe copyright on pre-recorded tapes. Unlike digital copying, copies made using tape equipment would degrade with each generation, and the House of Lords dismissed the arguments of CBS on the grounds of remoteness of damage. A further case to consider is the 1999 case of *RIAA* v. *Diamond Multimedia Systems Inc*, where it was stated that the portable MP3 player known as Rio 'merely makes copies in order to render portable, or "space shift" those files that already reside on a user's hard drive'. The Appeals Court in the Napster case distinguished between it and the Sony and Diamond cases. It said the methods of shifting in those cases did not also simultaneously involve distribution of the copyright work to the general public. The Court found that the complaints would most likely succeed at trial in establishing that Napster users did not have a fair use defence. The Court went on to find Napster liable for contributory infringement, as the evidence was sufficient to show that the complainants were likely to establish at trial that Napster knew or had reason to know of its users' infringements of their copyrights. The evidence was to show that the complainants were likely to succeed at trial in holding Napster vicariously liable for its users' infringements. A preliminary injunction was granted. The ambit of the ruling is to prevent Napster from 'engaging in, or facilitating others in, copying, downloading, uploading, transmitting or distributing music tracks which are the subject of copyright protection'.

2.12.1.4

So what is the future for Napster and mass reproduction and distribution of copyright works online? According to an article in the *Financial Times* in June 2001, one of Napster's opponents, Bertelsmann (a German Media conglomerate and one of the major record companies in the action against Napster), announced that it was planning a subscription service of music that Napster downloads over the Internet. In the terms of the agreement with Napster, users would be charged a membership fee and royalties will be paid to artists whose material was swapped over the Internet with the help of the Napster software. Napster formed a link with the online retailer CDNow (part of Bertelsmann) to promote music sales. CDNow can track the origin of a user to the Napster site and can also track whether that user makes a purchase. It has yet to be announced whether Napster will benefit financially from any sales. Napster was close to signing a technology deal that would turn it into a commercial service on 5 June 2001. Executives at Napster were also negotiating to license software from MusicNet, an alliance between Real Networks and leading record labels Warner Music, EMI and Bertelsmann's BMG entertainment. The software would let Napster work out which labels owned copyright on the songs on its system, giving the technical ability to make royalty payments and trade in music legally. However, both Warner and EMI stated that they would only consider distributing their songs through Napster once they were satisfied that it was willing and able to comply with copyright law. Napster announced that it would launch a paid–for version of its site in July 2001 but it did not materialize. The alliance with MusicNet was to be an important part of that move. Since the case against it in the USA, Napster saw downloads fall dramatically. According to the Bertelsmann Web site, Jan 2002, Napster plans to launch its new service in the first quarter of 2002.

Figure 2.3   Financial Times *Web site*

2.12.1.5
The cases outlined above are those that have caught the imagination of the media. This might give a misleading impression of the state of copyright disputes related to the advent of the Internet. An industry report published on 12 June 2001 concluded that Internet recordings contributed significantly to a booming pirate music market in 2000. The IFPI, the music's trade body, said fighting online piracy was a growing priority, apart from the need to address the exponential increase in the number of illegal physical recordings, which according to the IFPI cost copyright owners \$4.2 billion (£3 billion) in lost sales. New legitimate online distribution services run by music companies and successful court cases against pirate providers should help limit illegal activities, according to the IFPI's 2001 music piracy report. The average worldwide piracy rate for CDs and cassettes is 36 per cent, while the Internet is almost wholly a pirate medium. The IFPI and its national affiliates last year closed down 15,000 illegal Web sites containing 300,000 music files. Four successful court cases were brought against pirate operators in Belgium, France, Denmark and China. Jay Berman, the chairman of the IFPI, was quoted as saying, 'it is difficult to make an assessment of either the value or the cost to us except to say that virtually all of the billions of downloads that occurred in 2000 were illegal'. The IFPI called on all national governments to modernize laws on physical and online music distribution. European Union member states have 18 months to comply with an EU copyright directive (Directive 2001/29/EC on the harmonization of certain aspects of copyright and related rights in the Information Society, 22 May 2001) adopted in April 2001 that provides a legal basis to pursue Internet pirates (please see 2.13).

2.13 THE CURRENT LAW

2.13.1
Until the EU Copyright Directive 2001 is implemented into local law, UK law does not currently expressly cover 'on demand' transmissions of copyright works. In 1997 the commissioners harmonized certain aspects of copyright and copyright related rights in the information society. This was based on two World Intellectual Property Organization treaties, the WIPO Copyright Treaty 1996 and the WIPO Performances and Phonograms Treaty 1996.

As a copyright holder you have the following rights:

■ The exclusive right to authorize or prohibit reproduction of your Web pages or/and the storage of your copyright material in hard drive or on disk.
■ The exclusive right to authorize or prohibit communication of

your work to the public over the Internet. The work does not have to be accessed, it is enough that it is made available to the public. The use of the word 'public' excludes a private communication.

■ The exclusive right to authorize or prohibit the distribution of the original of your works and any copies. The exceptions to these exclusive rights are set out in paragraph 2.17.

Also, see Appendix 6.

2.14 ISSUES TO WATCH OUT FOR WHEN SETTING UP A WEB SITE

2.14.1
This issue is complex, since the very point of the Internet is to share information and you will need to draw from many industries to create your product. Using these materials on your Web site raises a number of special issues:

■ Any licence you obtain to use third party rights must be worldwide in scope because of the international nature of the Internet. It may be difficult to obtain such broad rights, because different parties may own them. (For example, many book publishers exclusively license or assign copyrights to different companies for distribution in different countries.) Consequently, you may have to obtain clearances from several different companies for a single work.

■ You will need to obtain a licence for public display rights for text and photographs, and public performance rights for video clips and music.

2.15 LITERAL ELEMENTS, NON-LITERAL ELEMENTS AND MORAL RIGHTS

2.15.1
Literal elements are computer programs, whether source code, object code, both, or micro code. These are broadly protected by US legislation following the 1980 amendments to the US Copyright Act and the work of CONTU (National Commission on New Technology Uses of Copyright Work) and the US Court case *Apple Computers Inc* v. *Formula International* [1983]. (Computer programs are protected in any form, fixed in any medium, regardless of their purpose and function.) They are also protected in the UK by the 1988 Act.

2.15.2
Non-literal elements include the structure, sequence and organization of software elements, interfaces and interface specifications of a computer program. Following the US case *Lotus Development Corporation* v. *Paperback Software* [1990], the user interfaces, menus, function key assignments and so on of LOTUS 1-2-3 were protected by copyright in the United States. In the European Union, although the originator's exclusive right of reproduction is important within all the Member States' laws, some Member States provide a narrow definition of 'reproduction' and it is unclear whether these narrow definitions include non-literal elements of a computer program.

2.15.3
Moral rights may apply to the preparatory design materials as literary works, but neither the right to be identified as author nor the right to object to derogatory treatment applies to the Internet. An anomaly arises, as the right to false attribution does apply to the Internet since it is not excluded by the 1988 Act. It is difficult to see why an author would need protection from the work being falsely attributed but not from being acknowledged as the author in the first place.

2.16 A TYPICAL WEB CONTENT LICENCE AND DISTRIBUTION AGREEMENT FROM THE POINT OF VIEW OF THE LICENSOR

2.16.1
- Be careful only to grant those rights that you want to grant.
- Consider any restrictions.
- Negotiate over moral rights.
- Consider third party rights.
- Consider the positioning of the hypertext links on the licensee's Web site.
- Settle how your content is to appear on the Licensee's Web site.
- Set out all distribution affiliate Web sites.
- Set out who owns the copyright to any developed Web site.
- Consider new distribution channels, distribution modes and distribution technology.
- The licensee is likely to want right of first refusal to additional content. Consider whether this will be profitable for you.
- Negotiate your marketing contribution for advertisements (if any).

- Negotiate for sharing subsequent usage data.
- The licensor must maintain an active Web presence.
- State the payment schedules for any transaction revenue or/and advertising revenue.
- Set a minimum quality of service if this is applicable.
- Include termination provisions in the event of a breach or/and insolvency. (Make sure the Licensee stops using your content in the event of termination of the contract.)

2.17 DEFENCES AND PERMITTED ACTS

2.17.1
Fair dealing: some EU Member States provide exceptions for fair dealing and others do not. Basically copyright material can be copied and communicated to the public if it is for research, teaching and other private non-commercial purposes. Temporary acts of reproduction, such as retrieving data immediately before transmitting it, do not infringe copyright. If you sell the data, however, then it does infringe copyright. Also a back-up copy of a video or CD ROM is not copyright infringement, but this provision is optional for Member States. Libraries may make specific acts of reproduction for private purposes but not to the general electronic marketplace.

2.17.2
The role of implied licences is an unresolved issue of Internet copyright in Europe. The technical ethos is such that linking and browsing are activities which are part of the Internet, and users must reasonably require an implied right to make necessary reproductions in effecting the main purpose of the Internet. For example, following *Roberts* v. *Candiware* [1980], knitting patterns carry the implied rights to reproduce the pattern for domestic purposes but not commercial purposes, and following *Hall-Brown* v. *Little & Sons Ltd* [1928], where a letter is written to a newspaper with a view to publication, with copyright remaining with the writer, a licence to publish is clearly implied, subject to payment of the usual fee. However, as is examined in detail in paragraph 2.15, Web site owners and the courts have shown that they are not prepared to have unlicensed third party links.

2.18 SUMMARY

2.18.1
The kind of business environment created by the Internet means greater opportunities for the ownership and exploitation of intellectual property. However, the same elements that offer these opportunities, such as speed

and globalization, also create challenges. Intellectual property laws are local to individual countries. For example, UPN does not own global copyright in the television series *Moesha*: it owns US copyright, UK copyright and so on. The same principle applies to trade marks, so a system of harmonization of intellectual property laws is badly needed. In fact in Europe the process has already begun. However, it needs to be speeded up as there are many unresolved issues, such as the relationship between trade marks and domain names in multiple jurisdictions.

Action checklist

■ Be proactive in dealing with intellectual property related legal issues.
■ Make sure that there is text attached to your Web pages indicating that they are subject to copyright.
■ Consider the use of 'watermarks' or/and 'tattoos' to prevent, or at least enable the tracing of, unauthorized digital copying.
■ Make sure you have a good idea of your copyright property and make sure infringers do not get away with it.

NOTES

1 Slogans and titles may not qualify. In *Exxon Corporation* v. *Exxon Insurance Consultants Intl Ltd* [1982], the name 'Exxon' was not copyrightable as it provides no information, no instruction and no pleasure; in *Francis Day and Hunter* v. *20th Century Fox* [1940], the title of a film did not infringe the title of a song; in *Green* v. *Broadcasting Corp. of New Zealand* [1989], the television programme *Opportunity Knocks* could not be protected, as it was too imprecise; in *Donoghue* v. *Allied Newspapers Ltd* [1938], business letters may not qualify, and in *Kenrick* v. *Lawrence* [1890], a hand pointing was not protectable.

3

Domain names and trade marks

3.1 DOMAIN NAMES AND TRADE MARK ISSUES

3.1.1
The seminal source of trade mark law in the UK is the Trade Mark Act 1994 ('the 1994 Act'). A trade mark means any sign capable of being represented graphically that is capable of distinguishing goods or services of one undertaking from those of other undertakings. It may include words, designs, letters, numerals or the shape of goods or their packaging. The absolute grounds for refusal of registration of a trade mark include the following:

- not capable of being a trade mark;
- devoid of distinctive character;
- consists exclusively of signs or indications that may serve, in trade, to designate the kind, quality, quantity, intended purpose, value, geographical origin, the time of production of goods or of rendering of services, or other characteristics of goods or services; and
- exclusively customary in established practices of trade.

3.1.2

Registration of a trade mark may also be refused on relative grounds. A trade mark will not be registered if it is identical or similar to an earlier mark and with the underlying goods and services, if because of the similarity there exists a likelihood of confusion including an association with the earlier mark. The owner of a mark has exclusive rights in the mark which are infringed by its use in the UK without consent.

3.1.3

Once an application for trade mark registration is submitted, the registrar examines it and decides whether to accept or refuse it. If he or she does not accept it, he/she writes to the applicant giving the opportunity to make representations or amend the application. If the application is accepted, the registry publishes it in the trade mark journal. Any third party may file an opposition against the registration within the prescribed time, currently three months after the date of publication. If no opposition is filed by a third party, the mark is registered and the applicant receives a certificate. The mark is registered for 10 years from the date of registration.

3.2 REVOCATION OF REGISTRATION

A registration can be revoked if:

- within five years the mark has not been put to genuine use in the UK, and there are no proper reasons for non-use;
- use has been suspended for five years, and there are no proper reasons for non-use;
- in consequence of inactivity it has become a common name in the trade for the product; or
- in consequence of the use made of it by the owner or with the owner's consent in relation to the goods and services for which it is registered, it is liable to mislead the public, particularly as to the nature, quality or geographical origins of goods and services.

3.3 THE RELATIONSHIP BETWEEN TRADE MARKS AND DOMAINS

3.3.1

The point of a trade mark is to identify the origin of a product or service, and the cornerstone of liability is confusion. Unlike in the US, in UK law a trade mark cannot be infringed by dilution only; there must be an element of confusion. Generally, a holder of a domain name and the holder of a trade mark to that name can have equal entitlement to that name (except when the brand name is so established that a domain name is no longer just an address). Two UK cases best illustrate the legal position. The first one concerns a world famous company holding registered trade marks to its brand name *Harrods Ltd* v. *Harrodian School Ltd*, [1996]. Harrods, the well known department store, held the trade mark to the name 'Harrods'. The domain name 'harrods.com', registered to Michael Lawrie, had to be returned to Harrods since the potential use of the name constituted 'trade mark infringement and passing off'. The second case concerns a situation where one company has a registered trade mark in respect of a name and the other party has registered a domain name in respect of the same name *Prince plc* v. *Prince Sportswear Group Inc (Prince)* [1998]. The courts decided that there was no infringement or dilution of the Prince Sportswear trade mark constituted by the use of the domain name prince.com by Prince plc. Prince plc was a reputable IT company which had been operating the prince.com Web site for two years before being notified of the Prince Sportswear objections. The products and services provided by the companies were completely different, therefore there was no possibility of confusion between the two companies. The case was thrown out on the technical ground that Prince Sportswear had no grounds to threaten litigation under the Trade Mark Act 1994.

3.3.2

As mentioned in Chapter 1, there are question marks about ICANN's effectiveness. The problems generated by misregistration (as illustrated above) continue to escalate. The extent to which the registration system has become abused is arguably reflected by the practice of 'reverse name hijacking'. This is where a complainant is keen to obtain the respondent's domain name for its own use. For example, in *Deutsche Welle* v. *DiamondeWare Ltd* (administrative panel descision case no: D2000–1200), the complainant knew that the respondent was using the domain name connected to an active Web site and in relation to a bona fide offering of goods and services. It also knew that the date of registration of the domain name preceded the dates of all its trade mark registrations outside Germany. Claims like these are becoming increasingly common and the boundaries of the ICANN dispute policy are therefore constantly expanding to keep up. In April 2001, novelist Julian Barnes was among a group of writers awarded a right to use their own names as domain names, in a series of cases brought by the Society of Authors. This follows the *Jeanette Winterson* case (case no. D2000–0235) which made it clear that the dispute policy was not just limited to considering domain names using registered trade marks. Names that have not been registered may also be considered, where it would be in breach of the legal rights of a third party to register or use the name. Hopefully the new '.biz' second level registration process will be handled more skilfully as ICANN will learn from its mistakes. The second WIPO process to study domain name abuse, which began in July 2000, is at the time of writing holding regional consultations looking, among other issues, at bad faith, unfair use of personal names, trade marks and geographical terms. The results will form the basis of recommendations expected to be published in 2001. A report of the second WIPO Internet domain name process was produced on 3 September 2001; however, this is a consultation document.

3.3.3

The important thing to remember in the relationship between domain names and trade marks is that a domain name is not associated with the underlying goods and services in the same way as a trade mark, so it does not cause confusion in the minds of customers in the same way. If another organization tried to use a domain name similar to your trade mark, to confuse your customers into buying its product or service because they associated it with your stronger brand, it is certainly possible that the customers would log on to the rival Web site, but once they accessed the site (assuming your trade mark itself was not infringed in its contents), they would no longer be confused as to what it offered. Therefore, as in *Prince*, the legal position is that so long as the underlying goods and services are different there is no question of a domain name causing confusion in the minds of customers in respect of a trade mark. However, you would doubtless prefer to avoid the risk of another entity using a domain name that is very similar to your own trade mark. The way to do so is to register a domain name effectively as a trade mark, under Class 38 of the UK Register of Trademarks. If you register under Class 38, an attempt by any other body to register a domain name very close to that mark should be disallowed on the basis of similarity of services. Remember that to register the domain name under Class 38 and do nothing more could leave the mark open to revocation for non-use. You have to show use of the domain/mark. This means an active 'live' Web site.

3.4 DILUTION

3.4.1

Clearly if you owned a famous mark that was synonymous with high quality fashion, you would be justifiably upset if your brand image was being diluted through an unwarranted association with mass produced low quality fashion. In the United States, dilution is seen as a separate ground for arguing that a trade mark has been infringed. This is not the case in the UK, where dilution is part of the confusion. However, the UK courts have shown a robust approach against companies seeking to profit by registering as domain names the brand names of famous marks, with the intention of either setting up inferior rival companies or selling the names on (so called 'cybersquatters'). The UK case of *Direct Line Group Ltd* v. *Direct Line Estate Agency* [1997] illustrates this clearly. Registration of names such as YSL, Virgin Jeans, Nike and Direct Line was said to be designed to make illegitimate use of other companies' trade marks. As pointed out in Chapter 1, the cybersquatter must be differentiated from the innocent Web site owner. The cybersquatter should not also be confused with Internet businesses which trade in Internet addresses. For example, Goldnames.Com has launched an investment bank for Web site names. It offers market making and trading on its own account, as well as advisory services for those seeking valuable addresses.

3.4.2
You should make sure that your domain names are at a high level of priority. Domain names are big business. The name 'business.com' attracted a record $7.5 million bid and was eventually sold for billions of dollars, and Intelligent Finance, owned by Halifax, reportedly paid $1 million for if.com.

3.5 SUMMARY

3.5.1
The issues here are complex and specialist legal advice is needed. Generally if a domain name and a trade mark relate to the same type of underlying goods or services, then an action for confusion is sustainable under trade mark law. If the issue becomes more complicated, as would be the case, for example, if it concerned two companies providing similar goods or services that both had rights to the same marks in different jurisdictions, the outcome is uncertain. (Please see Chapter 1, page 24, for action checklist.)

Part II

Managing Your Business

4

Strategic analysis

4.1 A STRATEGY TO ACHIEVE SUCCESS ONLINE

4.1.1

In the end your strategy will depend on the strength of your concept and your business plan. Remember before you start your Internet company that whatever strategy you decide on, the Internet is not a way to carry out a terrestrial business online. If you take this approach you will face strong competition from older established brands competing for the same market share, with the added benefit of much greater economies of scale. With the right concept the Internet industry is a dynamic industry with great growth potential. If you have this kind of concept, then you may think that a short term strategy solely for market share is inappropriate. You may wish to concentrate on organic growth techniques such as pricing, brand building, employment and good quality control. Alternatively, you could concentrate on building scale quickly through joint ventures, other strategic partnerships and acquisitions. As an early entrant you can set the standard of quality, set up exclusive arrangements with content providers and key portals. Another advantage is in the theory that once users are registered with your Web site they may not want to incur the costs of switching to another, or may not want to switch for loyalty reasons.

4.2 ORGANIC GROWTH: PRICING

4.2.1

Goods and services are generally sold at their demand price; that is, the maximum price that buyers are willing and able to pay for them. Generally, buyers would gladly buy at below their maximum price. If you start using e-commerce you should find your costs are lower than with conventional commercial methods. You can reflect your lower operating costs in your prices and attract customers from your competitors. Online travel is a good example of how the Internet can bring a more affordable service to the consumer. It is also no coincidence, therefore, that it is one of the most profitable. Almost 8 per cent of airline tickets are now bought over the Internet. Orbitz, the online travel agency funded by the United States' five largest airlines (American, Continental, Delta, Norwest Airlines and United Airlines), was launched on 4 June 2001 with a prediction that it would take up to 30 per cent of the market from rivals. Other online travel agencies such as Expedia and Travelocity are quite successful, each reporting their first quarterly profits before non-cash items in April 2001, and Orbitz intends to break even by the first quarter of 2003.

4.2.2

Several other companies are taking advantage of the cost savings of operating through the Internet. Examples include Easyjet plc, a low-fare scheduled passenger airline business. It offers a no frills service at fares which are on average significantly below those offered by traditional full service airlines. Advance bookings for Easyjet must be made on the Internet. The company has even closed down its call centres. Easyjet's operating costs are far below those of traditional airlines such as British Airways. Also T-online, Europe's largest Internet service provider, launched the T-online travel venture, with C&N and Preussag. The online travel agency is integrated into the ISP's existing portal and operates under its brand name.

4.3 GROWTH AND COMPETITION

4.3.1

Whatever strategy you adopt to take costs out of your business, you need to be careful not to fall foul of anti-competition laws. As soon as Orbitz was launched it came under heavy criticism that the carriers would have an incentive to offer their best fares exclusively to Orbitz, and this would stifle competition. The US Justice Department began an examination of the Web site and the Department of Transport promised to review the impact on competition at the end of 2001. Similar laws apply in the UK, and ignoring them could mean that you may be facing a costly fine from the Office of Fair Trading. According to the Competition Act 1998, which came into effect on 1 March 2000, any agreements and business practices that have a damaging effect on competition in the UK are prohibited. The 1998 Act applies to any company whatever the size, and includes a wide range of agreements in its scope. It applies to formal or informal agreements, oral or written. It applies to agreements that have an appreciable effect on competition and agreements that abuse a dominant position in a marketplace. Where both parties to the agreement have a combined market share of 25 per cent or over, an appreciable effect is more likely to be apparent. However, agreements to fix prices or to impose minimum resale prices will generally be seen as capable of having an appreciable effect even when the combined market share of the parties is less than 25 per cent. This also applies where an agreement is one of a network of similar agreements that have a cumulative effect on the market in question. There is an exception if it can be proved that the agreement benefits consumers. This was one of the arguments used by Microsoft's legal team, and was one of the reasons influencing the decision by the US courts not to break up Microsoft. Generally an entity that holds 40 per cent or more of the market share of a particular market is considered to be in a dominant position. However, in certain circumstances it may be considered dominant without 40 per cent of the market share. You could be seen to abuse your dominant position if, say, you charge excessive prices or use price fixing to reduce your competition by selling at different prices to different customers. Another example is if you deliberately incur losses in order to eliminate a competitor, so as to charge excessive prices in the future.

4.4 ORGANIC GROWTH: BRAND BUILDING

4.4.1

Generally speaking all Web sites look pretty much alike. Since an important element for business success is almost always a strong brand and customer loyalty to it, you need to think carefully about the development and maintenance of your brand. Any comprehensive Internet marketing campaign must include Internet advertising. In my opinion it is the most important part of any Internet company's marketing strategy, as most of the users who will see Internet advertisements also use the Internet. It also means that consumers become customers, since they can click on your banner ad and buy instantly whatever it was that attracted them.

4.5 ORGANIC GROWTH: QUALITY CONTROL

4.5.1

In every successive wave of Internet technology, quantity has been privileged over quality. The so called 'gold-rush' of 1998–99 was driven by the exponential growth in total online users. Venture capital firms valued companies by their number of registered users. Internet service providers fought to sign up more customers. In the meantime pricing packages were not viable, customer service was poor and Web sites were cluttered and difficult to navigate. Providing a quality service that generates quality revenues achieved at viable margins will be the hallmark of the successful Internet company of the future. You need to constantly monitor that you are delivering the service level required by your users. You need a quality measurement and monitoring system. Conduct consistent feedback exercises with your users. Make sure that you manage your legal risk in respect of data protection, privacy and advertising online when conducting these research exercises. Compare your delivery of service with that of your competitors.

4.6 ORGANIC GROWTH: RECRUITMENT

4.6.1

To grow the business in the long term you will need good people. You will need to set out sustainable company values in your relationship with your people. You may wish to consider employing a human resources director to manage this aspect of your business. You may wish to incentivize employees with share options related to their performance. This is a highly specialized area of the law and it is vital to get good legal advice.

4.7 SUMMARY

4.7.1

There are several different strategic tools at your disposal. Make sure you select the ones best suited to the Internet. In the next chapter the operational side of your business will be examined, particularly valuing your business.

Action checklist

- ■ Is your idea best suited for the Internet?
- ■ Make sure you are not being anti-competitive.
- ■ Quality of service includes complying with legal obligations.
- ■ Seek legal advice regarding employee contracts and share options.

5

Business operations

5.1 WORKING CAPITAL AND CASH FLOW MANAGEMENT

5.1.1
You must have efficient cash flow management. To illustrate the cost of cash management, if you take the annual turnover of cloudcuckoo.com which is US$1,000,000, the turnover per day is US$3,000. If it proves possible to increase the turnover per day by optimizing efficiencies in collecting cash, this saves a substantial amount of interest on the cash. Your working capital is your current assets less current liabilities. You should take a vigorous attitude to debt collection. In Appendix 4, page 202, there is an example of cash flow forecasts for cloudcuckoo.com. You can see that cash flow steadily increases over the five year projection. It is vital that you plan out your cash flow procedures. Investors will expect you to have thought through this, and the efficiency of your planning will be important to them in making their investment decision.

5.2 METHODS FOR VALUING YOUR INTERNET BUSINESS

5.2.1
This section discusses a number of the practical approaches to valuing your Internet business. The valuation of your business is very important

from your operational perspective, as knowing what you are worth helps you to gauge your position in the marketplace and to strategize going forward. However, how do you determine the value of your Internet company? The first thing to note is that traditional methods of valuing business can also be used for valuing your Internet company. The traditional methods I refer to are discounted cash flow, comparable company analysis and comparable transaction analysis. I am not including the net asset value method as generally the balance sheet of an Internet business has little or no effect on its potential performance. Your Internet company is not a traditional company. Your company is probably in a very early stage of its development and it is unlikely that you will have a profit and loss and balance sheet over three years showing profits. Your Internet company is also unique in its network effect. As every new user joins, the average cost of a transaction drops. Your company's potential as a distribution portal is staggering. From a valuation perspective your company should be evolving constantly, with new ways of generating and delivering business. This makes projections a very relevant part of your valuation. The problem is that it is difficult to tell the future. Careful! under the Companies Act 1985 as amended by the Companies Act 1989 there are solvency requirements. So your company must be technically solvent, and there is a risk that the directors may become personally liable if your company is trading while it is insolvent.

5.2.1.1

Discounted cash flow. This method indicates the current value of all future earnings generated by your company. You need to set out all the projected income and expenses of the company. You do this by projecting future financial ratios, on the basis of a number of key variables such as market size and growth, unique visitors, click rates, customer acquisition and retention costs. You check if these ratios are plausible against industry benchmarks. Once you have determined the future earnings, you then determine the cost of capital rate to discount future earnings to determine the present value. Methods of determining cost of capital include looking at listed and private companies that have a similar business strategy and are in a similar situation. It is important to consider any unforeseen possibilities. You should then end up with a fairly moderate valuation which can be adjusted according to your experience.

5.2.1.2

Comparable quoted company analysis. The basis of this is the determination of multipliers: for example, you could compare your share price with your profit. This is by no means conclusive, as multiples can only determine the value of a company relative to that of competitors. Adjustments are not made as to whether the market as a whole is overvalued or undervalued. The size of the multiple depends on the current stock market price. A look at the strong price fluctuation of Internet stocks reveals the problems associated with the use of multiples, as such fluctuation is often caused by speculative effects or technical circumstances. In order to adjust for this problem you need to observe the medium strike price over a reasonable period of time to level the fluctuation. It is important to remember that Internet companies generally have very high growth rates. Your sales in a previous year say little about developments going forward, so projections of sales, or the sales for the last quarter rolled forward to one year, should therefore be used as a reference value. Since Internet companies also have highly divergent future growth prospects, you need to try to adjust for growth rates and market shares in the valuation. A higher growth and higher market shares justify a higher multiplier. Uniquely, losses incurred by Internet companies do not appear to have the same effect on their share price as with offline counterparts. This results in Internet companies receiving much cheaper capital for their investments than conventional companies. Apart from the desire to create transaction revenue, this uniqueness is one of the principal drivers behind businesses like T-online being spun off as stand-alone companies. Due to the nature of the comparable listed company valuation method, a valuation range is provided, and you should combine this method with the discounted cash flow method for greater accuracy in arriving at an appropriate valuation.

5.2.1.3

Comparable transaction analysis. The difference between the comparable listed company analysis and the comparable transaction analysis is that the price for the acquisition of a majority shareholding, not the stock market price, is used as a basis for the calculations. This method is generally aimed at quantifying the control premium for takeovers. A problem with this method is the scope and quality of the market information. First of all, there have been few takeovers in the Internet sector to date and the purchase price is only made public in a few such transactions. Further, in the Internet area the purchase price is often paid entirely in the form of stocks or in combination with cash, making it more difficult to determine the relevant ratios. What is important is that not only the implied prices at the announcement of the purchase, but also the price at the closing of the transaction, can be used for the purposes of comparison. A possible alternative is a comparison with companies from similar high growth and innovative industries such as certain mobile network providers.

5.3 VALUE VERSUS PRICE

5.3.1

Since value is highly dependent on subjective aims and ideas, you should not specify one single value, but a valuation range. How the price behaves in relation to this valuation range is dependent on many factors. The current stock market prices are at an all-time low, due to the current structure of supply and demand. The combination in the second quarter of 2001 of the high number of Internet stocks and the low demand from institutional and private investors, all wanting to drop their portfolios in the Internet segment, led to the supply of Internet stocks far exceeding the demand for them. More realistic prices and lower volatility are the result of these changes. In a takeover or merger, your share price is determined by your negotiating position. Your liquidity, strategic options and available resources will play a central role. In transactions involving Internet companies the 'transaction currency' is also very important. As the stock market conditions prevailing are at the time of writing not favourable to your Internet company, you will find it very difficult to pay for your takeovers using your own stock. If your stocks are offered they almost certainly will only be accepted in lieu of cash payment in return for a huge discount.

5.4 THE IMPLICATIONS OF THIS IN ARRIVING AT A VALUATION

5.4.1
From a practical point of view, the same valuation methods applied to conventional companies can be used for your Internet company. However, you need to give a large number of features further consideration. You need to consider that at the moment, future prospects for many Internet-based business concepts are uncertain. You need to apply risk discounts to account for this situation. Generally you need to make your own 'call' on the basis of your own impressions. Since valuation is such an uncertain art form, you need to work with a combination of valuation methods and not use them as alternatives.

5.5 SUMMARY

5.5.1
A strong business operation will have a good grasp of working capital and cash flow requirements at all times. Also the flow of information around the company is important as it enables operations to run smoothly and efficiently.

Action checklist

- Do not wait until the last minute. Forget about bridging loans. It is better to know that you can get through a first round of funding than to go through several bridging loans and then not be able to close on funding.
- Think big. Think global. Say you want to grow from US$1 million turnover to US$500 million.
- Know your financials thoroughly. Your working capital and cash flow requirements are very important to your business and to potential investors.
- You must have enough working capital to ensure you can pay for, at any given time, your premises, staff and hardware leases. You must make sure that your cash flow allows you to carry on being able to meet the demands of your creditors.
- Sell your site. Make sure you can deliver a slick presentation of the following things:

  - A brief summary of what your site is about and its users.
  - A brief summary of your revenue streams (subscription revenue, transaction revenue) and strategic partners.
  - The unique features and popularity of your site.
  - How you are marketing your ideas. You should be advertising, have a public relations team and know your demographics thoroughly.
  - The uniqueness of your users and why advertisers and sponsors want to reach them.
  - How your site has the latest technology capabilities.

- Don't rely on just one venture capital firm. Have plans B and C ready.
- Let the venture capitalist know that you have other interested venture capitalist firms.

6

Fundraising

6.1 INTRODUCTION

6.1.1
So you want to succeed in the Internet industry. Two things are certain: you will need to raise funds and have some knowledge of company law.

6.2 FUNDRAISING

6.2.1
We are currently in a bear market; however, investment by venture capitalist firms in good business plans continues, so be positive about your fundraising.

6.3 FINANCIAL PROMOTIONS AND TIPS FOR YOUR FIRST ROUND OF FUNDING

6.3.1
Careful! Section 21 of the Financial Services and Markets Act 2000 prohibits unauthorized persons from issuing financial promotions, unless the content of the promotion is approved by a person authorized by the Financial Services Authority: that is mostly bankers and brokers. Since it is

a criminal offence to 'invite' or 'induce' person(s) to engage in investment activity, unless the contents of such are invitation or inducement is either issued or has been approved by an authorized person, it would be prudent to seek professional advice on this issue. Make sure you do not say anything in the business plan that is misleading, false or deceptive, or designed to conceal material facts. If you do, you could be sued for misrepresentation or negligent misstatement.

6.4   THE BUSINESS PLAN

6.4.1
Before you start seeking funding for your Internet venture, you need a good business plan. Seed funding for an Internet start-up could be any amount. For the purpose of this chapter I will use US$700,000. A draft business plan is given in Appendix 4, page 185.

6.5   CONFIDENTIALITY AGREEMENT

6.5.1
You need to minimize the risk that your business plan will be used wrongly to gain a strategic advantage. Make sure that anyone who reads the business plan, including colleagues, signs a confidentiality agreement.

6.5.2
Some of the clauses that you might consider having in your confidentiality agreement are:

- A clear definition of your confidential information, and the duration of the period of confidentiality. This should include when the disclosure begins and when the duty of confidentiality ends. You should state that the duty of confidentiality is in place throughout the disclosure and confidentiality period.
- Make sure that the purpose for which the confidential information is disclosed is clear and that the receiving party cannot use the information for any other purpose.
- Make sure there is no implied licence to the intellectual property in the confidential information.
- Protect yourself from any potential liability for the confidential information. Make sure that you state that you do not give any warranties in relation to the confidential information.

6.5.3

The duty to respect confidence is one that exists whether there is a contract or not, so long as:

- the information is inaccessible to the public;
- the information is given for a limited purpose; and
- you can show that the information has been used for some other purpose.

Knowing that you are protected irrespective of a contract is important, because a contract does not protect against third parties directly, but the equitable doctrine of confidentiality does.

6.6 KNOWING YOUR FINANCIALS

6.6.1

Investors will read a proposal inviting funding from the back to the front. You will have to produce good quality accounts: this means easy to read and explain, preferably with graphs. So you will need balance sheets, detailed profit and loss statements, cash flows and financial ratios.

6.7 THE VALUATION AND SHARE CAPITAL

6.7.1

(See Chapter 5 for more information on valuation.) Clearly the concept of valuation is an illusion; it is not an exact science. Even with a publicly traded company, multiplying the share price by the number of shares issued only gives an indication of what a large group of investors think about the company and its prospects at that time. Valuing a privately owned Internet company needs even more conjuring based on expert forecasts and estimates. Your company probably has no net income and very few tangible assets.

6.7.1.1

Your pay-off is in maintaining the valuation levels that you have set for yourself. The venture capitalist will try to reduce the valuation levels. Let us say you think your pre-money valuation should be US$2,800,000 and a venture capitalist firm is willing to invest US$700,000. Your post-money valuation would be US$3,500,000. The venture capitalist would receive only 20 per cent of the company. However, if the venture capitalist had invested at a US$2,100,000 pre-money valuation it would own 25 per cent of the post-money valuation. You should also make sure that you are selling your existing shares to new investors. This gives you more control over the company than issuing new shares. Let us say you incorporate the company with an authorized share capital of US$1,000,000 divided into 1,000,000 shares of US$1 each. At this time you acquire all 700,000 ordinary shares issued in the company through cash or non-cash consideration. (It is important to remember that shares issued for non-cash are processed through Companies House using different formalities from shares issued for cash.) Since your valuation is now US$3,500,000, your US$1 shares are now worth US$5 each, and you sell 140,000 shares of your holding to venture capitalists, retaining an 80 per cent controlling interest in the company. The venture capitalist firm is usually a long-term investor. However, it will want exit routes: that is, ways of realizing some of its investment in the long term. It is worth considering some form of redeemable preference share or loan stock for the institutional investor. The deal may be structured so that the investment is made in return for loan stock or preference shares. At the occurrence of a key event such as a flotation or disposal, then the loan stock or preference share are converted into equity and accordingly into capital gain. The venture capitalist firm will also want to see that senior staff are tied into the company. Accordingly some reserve shares related to management performance are seen as an attractive carrot to retain key management. You may also be prevented from selling your shares for a specified period, or the value of your shares may be reduced substantially if you sell within a specified period.

6.8 SUMMARY

6.8.1

The funds under the control of venture capitalists are provided either by themselves, through large pension funds and other institutions, or through high net worth individuals. If you are seeking funding from venture capitalists, remember that these funds have to be invested, as the institutions backing the venture capitalists expect a return on their funds.

Action checklist

- Make sure you have a business plan.
- Contact funders.
- Get a subscription agreement.
- Check your Articles of Association.

NOTE

1 Since the case of *Prince Albert v. Strange* [1849], English courts have protected the relation of trust or intimacy created by the communication of confidential information for a limited purpose.

7

Company law

7.1 SEMINAL STATUTES

7.1.1
The seminal statute governing company law in the UK is the Companies
Act 1985, as amended by the Companies Act 1989 ('the 1985 Act').

7.1.2
To incorporate a private company having a share capital there must be:

- at least one director;
- a director can be a company;
- at least one secretary and a sole director cannot also be secretary;
- a registered office;
- at least one initial shareholder (subscriber);
- a Memorandum and Articles of Association;
- a completed Form 10 (statement of first directors and secretary
  and intended situation of registered office);
- a completed Form 12 (statutory declaration of compliance with
  requirements on application for registration of a company); and
- payment of the fee, which is £20, or £100 for same-day incorporation.

7.2 GETTING STARTED

7.2.1

Essentially you cannot conduct any order of business without getting the approval of either the directors or the shareholders. Generally if the matter to be resolved involves altering the company's articles, consolidation, division, subdivision and so on of its share capital, or re-registration as a public company, a shareholders' meeting is needed. If the matter is about the day to day management of the company, a board meeting is appropriate. Some of the basic issues directors must consider and approve are:

- appointment of directors and approval of their service agreements, secretary and registered office;
- appointing non-executive directors and approving their service letters or agreements;[1]
- appointing the chairman;
- appointing accountants;
- fixing the accounting date;
- appointing bankers;
- authority limits for directors;
- approving the payment of commissions;
- granting of option or warrants to subscribe for shares;
- approving the lease of hardware, office premises and so on;
- issuing shares and signing share certificates;
- registering for VAT;
- approving directors' authorization limits for contracts;
- approving the share application for the first round of funding.

7.3 THE ARTICLES OF ASSOCIATION ('THE ARTICLES')

7.3.1

An Internet company works in a different way from offline companies. It should be free to function quickly, to accommodate the nature of Internet business. Make sure you incorporate the company with the right articles: get it right once and save a lot of time and money. Some of the provisions you might consider having in the articles are providing for lost shareholders and providing for preferential pricing of shares. There are many other provisions that you could make, and I would encourage you to seek legal advice.

7.4 MEETINGS

7.4.1

Both board meetings and shareholders' meetings require notice of the meeting to be sent out. With a shareholders' meeting the notice period depends on the subject matter. If the subject matter requires an ordinary resolution to be passed, that is a majority of 50 per cent plus one of the shareholders, the notice period is 14 days. If a special resolution is needed, that is a majority of 75 per cent of the shareholders, the notice period is 21 days. Some resolutions require special notice of 28 days. A directors' meeting requires a separate notice. There is no specific notice period, and 48 hours has been accepted as sufficient. Careful minutes should be taken and properly filed of the important things said and any resolutions. The board minutes should be kept separately from the minutes of share-holders' meetings, since shareholders are entitled to inspect only minutes of shareholders' meetings. There are two types of shareholders' meetings, an annual general meeting (which happens once a year) and an extraor-dinary general meeting (which happens whenever it is necessary).

Figure 7.1   *Companies House Web site*

7.5   COMPANY FILING AND OTHER FORMALITIES

7.5.1

The company secretary should manage the filing and handle formalities at Companies House. Table 7.1 sets out some of the procedures.

Table 7.1   Company formalities

Action	Internal (company's statutory books)	External (Registrar of Companies)
Appointment/removal of directors	Minutes etc Register of Directors Register of Directors' interests (S324 declaration)	Form 288 (incl. consent to act signed by new directors) (within 14 days)
Directors' service contract (term in excess of five years (S319 CA	Minutes etc (O/R) Copy service agreement at registered office	
Purchase of material asset from director CA	Minutes etc (O/R) Copy contract	
Increase in authorized share capital	Minutes etc (O/R) Amended Memorandum of Association	Form 123 Print of O/R Print of amended Memorandum of Association (within 15 days)
Disapplication of pre-emption rights on issue of shares for cash S89CA S95CA	Minutes etc (S/R) (NB directors' recommendation circulated with notice of meeting)	Print of S/R (within 15 days)
Authorization of directors to issue shares S80CA	Minutes etc (O/R)	Print of O/R (within 15 days)
Allotment of shares	Copy of letter applying for shares Minutes etc (board resolution Register of Members Register of Allotments Register of Directors' Interests (plus S324 declaration if approriate) Share certificate issued within 2 months	Return of Allotments form 88(2) (If non-cash consideration include stamped contract or, if no written contract, use stamped From 88(3)) (within 1 month)

7.6 SUMMARY

7.6.1

Knowledge of company forms and formalities is vital to the efficient running of any company. This area should be raised to a high management level. In the long term this investment will bring great rewards, especially where the company attempts a private placement or a listing.

> ### Action checklist
>
> To accept the application by the venture capitalist for the 140,000 shares in your company you will need the following documents:
>
> ■ a subscription agreement (a sample precedent subscription and shareholder agreement is on page 205);
> ■ shareholder agreement;
> ■ stock transfer form;
> ■ share certificate;
> ■ register of members.

NOTES

1 There is no fixed rule but non-executive director remuneration is usually between £12,000 and £18,000 a year. The chairman gets toward the top of that. It depends on the time commitment and supply and demand. The investment community tends not to be keen on share options for non-executive directors and would rather see them subscribing for shares as part of an open offer.

Part III

Internet Business

8

The Privacy and Regulation of Investigatory Powers Act 2000

8.1 INTRODUCTION

8.1.1
In this part of the book I examine the Regulation of Investigatory Powers Act 2000 (RIPA), Data Protection Act (DPA) 1998 and related privacy issues. Privacy is difficult to achieve in a world driven by information and communication. Directive 1997/66/EC, concerning personal data and privacy in the telecommunications sector, confirmed that individual human rights regarding information and communication have become a very important part of human rights as a whole. The right of an individual to privacy is embodied in the European Convention of Human Rights. However, as ever, human rights have to be balanced with public policy issues such as crime. Governments realized that the existing framework for combating crime was not sufficient for dealing with the Internet and other new technologies. Several new issues arose with the emergence of the Internet and Intranet and the way in which they were used. The greater needs for law enforcement led to the Council of Europe Draft Cybercrime Convention. There was and is now an urgent need for monitoring usage of these networks.

8.1.1.1

The case of *Western Provident Association* v. *Norwich Union* (1997) demonstrated that companies can be required to make a very costly payment should their Intranet be used in a way prejudicial to another company. This case is a landmark 1997 libel case which involved two competitors in the medical insurance industry. At Norwich Union, employees were circulating e-mails among themselves alleging that Western Provident was in financial difficulties. Western Provident got wind of this and sued for libel, forcing Norwich Union to part with £450,000.

8.1.1.2

There is a distinction to be drawn between the content of a communication and its attributes (the content is the body of the communication, for example an e-mail, and the attributes are details of its sender and recipient). I examine later how this distinction is important in practice. In any event it is important to see this body of law relating to privacy as linked, since the regulations all in some way overlap with each other.

8.1.2

The Telecommunications Act 1984 gave telecommunications operators (telco) the right to monitor systems to protect against fraudulent or improper use. However, the UK had no other regulatory regime regarding messages sent via telecomms.; therefore it was found wanting by the European Court of Human Rights (ECHR). As a result the Government tabled the Interception of Communications Act 1985 (IOCA). In addition the DPA 1984 and now the DPA 1998, the Telecommunication (Lawful Business Practice) (Interception of Communications) Regulations 2000, and the Human Rights Act 1998 impact on the monitoring of communications. The RIPA 2000 has now replaced the IOCA.

8.2 THE RIPA 2000

8.2.1

The IOCA made it an offence to intercept transmissions over a public telecommunication system. The RIPA extends the offence to a private system. *Halford* v. *United Kingdom* [1997] confirms the position. Ms Halford sued Merseyside police on the grounds that she had been discriminated against on grounds of sex. She alleged that a 'dirty tricks' campaign had been launched against her, including leaks to the press, interception of her telephone calls and the decision to bring disciplinary proceedings against her. As an Assistant Chief Constable, Ms Halford had two phones, one of which was for her private use. Both phones were part of the Merseyside police internal network, a telecommunications system outside the public network. Ms Halford was given assurance that she could attend to the case using her private phone. She subsequently alleged that calls made from her home and office telephones were intercepted for the purposes of obtaining information to use against her in the discrimination proceedings. However, the IOCA 1985 did not apply to telecommunications systems outside the public network, such as the internal system of Merseyside police, and there was no legislation to regulate the interception of communications on a private system. Ms Halford appealed to the ECHR on the basis that the interception of the calls amounted to unjustifiable interference with her rights to respect for her private life and freedom of expression, contrary to Articles 8 and 10 of the Convention, that she had no effective domestic remedy in relation to the interception, contrary to Article 13 of the Convention, and that she was discriminated against on grounds of sex, contrary to Article 14 of the Convention in conjunction with Articles 8 and 10. The court held by unanimous decision that there had been a violation of Article 8. Telephone calls made from business premises may be covered by notions of 'private life' and 'correspondence', Ms Halford had a reasonable expectation of privacy, and she had been discriminated against on grounds of sex. RIPA therefore confirms the position in the Halford case. The exception is that for a system controller (in effect, an employer) to intercept a private communication is not an offence, even if the system is outsourced. RIPA creates a new tort of unlawful interception. For an employer to intercept an employee's communication is not a criminal offence, but it may be a civil offence. There conditions under which it is permissible to intercept communications are governed by the Lawful Business Practice Regulations (SI 2000/2699) – Directive 1997/66/EC Article 5(2), 'for the purpose of providing evidence of a commercial transaction or of any other business communication'.

8.2.1.1
The authorized purposes for monitoring or keeping a record of communications are:

- to establish facts;
- to ascertain compliance with regulatory or self-regulatory practices or procedures;
- to ascertain or demonstrate standards achieved by the person using the system in the course of his or her duties (the classic call centre situation);
- in the interests of national security;
- in the course of preventing or detecting crime;
- in investigating or detecting authorized use of that or any other telecommunication system; and
- to secure an inherent part of the effective operation of the system (operation of firewalls as they monitor communication).

8.2.1.2
Other authorized purposes are:

- monitoring to determine whether messages are relevant to the system controller's business (the right to open up messages to see if they are relevant for business);
- monitoring communications made to a confidential voice telephony counselling or support service.

The interception must be made solely for the purposes stated: for example, if the monitoring takes place 'as a self-regulatory practice or procedure', the information gathered could not then be used in setting up an employee incentive scheme. In addition, if monitoring takes place the monitor must make all reasonable efforts to inform all the individuals who may use the communication system that their communications could be monitored. (It is necessary to inform internal users of the system but not external users.)

8.2.1.3

'Interception of communication' is making the content of the communication available to a person other than the sender or intended recipient, while it is being transmitted (but this includes storage under section 2(7)). So if one person stores a message and somebody else retrieves it, this is interception. To retrieve a message that has already been read is not interception. Interception of communication does not cover traffic data (see below).

8.3   WHAT IS TRAFFIC DATA?

8.3.1

The offences are concerned with the content, not its attributes. Its attributes are termed 'traffic data' by the RIPA.

8.3.1.1

Traffic data includes:

- data identifying any person, apparatus or location to or from which a communication is transmitted (note that traffic data is covered by the Data Protection Act 1998, since it is possible to, for example, identify a person by their e-mail address);
- data identifying or selecting an apparatus through which a communication is transmitted;
- data comprising signals for actuation of apparatus used for effecting the transmission;
- data identifying the data comprised in or attached to a communication, such as packet headers, computer files and programs (this includes cookies from which a trail on the Internet can be traced.

The US case *US Telecom Assoc. et al* v. *FCC and United States* [2000] concerns the Communication Assistance for Law Enforcement Act of 1994 (CALEA) requiring carriers to ensure that their systems are technically capable of enabling law enforcement agencies operating with proper legal authority to intercept individual telephone cases and to obtain certain 'call-identifying information'. According to CALEA, if a government agency or person believes that standards required of carriers are 'deficient' it can petition to have those standards corrected. In this proceeding, telecom industry associations and privacy rights organizations challenged those parts of the FCC's implementing order that require carriers to make available to law enforcement agencies the following capabilities:

- antenna tower location information;
- packet mode communication;
- dialled digit extraction;
- party hold/join/drop;
- subject–initiated dialling and signalling; and
- in band and out of band signalling.

The petitioners contented that the commission: first, exceeded its authority under CALEA because at least some of the information required to be made available to law-enforcement was neither call content nor 'call identifying information that is reasonably available to the carrier'; second, failed adequately to 'protect the privacy and security of communications not authorized to be intercepted as required by statute'; and third, failed both to ensure that the capability requirements are implemented 'by cost effective methods' and to 'minimize the cost of such compliance as residential ratepayers'.

The court first considered the required capabilities, and decided that whether CALEA requires carriers to make these available turns on what the Act means by 'call identifying information'. CALEA defines 'call identifying information' as 'dialing or signalling information that identifies the origin, direction, destination, or termination of each communication generated or received by a subscriber by means of any equipment, facility, or service of a telecommunications carrier'. The court decided that 'call identifying information' includes more than telephone numbers and so this part of the petition was declined. In respect of dialled digit extraction, party hold/join/drop, subject–initiated dialling and signalling and in band and out of band signalling, the court held that these requirements did not meet the requirements of privacy or cost that the commission's rules must satisfy under CALEA. The matter was remanded for further consideration. I believe that there has not yet been a published report of the results of the further consideration, or that it has taken place.

On the issue of packet mode communication, it was contended by the carriers that a packet header contains 'call identifying information' but it cannot be separated from its body or payload which contains call content. So disclosing a packet mode-data will also include call content, violating CALEA's privacy protection provisions. The court declined this ground. It was possible for the carriers to only include 'call identifying information' in their disclosures to LEAs. Also the commission had observed privacy requirements under CALEA.

In the UK the subject of what constitutes traffic data under RIPA has not yet been challenged. In respect of packet mode data this may well be content rather than attributes of a communication. It is a subject that needs further examination as technology constantly evolves.

8.4   INTERCEPTION UNDER A WARRANT

8.4.1
The RIPA also authorizes interception under a warrant (section 5). This is concerned with interception by the police which is only legal when it is done under a warrant. A warrant is likely to be granted for reasons of national security, to prevent a serious crime or for the economic wellbeing of the UK. The warrant is very wide in scope as it may be served on a person or an address (section 8(1)), so an individual with several e-mail addresses can simply be served in person. The warrants are scrutinized by a commissioner and a tribunal (part IV) and an annual report is made to Parliament.

8.5   EXCEPTIONS TO THE NEED TO COMPLY WITH THE RIPA RESTRICTIONS

8.5.1
It is permissible to intercept communications that are not within the authorized classes of interceptions under the RIPA where both parties consent. If an employer obtains its employees' consent to intercept their communications, then it is lawful for it to do so.

Separate rights to intercept communications are granted to telecommunications operators (telco) under the Telecommunications Act 1984.

8.6 CRIMINAL AND CIVIL EXCEPTIONS

8.6.1
Under section 17 of the RIPA, any material gathered through an interception warrant is not admissible as evidence in court. This is because interception under a warrant is an investigatory power. To make the intercepted communication evidence admissible in court would cause investigative methods to become public knowledge, and as a matter of public policy this is undesirable. However, interception evidence from elsewhere in Europe is admissible as evidence. The governments that are members of the Council of Europe adopted common rules in the field of mutual assistance in criminal matters to achieve greater unity among their members (European Convention on Mutual Assistance in Criminal Matters (2000); OJ 1971/1, 12 July 2000).

8.6.2
Another exception to the laws against disclosing personal data is under section 29(3) of the Data Protection Act 1998, which concerns civil or criminal litigation. A person or organization served by the police with a section 29(3) order may voluntarily submit the information requested, although under the RIPA the police cannot demand communications data. In a civil action a third party can be made to disclose data *Totalise plc* v. *Motley Fool Ltd and another* [2001]. Section 21(4) of the RIPA defines communications data as traffic data, usage data and any information 'that is held or obtained in relation to the persons to whom he provides the service'.

8.7 TELECOMMUNICATIONS COMPANIES

8.7.1
The RIPA specifically requires telcos to build into their systems the ability to intercept communications. Before any communication is intercepted the government must issue a specific order to the telco called a Section 12 order. The order requires an interception capability to be:

- built in a reasonable time frame;
- capable of enabling transmissions to be intercepted in near real time;
- filtered where necessary;
- free of any Certificate Service Provider applied protection such as encryption;
- capable of simultaneous interception of one in 10,000 end users;
- auditable;
- secure.

8.7.2

The Act provides for the Secretary of State to assess and make a contribution to the costs of incorporating interception capability as he thinks necessary. A big communications company might be granted a lesser contribution to its costs than a smaller one. The installation cost could run into millions of dollars, and there is not yet a set standard for the technology. The Internet Engineering Task Force Policy 1999 has not set a standard for the Internet.

8.8 SUMMARY

8.8.1

Your key concerns about RIPA will depend on your own position and activities. RIPA applies to circuit switched systems as well as packet switched systems, on a physical level (ie bit-stream) and at an application level (eg e-mail). Only telcos need worry about Section 12 orders, and they will not be required to comply right away, although they should start making preparations now. You can ignore the provisions on encryption if you are not a key holder. In any event if you are providing end to end encryption facilities, RIPA may not apply to you. In respect of interception warrants, RIPA only requires you to take 'reasonably practicable' steps to comply. It does not require you to succeed. However, a knowing failure to comply is a crime punishable by up to two years' imprisonment and a fine (section 1(7)). If as an employer you decide to intercept communications, make sure you identify your purpose for monitoring. Also tell your staff you are doing it (unless they are suspected of criminal activity). Further, use the information obtained from interception for the notified purpose only. You will need to consult an expert in this area when setting up your system. Organizations like Amtec Consulting plc specialize in data protection.

8.8.2

The government has published the Accessing Communications Data Draft Code of Practice under section 71(3)(a) of the RIPA, laying down procedures to be followed by public authorities when obtaining information. A detailed report on this code of practice is beyond the scope of this book. You can view the code of practice at www.homeoffice. gov.uk/rtpa/pcdcpc/htm.

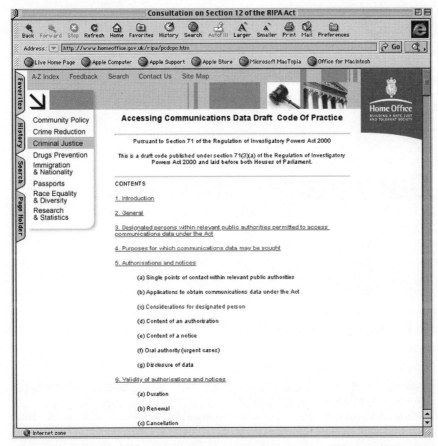

Figure 8.1   *Accessing Communications Data Draft Code of Practice on the Home Office Web site*

Action checklist

- Highlight your concerns about RIPA.
- Make sure you have a privacy and security policy on your Web site(s).
- Treat the RIPA and the Data Protection Act 1998 as linked.
- Get experts such as Amtec Consulting plc to give advice on setting up your system.
- Where relevant, get consent before intercepting communications.
- If you are monitoring communications, state the purpose for which you are doing the monitoring. Do not use the information for another purpose.

9

Data protection

9.1 INTRODUCTION

9.1.1

Although there are several laws in respect of privacy and data protection, the Data Protection Act 1998 ('the 1998 Act') is the seminal statute in UK data protection law. The term 'data protection' is a misnomer, as the 1998 Act does not try to protect the information itself. What it does is to give control back to individuals over the use of their personal information. Individuals are now able to prevent unforeseen use of their information and have been provided with protection from unlawful or harmful use of their information.

9.1.2

The 1998 Act is not there to stop the flow of information but to encourage it. As an Internet business you want some 'stickiness' on your site. You want site users, registered users and subscribers to have increased confidence in the service that you provide. You will almost certainly need terms and conditions for your Web site, and an understanding of how the 1998 Act affects you and what systems you need to put in place. The 1998 Act affects everyone who maintains personal records, whether manually (paper files) or automated. As an Internet business you are exposed to spot checks by the Office of the Data Protection Commissioner. If you are collecting just the e-mail addresses of site users, you will fall within the ambit of the 1998 Act. Anyone is entitled to apply to you to have access to any data which you hold relating to them. It is very important that your existing systems comply with the standards set down by the 1998 Act regarding the way you compile and access the content of personal files. At the time of writing, the latest Department of Trade and Industry report on information security states that a single security breach can cost an organization more than £100,000. The impact on your organization's reputation can be much greater, and investors are becoming increasingly concerned about such risks. Failing to comply with the 1998 Act could also be construed as corporate negligence which could mean, if you are a director of your company, personal liability.

9.2   THE DATA PROTECTION ACT 1998

9.2.1
The 1998 Act came into force on 1 March 2000. The Act supersedes the Data Protection Act 1984 which only covered personal data held in an automatically processable form (and not paper files). The Act expands the definition of data to include some paper files.

9.2.2
The principal points are:

- the application of the data protection regime to manual files;
- the widening of the scope of 'processing';
- the widening of the scope to all forms of processing, including telephone conversations and CCTV surveillance as processing;
- requirements to notify the individual of the personal data content and that the processing will take place (whoever the data is obtained from), and to identify all the purposes for which the data will be used;
- the limitation of processing to circumstances where specific criteria are met: you must be able to justify reliance on specific criteria;
- tightened security requirements;
- restrictions on the use of automated decision-making systems;
- special restrictions on processing certain sensitive data;
- the ability of individuals to prevent or stop use of their personal data in direct marketing.

9.3   TERMS USED IN THE 1998 ACT

9.3.1
'Personal data' means information that relates to a living individual identifiable from that information, or identifiable from that information and any other information likely to come into the possession of the data controller.

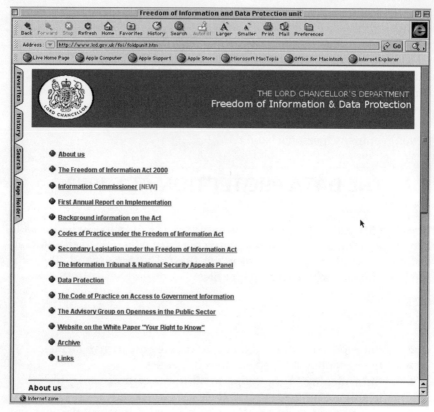

Figure 9.1   *Freedom of Information and Data Protection Web site*

The 'data controller' maintains the personal data and may also process it. The 'data subject' is the person about whom the personal data is held.

9.4   THE IMPACT OF THE 1998 ACT ON E-COMMERCE

9.4.1

The 1998 Act places obligations on those who process personal information. It does not just apply to Internet companies, and the personal information includes (but is not limited to) sensitive personal information. These obligations fall into two groups:

■   Data controllers must notify the information commissioner of their intention to gather personal information online. Their application must include reference to the technical and organizational measures they have taken against unauthorized or unlawful processing of personal information, as well as against accidental loss or destruction of or damage to the information. The notification can be made online, by completing an electronic form. The notification is usually approved within two to four weeks.

■ Data controllers must have systems in place to comply with a further eight data protection principles or obligations and with the terms of the notification.

Notification covers such matters as:

■ the personal data being processed and the data subject to which it relates;
■ the purposes or purposes for which the information is to be processed;
■ who the personal data can be disclosed to;
■ any countries outside the EU or European Economic Area to which the data might be transferred.

9.5 COMPARISON OF THE 1998 ACT AND THE DATA PROTECTION ACT 1984 ('THE 1984 ACT')

9.5.1
The 1998 Act has broadened the scope of the 1984 Act, which covered automatically processed personal information, to cover manually processed files ('paper files') that are 'readily accessible'. This means that if the organization stores personal information with a referencing system to individuals, or referring to criteria from which individuals can be identified easily, that information falls under the scope of the Act.

9.5.2
In an e-commerce business it is likely that most if not all files will be stored electronically, and that there will be a robust system to keep personal information secure. However, if you do have paper files then I suggest you do the following:

■ Carry out a 'house-clean' for your paper files.
■ Verify those systems to which the 1998 Act will apply.
■ Verify the standards, purposes and security measures which apply to each system.
■ Consider notification to the Information Commissioner in relation to those systems.

- Ensure those systems comply with, or are used in accordance with, the data protection principles set out in the 1998 Act.

There are transitional periods which relate specifically to paper files. With regard to new processing in particular, a failure to take the necessary steps could expose you to an enforcement notice being issued by the Information Commissioner, and an inability to provide requisite information to an enquirer within the timetable set out in the Act could expose you to criminal sanctions.

9.5.3
The definition of processing in the 1998 Act is very wide. Just about everything that you may choose to do with personal data is covered, including collecting, recording, using, retrieving, consulting, disclosing, adapting, altering, combining, destroying and erasing. 'Obtaining', 'recording', 'using' and 'disclosing' cover both the information and any conclusions or opinions you may draw from such information.

9.5.3.1
The 1998 Act requires that for processing to be fair, certain information must, where you are able to do so, be provided to the subscriber. This is the case even if the information is obtained from a third party.

9.6 INFORMATION TO BE PROVIDED TO THE DATA SUBJECT

9.6.1
When information is obtained from data subjects you must make sure that they have, or are provided with, or have made readily available to them, the following information:

- your identity, and for a group of companies, the appropriate group member;
- the identity of your nominated data protection representative;
- the purpose or purposes for which the information is intended to be processed;
- any further details necessary, taking into account the specific circumstances in which the information is or is to be processed, to enable processing in respect of the data subject to be fair.

9.6.1.1
In deciding whether and, if so, what further information is 'necessary' to satisfy the last of these points, you should consider what processing of personal information you will be doing and whether your data subjects

are likely to understand:

- the purposes for which their information is going to be processed;
- the likely consequences of such processing;
- more particularly, whether the particular disclosures can reasonably be anticipated.

9.6.1.2
The fair processing of information should also be provided to data subjects where the information has been obtained from third parties, unless one of the exceptions below apply.

9.6.2
When disclosing personal information to third parties you are obliged to make sure that your subscribers have been appropriately notified. You should make sure that you enter into a contract with that third party that obliges it to comply with the 1998 Act as a 'processor'.

9.6.3
In summary, you need to ensure that all purposes are explicit at the time of getting the information from your subscribers. You must not change the purpose(s) without getting the consent of the data subject. You should make sure your purpose(s) is/are sufficiently wide that you do not have to keep going back for consent.

9.7 OBLIGATIONS OF INTERNET COMPANIES

9.7.1
Internet companies must comply with the following eight data protection principles or obligations in maintaining personal information. These principles apply to both registered and unregistered users of personal information. Personal information shall be:

- processed fairly and lawfully;
- obtained and used only for specified purpose(s);
- adequate, relevant and not excessive;
- accurate and kept up to date;
- not kept for longer than is necessary;
- processed in accordance with the rights of the data subjects;
- kept secure;
- not transferred outside the European Economic Area unless the country to which it is transferred has adequate protection measures in place.

9.7.2

There are many legitimate purposes for the processing of personal information, even where the data subject does not wish it to happen. The essential element here is ensuring fairness in the relationship between you as processor and the data subject. Accordingly where you identify a particular purpose for processing personal information, you must also consider its fairness. Ideally, you should take as broad an approach as possible to your fairness criteria in assessing each processing operation, with the aim of reducing any likely discontent with that processing by the data subject.

9.7.2.1

The letter of the 1998 Act states that at least one of the following conditions must be met in the case of all processing of information for it to be fair and lawful processing:

- The data subject has given his/her consent to the processing.
- The processing is necessary:
  - for the performance of a contract to which the data subject is a party; or
  - to the taking of steps at the request of the data subject with a view to entering into a contract.
- The processing is necessary to comply with any legal obligation to which you are subject other than an obligation imposed by contract.
- The processing is necessary in order to protect the vital interests of the subscriber, ie a life or death scenario.
- The processing is necessary for the:
  - administration of justice;
  - exercise of any functions conferred by or under any enactment;
  - exercise of any functions of the Crown, a minister of the Crown or a government department;
  - exercise of any other function of a public nature exercised in the public interest.
- The processing is necessary for the purposes of legitimate interests perceived by you or by a third party or parties to whom the information is disclosed, except where the processing is unwarranted in any particular case because of a prejudice to the rights of freedoms or legitimate interests of the subscriber. (In other words, the processing is in your legitimate interests and in the data subject's legitimate interests.)

9.7.2.2

You need to have opt-out clauses, which imply consent by lack of objection, incorporated into your terms and conditions. You will obviously have to define clearly what the data subject is opting out of.

9.7.2.3

'Sensitive data', as the name implies, is personal information that is acutely private, the misuse of which has the potential of easily adversely affecting the subscriber. The processing of such information is only permitted where the registered user or subscriber has given express consent. Such consent cannot be implied by lack of objection (you must get opt-in consent). Sensitive information relates to the following:

- racial or ethnic origins;
- political opinions;
- religious beliefs;
- trade union membership;
- physical or mental health;
- sex life;
- commission or alleged commission of any offence;
- any proceedings for offences or disposal of those proceedings.

For processing of sensitive information to be lawful, at least one of the following stringent conditions must be complied with, in addition to at least one of the conditions for processing more general personal information:

- The subscriber has given his or her explicit consent to the processing of the information.
- The processing is necessary for the purposes of exercising or performing any right or obligation which is conferred or imposed by law on you in connection with employment.
- The processing is necessary:
  - in order to protect the vital interests of the data subject or another person in a case where consent cannot be given by or on behalf of the subscriber or you cannot reasonably be expected to obtain the consent of the subscriber;
  - in order to protect the vital interests of another person in a case where consent by or on behalf of the subscriber has been unreasonably withheld.
- The processing meets one of the following conditions. It:
  - is carried out in the course of its legitimate activities by any body or association which exists for political, philosophical, religious or trade union purposes and which is not established or conducted for profit;
  - is carried out with appropriate safeguards for the rights and freedoms of subscribers;
  - relates only to individuals who are the members of the body

or association or who have regular contact with it in connection with its purposes;
- does not involve disclosure of the information to a third party without the consent of the subscriber.

■ The information has been made public as a result of steps deliberately taken by the data subject.
■ The processing:
- is necessary for the purpose of or in connection with any legal proceedings (including prospective legal proceedings);
- is necessary for the purpose of obtaining legal advice;
- is otherwise necessary for the purposes of establishing, exercising or defending legal rights.

■ The processing is either:
- necessary for the administration of justice;
- necessary for the exercise of any functions conferred by or under any enactment;
- necessary for the exercise of any functions of the Crown, a minister of the Crown or a government department.

■ The processing is necessary for medical purposes (including the purposes of preventative medicine, medical diagnosis, medical research, the provision of care and treatment and the management of health care services) and is undertaken by either:
- a health professional; or
- a person who owes a duty of confidentiality which is equivalent to that which would arise if that person were a health professional.

■ The processing meets the following conditions:
- it is of sensitive information as to racial or ethnic origin;
- it is necessary for the purpose of identifying or keeping under review the existence or absence of equality of opportunity or treatment between persons of different racial or ethnic origins with a view to enabling such equality to be promoted or maintained;
- it is carried out with appropriate safeguards for the rights and freedoms of the subscriber; and
- the Secretary of State may by order specify circumstances in which processing of information as to racial or ethnic origin claimed to be necessary for maintaining or promoting equal opportunities is or is not carried out with appropriate safeguards for the rights and freedoms of subscribers.

■ The personal data are processed in circumstances specified in an order made by the Secretary of State.

9.7.2.4

One of the conditions for processing personal information is that the processing is carried out with the consent of the data subject. Consent is not defined in the Act. The Data Protection Directive defines consent as any freely given specific and informed indication of the data subject's wish for information about or relating to him or her to be processed. Accordingly, the data subject must actively demonstrate consent. This is the so called 'opt-in' clause. In practice however, until there is clarification in UK law, companies regularly use an 'opt-out' clause: if data subjects do not indicate otherwise then they are deemed to have consented. At the time of writing this method remains unchallenged in the courts.

9.7.2.4.1
However, in respect of 'sensitive' information, a higher standard of consent is needed. The process or disclosure of such information is only permitted where the data subject has given 'explicit' consent. Such consent cannot be impaired by lack of objection (that is, the data subject must opt in). In appropriate cases such consent should cover the specific detail of the processing, the particular type of data to be processed, the purposes of the processing and any special aspects of the processing which may affect the individual, such as disclosures which may be made of the information. Compliance with 'the fair processing code' (see below) should in most cases ensure that consent is both 'specific' and 'informed' where appropriate.

9.7.2.5
The fair processing code is as follows.
1. In determining whether information is processed fairly for the purposes of the first principle, regard must be had to the method by which it is obtained including, in particular, whether any person from whom it is obtained is deceived or misled as to the purpose or purposes for which it is processed. In addition a subscriber should be provided with any information which is necessary in the circumstances to enable the processing to be fair. In *Innovations (Mail Order) Ltd* v. *Data Protection Registrar*, September [1993], the data protection tribunal held that data subjects should be informed of any non-obvious purpose for which the data is to be used before it is used for that purpose.
2. Subject to (3) below, for the purposes of the first principle information is to be treated as obtained fairly if it consists of information obtained from a person who is:
   – authorized by or under any law to supply it; or
   – required to supply it by or under any enactment or by any convention or other instrument imposing an international obligation on the UK.
3. Subject to (5) below, for the purposes of the first principle personal information is not to be treated as processed fairly unless in:
   – the case of information obtained from the data subject, you ensure that the data subject is provided with, or has made readily available to him or her, the information specified in(5) below; and

- any other case (that is, for information obtained from a third party), you ensure that before the relevant time or as soon as practicable after that time the data subject is provided with, or has made readily available to him or her, the information specified in (5).
4. In (3) above 'the relevant time' means:
    - the time when you first process the information; or
    - in a case where at that time disclosure to a third party within a reasonable period is envisaged, or if the information is in fact disclosed to such person within that period, at the time the information was first disclosed to the third party, or within that period you become, or ought to become, aware that it is unlikely to be disclosed to such person within that period, the time when you become or ought to become so aware; or
    - in any other case at the end of that period.
5. The information referred to in (3) above is as follows:
    - your identity;
    - the identity of a nominated person who acts as data protection officer;
    - the purposes for which the information is intended to be processed; and
    - any further information which is necessary having regard to the specific circumstance in which it is to be processed to enable processing in respect of the data subject to be fair.
6. Point (3) does not apply where either of the primary conditions in (7) below are met, together with such further conditions as may be prescribed by the Secretary of State by order.
7. The primary conditions referred to in (6) above are that:
    - the provision of that information would involve a disproportionate effort; or
    - the recording or disclosure of the information by you is necessary for compliance with any legal obligations which you are subject to other than an obligation imposed by contract.
8. Personal information which contains a general identifier falling within a description prescribed by the Secretary of State by order is not to be treated as processed fairly and lawfully unless it is processed in compliance with any conditions so prescribed in relation to general identifiers of that description.
9. In (8) above 'a general identifier' means any identifier (such as, for example, a number or code used for identification purposes) which:
    - relates to an individual; and
    - forms part of a set of similar identifiers which is of general application.

9.7.3

Information obtained and used for a specified purpose. Purpose forms the cornerstone of the control the 1998 Act gives to the data subject. You must notify the Commissioner of the full registrable particulars, which include the purpose for which data is processed, and you should not deviate from that without amending your particulars. You should only process personal information where there is a clear purpose for doing so, and then only as necessitated by that purpose. Accordingly your purpose for any information processing operation should be set out clearly before any processing, and should be readily demonstrable to the data subject and third parties. If you disclose personal information to third parties you must make sure that the purposes for which they use the information are compatible with the purpose for which it was obtained. You need to think about not only how you will use the information, but how third parties will use it as well.

9.7.4

Adequate, relevant and not excessive. The information must be obtained and used only for the purposes for which it was obtained. This means that information may not be obtained or held on the basis that it might at some time be useful for some as yet unidentifiable purpose. There is also a necessity to review the holding of information periodically to see whether it is still relevant or whether some or all can be discarded.

9.7.5

Accurate and kept up to date. You should state in your terms and conditions that in order to ensure the smooth running of your service you need accurate up-to-date information. If you then give out inaccurate information you will not be in breach of this principle, as you will have taken reasonable steps to ensure the accuracy of the data. Also if the information is inaccurate and you have been notified by the data subject that it is inaccurate and your information bears out this fact you will not be in breach of this principle. An opinion cannot be challenged due to inaccuracy if it is clear that it is an opinion and not fact. The court can however order rectification or destruction of an opinion which is based on inaccurate facts. There may also be grounds for defamation.

9.7.5.1

I suggest the following procedures for maintaining accurate information:

- good procedures for creating and updating records;
- reliable programmes and procedures for matching/duplicating information;
- effective staff training in such procedures;
- the establishment and maintenance of standards of accuracy;
- adequate testing and monitoring procedures.

9.7.6

Not kept for longer than necessary. You decide what is necessary. In deciding this I suggest that you bear in mind other laws relating to the keeping of records and time limits for bringing lawsuits. There is a legal time limit of six years for bringing a lawsuit based on a contract and 12 years where the contract has been signed as a deed (see general contract tips in Part I, page 16).

9.7.7

Processed in accordance with rights of data subjects. You will also breach this principle if you fail to comply with the following rights of a data subject: subject to access rights, right to prevent processing, right to prevent a solely automated decision and right to be notified.

9.7.8

Kept secure. The level of security must match the harm that might result from unauthorized processing or from loss of destruction of or damage to the information, and the nature of the information to be protected. You need to develop a risk assessment process involving those dealing with technology, human resources and any other aspect of your operations that may be affected.

9.7.8.1

The obligations imposed on data controllers in processing personal information under the 1998 Act are onerous. As this is a non-core competency you may wish to outsource it as a means of making the most of limited resources. You need to both select a data processor who can guarantee adequate security measures governing the processing, and take reasonable steps to ensure compliance with those measures. You will require a written contract stating that the data processor will act only on your instructions, and that security measures are required which are equivalent to those imposed on you by this principle.

9.7.9

The principle of trans-border data flow ensures no transfer of data to jurisdictions outside the European Economic Area ('the EEA') unless that country has adequate protective measures in place. As part of your notification requirements, you must inform the commissioner of any countries outside the EEA to which you, directly or indirectly, intend to transfer personal information. If you are already transferring personal information outside the EEA, say to the United States or Asia, then this might have to stop.

9.7.9.1

The eighth principle will not apply in the following circumstances:

■ The data subject has given his or her opt-in consent to the transfer.

- The transfer is necessary for one of the following reasons:
    - the performance of a contract between you and the data subject;
    - the preliminary steps with a view to entering into an agreement with the data subject at his or her request;
    - concluding an agreement between you and a third party at the data subject's request and in his or her interest; or to carry out that agreement; or for the performance of such an agreement;
    - for reasons of substantial public interest;
    - for a lawsuit or relating to a lawsuit;
    - for obtaining legal consent;
    - for defending yourself legally.
- The transfer is part of a public registry and the rules of that register are complied with by the receiver of the information.
- The transfer is made on terms which are of a kind approved by the information commissioner as being secure.
- The transfer has been authorized by the information commissioner as keeping safeguards for the rights and freedoms of the data subject.

9.8 RIGHTS OF DATA SUBJECTS

9.8.1
A data subject's rights can be divided into the following:

- rights of subject access;
- rights to prevent processing likely to cause damage or distress;
- rights to prevent processing for the purposes of direct marketing;
- rights in relation to automated decision making;
- rights to take action for compensation if the individual suffers damage by any contravention of the 1998 Act by you;
- rights to take action to rectify or block, erase or destroy inaccurate information;
- rights to make a request to the information commissioner for an assessment to be made as to whether any provision of the 1998 Act has been contravened.

9.8.2
An approach to rights for subject access is transparency. Much of the burden for ensuring enforcement of the data subject's rights lies with you as data controller. You are required to provide data subjects with a basic minimum amount of information about the collection, use and distribution of their personal information. Therefore the data subject needs to know

the purpose of the processing, and the measures that you have taken to ensure the processing is fair. Your processing operation needs to be transparent, without disclosing any more than is necessary. The more transparent your data processing operation, the less likely a data subject is to make a subject access request to elicit further information. A data subject may write to a data controller with the appropriate fee (set by the data controller to a maximum of £10), asking to be provided with the matters raised in points (1) to (5) below. Points (6) and (7) should also be considered in relation to subject access requests:

1. A description of personal information relating to the data subject which you are processing.
2. The purpose for which it is being processed.
3. Those to whom it has been or may be disclosed.
4. All the information, told in an intelligible manner, which forms any such personal information.
5. Any information as to the source of that information.

Other issues to consider in relation to subject access requests are:

6. Where a decision significantly affects data subjects or is likely to be made about them by fully automated means, for the purposes of evaluating matters about them such as their performance at work, their credit worthiness, their reliability or their conduct, they are entitled to be told of the logic involved in that process.
7. There is a qualification in respect of third parties. It is not permissible to disclose information relating to third parties as this would be a breach of confidence owed to that third party. You can only do so with their consent or where it is reasonable to do so without their consent. You may still comply with the request if you can disclose the information and still maintain the confidence of the third party. In deciding whether or not to disclose information relating to a third party as part of a subject access request, you should consider any professional duty of confidentiality you may have, whether or not the third party is able to give you consent or refuses consent.

9.8.2.1
You must respond to the data subject's request within 40 days of receiving the written request and appropriate fee.

9.8.3
The right to prevent processing likely to cause damage or distress. You may be served with a notice by the data subject asking you to stop or not to start processing personal data, where such processing is causing or is likely to cause unwarranted or substantial damage or substantial distress to that person or to a third party. You have 21 days to respond to the data subject

notice, by writing to the individual stating that you have complied or intend to comply with the data subject notice, or stating your reasons for regarding the data subject notice as to any extent unjustified, and the extent, if any, to which you have complied or intend to comply with it.

9.8.4
The right to prevent processing for purposes of direct marketing. You may be served with a notice to stop or not to start processing personal information relating to a data subject for the purposes of direct marketing. The data subject may apply to Court for an order to that effect if you do not comply with the notice.

9.8.5
Rights in relation to automated decision taking. You may be served with a notice by a data subject to ensure that a decision which significantly affects him or her is not based solely on the processing by automatic means of personal information. Where no notice has been effected and you are making a decision that significantly affects an individual solely by automatic processing, you must notify that individual that the decision was taken on that basis as soon as is reasonably practicable. There are two exceptions when the data subject cannot prevent such processing. The first is where the decision is taken for the purpose of considering whether to enter into an agreement with the data subject, with a view to entering into such an agreement, or in the course of performing such an agreement, if the decision is authorized or required by or under any law. The second is where the effect of the decision is to grant a request of the data subject or of steps that have been taken to safeguard the legitimate interests of the data subject (for example, by allowing them to make representations).

9.8.6
Rights to compensation. A data subject can sue you for damage or distress that he or she has suffered as a result of non-compliance with the 1998 Act.

9.8.7
Rectification, blocking, erasure and destruction. A data subject may apply to the Court for an order requiring you to rectify, block, erase or destroy such information relating to them as is inaccurate, as well as any other personal information which contains an expression of opinion which the Court finds is based on the inaccurate information. Information is inaccurate if it is incorrect or misleading as to any matter of fact.

9.9 EXEMPTIONS

9.9.1
There are exemptions, noted above, from the requirement to provide your subscribers with information under the fair processing code (see paragraph

9.7.2.5) and the rights for subject access (see paragraph 9.8.2). There are also exemptions from the main provisions of the 1998 Act that restrict disclosure of personal data, subject to satisfaction of certain conditions. Broadly, the 1998 Act does not apply to information processed for:

- The purposes of safeguarding national security.
- Purely recreational or domestic purposes.
- Prevention or detection of crime.
- The apprehension or prosecution of offenders.
- The purpose of assessing suitability for employment by the crown or ministerial appointments.
- The purposes of management forecasting or planning.
- In relation to an employer negotiating with an employee or potential employee, to the extent that an exercise of subject access rights would prejudice the employer during the negotiations.
- In connection with a corporate finance service provided by a relevant person, to the extent that an exercise of subject access rights could affect the price or value of particular instruments of a price-sensitive nature.
- A confidential reference given or to be given by an employer for specified purposes. Not available for such references where they are received by an employer, although an employer may not be obliged to disclose information that identifies a third party.
- As required by law.
- Under a 'special purposes exemption', see below.
- In connection with legal proceedings.

For the special conditions exemption to apply, the following conditions must all be present before processing of personal data for the special purposes can qualify for exemption. The personal information is processed only for the special purposes; the processing is undertaken with a view to the publication by any person of any journalistic, literary or artistic material; it is reasonably believed that publication would be in the public interest; and it is reasonably believed that compliance with the provision in respect of which the exemption is claimed is incompatible with the special purposes.

In the case of *Totalise plc* v. *Motley Fool Ltd and another* [2001], an Internet service provider (Totalise plc) brought a suit against Motley Fool and Interactive Investments for the removal of defamatory material from their Web sites and the disclosure of the identity of the offending party Z Dust. One of the defendants' argument for not disclosing the identity of Z Dust was that the exception to non-disclosure under section 35(2) of the 1998 Act only applied to the data controller. Accordingly the exception was not available to Totalise plc. Mr Justice Owen held that the exception was not limited to the data controller needing it for a matter he or she was directly involved with, and that the exception was available to third parties.

9.10 ENFORCEMENT

9.10.1

You may be issued and served with an enforcement notice by the Information Commissioner if he or she is satisfied that you are in breach of the 1998 Act. This is the Information Commissioner's right whether or not you have notified the register. The data subject can also request the Information Commissioner to assess the processing of personal data for compliance with the data protection principles. The Information Commissioner can also require you to supply information by issuing an information notice. Failure to comply with the terms of an information notice or supply of false information in response to an enforcement notice is a criminal offence. The Information Commissioner can obtain warrants to enter premises and to inspect and seize (Schedule 8). There are rights of appeal to the Data Protection Tribunal against enforcement notices and information notices.

9.10.2

The penalties for the offences are fines, whether on summary conviction or indictment. A director or other company officer can be personally liable for an offence committed by his or her company if the offence was committed with his or her consent or connivance or is attributable to that person's neglect.

9.11 COOKIES

9.11.1

A cookie is a program that records details of a data subject's visits on the World Wide Web on his or her hard drive. It is possible to access cookies from servers, read the information stored and analyse the information to build profiles of users. Developments in technology have meant that Web servers may now extend the lifespan of a cookie to several years. Data subjects' cookies are now accessible from a large number of other servers. Cookies are also useful for the data subject, as they act as the memory for the data subject's browser and enable a data subject to get to previously visited Web sites quickly. Being able to analyse and build personal profiles of your users through their cookie trail has obvious data protection implications. The current versions of most browsers, including Netscape and Internet Explorer, give users the option to be notified when a cookie is received and to reject all cookies. See Appendix 6 for the latest developments.

9.12 NOTIFICATION

9.12.1
In order to notify (see the obligations on Internet companies discussed above) (previously known as registering, under the Data Protection Act 1984) you have to notify the Information Commissioner of your name and address; the name and address of your representative (if any); a description of purposes; a description of recipients of data; any overseas transfers; any exempt data; and your security measures.

9.12.2
Renewals are required every 12 months and cost £35 to register, and existing registrations continue until they expire. The new and old procedures will run alongside each other over a three-year period. Conversion will take place when either the entry expires or the processing undergoes radical change.

9.12.3
Any manual data is exempt from notification. You need to make a statement that you hold exempt data. You have a duty to notify the Information Commissioner if your entry becomes inaccurate.

9.13 TRANSITIONAL PERIODS

9.13.1
Two transitional periods were outlined in the 1998 Act . The first transitional period started on 1 March 2000 when the Act came into force and ended on 23 October 2001. The second transitional period started on 24 October 2001 and ends on 23 October 2007.

9.13.2
The transitional period covers eligible data, manual data and automated data. 'Eligible data' means personal information subject to processing that was already underway immediately before 24 October 1998. If your processing was underway before that date you continue to benefit from the transitional provisions regardless of when your registered entry expires and whether or not you have notified under the Act. 'Manual data' which was being processed immediately before 24 October 1998 did not have to comply with the Data Protection Principles, notification, or the subject access requirements until 24 October 2001. This exemption applies to the whole processing system if the way information is processed has not changed since 23 October 1998. You may wish to carry out essential program and software changes to enable existing operations to continue

without risk of losing this exemption. Paper files held before 24 October 1998 are exempt from the first to the fifth data protection principles until 24 October 2007. 'Automated data': until 24 October 2001 information covered by the Act which is processed automatically will not be deemed to fall within the definition of processing unless the definition of processing is by reference to the individual (ie any reference to the individual is removed). They are therefore exempt from the Data Protection Principles, the notification requirements and the subject access requirements until 24 October 2001.

9.14 INTERNATIONAL DATA PROTECTION

9.14.1
As with all Internet legal issues, there is an international perspective going right through all the data protection issues. Several e-commerce businesses have their back-end systems in 'hotels' around the world such as Amsterdam and South Africa, even though their registered offices are in the UK. In this case I would say it is very difficult to know who is the data controller and who is the data processor. My view is that although a company in the UK may 'control' the information, it is the company that operates the servers and databases that is the 'processor'. In any event both the controller and the processor are regulated by the data protection principles.

9.14.2
Section 5 of the 1998 Act applies the data protection requirements to UK data controllers established in the UK, and also to data controllers established neither in the UK nor in any other EEA state, but who use equipment in the UK for processing information otherwise than for the purpose of transit through the UK. Such non-UK controllers must nominate a representative in the UK. The data protection rules which apply are those of the place of establishment of the data controller for whose purposes the processing is carried out. It is apparent, particularly for e-commerce businesses, that a data controller and processor may be established in several EC Member States at the same time. For example, a controller in the UK who is only processing in Amsterdam would need to comply with UK law. A controller in both the UK and Holland might have to comply with the data protection laws for each relevant country. However, a business that is not registered in Europe will not have to comply with European data protection legislation even if it has European subscribers.

9.15 SUMMARY

9.15.1

The 1998 Act is a very important piece of legislation because it tries to give individuals control over the use of their information. With increased globalization and ever increasing speeds of processing information, proponents of human rights are keen to protect the individual from abuses of these rights. However, the provisions of the 1998 Act still enable e-commerce directly and indirectly: directly by focusing on information and setting guidelines for efficient processing of that information, and indirectly by instilling confidence in the consumer with respect to the Internet environment.

Action checklist

The systems you need to put in place are as follows:

- Establish a data protection policy. You should allow for users to opt out of the processing of their personal data, and ensure that a data protection notice is incorporated with your terms and conditions, order forms, registration forms and so on.
- Include a privacy policy on your site, and ensure it is adhered to.
- Consider the British Standards Institution's Code of Practice for Information Security Management (BS7799). Information security is an important part of the Act. The BSI offers a number of different products and services to help you keep your information systems and electronic data secure. These include information security standards Part 1, ISO/IEC 17799, and Part 2, BS 7799, training courses and software. Part 1 contains over 100 security controls to help you identify elements of your business which impact on information security, while Part 2 is a standard for which your company can be measured and registered. BS7799 is a method of improving the efficiency of your information systems as it helps in identifying, managing and minimizing risks to which information is regularly exposed. You register by passing an assessment by a BSI auditor. To achieve this, you should establish a management framework as identified in BS7799. Ask the BSI for an estimate of costs and timescales for assessment before submitting an application form. The BSI auditor undertakes a desk-top review, conducts an on-site assessment and makes recommendations to your

organization. On successful completion of the audit the BSI
issues a certificate of registration. The certificate is valid for
three years.

10

Contract law and e-commerce

10.1 INTRODUCTION

10.1.1
You will want to sell goods or offer services through your Web site.
Although this chapter deals primarily with English law, it also addresses
the international scope of the Internet. It is sufficient for the purposes
of this book to mention the main points regarding contract law and
e-commerce, although the principles do need to be thought through
rather more carefully, and specialist advice taken in cases where circumstances require greater detail. The law in this area is concerned primarily
with matters of public policy: how to facilitate e-commerce while
protecting the public. For any regulatory regime to work on an international level the law in that area has to be harmonized, hence the European
Directives which are then implemented into Member States' law. (See
Directive 1993/13/EC on unfair terms in consumer contracts.) Leading from
the issue of harmonization is jurisdiction. The question is, as the Internet is
global by nature, which is the applicable law or court in the event of a
dispute? Once the laws are in place there also has to be an appropriate
procedure for effecting these laws.

10.2 GEOGRAPHY AND THE INTERNET

10.2.1

Back in the early 1990s the Internet was just emerging as a platform for elec-tronic business. At that time the medium was seen as a channel for freedom of information and expression. Since then the Internet has been brought within the ambit of government regulation and laws. Technologies have been developed to facilitate the commercial use of the Internet and to bring the medium under the auspices of both local and international law. This has happened through the speeding up of the delivery of content, protection of networks from intruders and applications for the targeting of advertising, depending on the user's country of origin.

10.2.2

Firewalls and filtering technology have been instrumental in bringing borders to the Internet. In China, the Chinese government has been able to limit political discourses online. Chinese citizens are encouraged to use the Internet, but access to overseas sites is strictly controlled and monitored. In other words, China has been able to effectively control accessibility to the Internet within its borders. Singapore and Saudi Arabia also filter and censor Internet content, and South Korea has banned access to gambling Web sites. In Iran, it is illegal for children to use the Internet, and access providers are required to prevent access to immoral or anti-Iranian material. In these countries, local standards apply, even on the Internet. In parts of the world where access to the Internet is not tightly controlled, local rules also apply. The Internet consists of information sitting inside computers which are located in the real world, and legal action can be taken. It is a reality, and is being taken, against Internet access providers and publishers, using existing laws, in existing courts. Libel and defamation laws have been applied to publications on the Internet in several countries (see *Laurence Godfrey* v. *Demon Internet*), and other laws are being applied across borders too. A particularly good example concerns Yahoo! (see also section 10.11), an Internet portal which includes an auction site, and which fell foul of French law banning the sale of Nazi memorabilia. A French judge ordered Yahoo! to find a way to ban French users from purchasing such items posted on any of its sites, including sites based in the United States, using 'geolocation'[1] technology. This technology can work out where individual Internet users are. Although it is not perfect, it can identify a user's country of origin within a 30 per cent margin of error.

10.2.2.1

There are bound to be more cases of this nature where the courts will require 'geolocation' technology to be used by Internet companies to comply with the judgement. Yahoo! appealed against the French decision on the basis that such a decision would set a precedent requiring that Web site owners to filter their content to avoid breaking country-specific laws. It also argued that the decision would curtail free speech, since a page posted online in one country might break the laws of another. Enforcing a judgment against the original publisher is now possible at least within the EU under the Brussels Convention, and the Hague Convention (see below) hopes to extend this internationally.

10.2.2.2
However, the Internet is not quite the physical world yet. Filtering and relocation are not unbeatable. Filters and firewalls can be defeated by dialling out to overseas Internet access providers. E-mail can be encrypted. Most Internet users are not able to carry out these measures, so at least for the majority of us, long live the regulated Internet.

10.3 THE PROS AND CONS OF A HARMONIZED REGULATED INTERNET

10.3.1
There is only a subjective answer to this. My view is that the imposition of local laws and a harmonization of laws worldwide (see below) is vital to build consumer confidence in the Internet, especially in the area of consumer protection. It should be possible to agree on common rules since there is already a degree of interdependency between countries for the effective functioning of immigration and taxation laws.

10.4 HARMONIZATION AND ORGANIZATIONS

10.4.1
There are many organizations which assist in the harmonization of trade and commerce by writing or discussing rules and procedures. These bodies are referred to throughout this book. They are not, however, the only international bodies set up to consider global issues. The Internet operates regardless of geographical distances, and as a result it is receiving particular interest from organizations which include those mentioned below.

10.4.2
The United States Commission on International Trade Law (UNCITRAL), based in Vienna (see section 10.7), has put forward a model law on e-commerce.

10.4.3

The Hague Conference on Private International Law is an intergovernmental organization which claims its purpose is 'to work for the progressive unification of rules of private international law'. It is currently working on a new convention on jurisdiction and foreign judgements in civil and commercial matters.

10.4.4

The Council of Europe, headquartered in Strasbourg, France, currently has 43 European Member States. Established in 1949, its primary goal has been to promote the unity of the continent through a wide range of initiatives, including many conventions designed to bring national legal practices into line with one another. Its current initiative is the final draft convention on cybercrime which was to be submitted to the Committee of Ministers for adoption in September 2001.

10.4.5

Other organizations that contribute to international policy making on an economic and political level include the Organization of Economic Cooperation and Development (OECD), the UN, the World Trade Organization (WTO) responsible for the TRIPS Agreement 1988, the World Intellectual Property Organization (WIPO) and the International Telecommunications Union (ITU).

10.5 HARMONIZATION OF CONTRACTUAL LAWS

10.5.1

A good example of how the European Commission is trying to harmonize contractual laws among Member States is the (UK) Unfair Terms in Consumer Regulations 1999, implementing EC Directive 19/13 which came into force on 1 October 1999. The regulations apply to unfair terms in contracts between a seller or a supplier and consumer. Regulation 5 states that a contractual term that has not been individually negotiated is regarded as unfair if it causes a significant imbalance in the rights and obligations under the contract to the detriment of the consumer. A term shall always be regarded as unfair where it has been drafted in advance and the consumer has therefore not been able to influence the substance of the term. The burden of showing that the contract was individually negotiated is on the seller or supplier. Schedule 2 to the regulations contains an indicative and non-exhaustive list of the terms which may be regarded as unfair. Regulation 5 states that the seller or supplier shall ensure that any written term of a contract is expressed in plain, intelligible language. If there is any ambiguity about the interpretation of a written term, an interpretation favourable to the consumer shall rule. This presumption does not apply in the case of injunctions to prevent continued use of unfair terms. You cannot contract out of these regulations through a choice of law clause.

10.6 ELECTRONIC CONTRACTS, DIGITAL SIGNATURES AND CERTIFICATES, SECURITY AND PUBLIC KEY INFRASTRUCTURE

10.6.1
There are specific legal form requirements for contracts. Generally contracts have to be in writing. Currently, in jurisdictions round the world electronic and digital signatures are gradually gaining the same legal weight as manuscript signatures.

10.6.2
In France,[2] a statutory instrument relating to the application of article 1316–4 of the French Civil Code on electronic signatures was published on 31 March 2001. This text creates the framework to guarantee the reliability of electronic signatures defined by the statute. According to Article 2, an electronic signature is deemed reliable until contrary evidence is presented when, first, the signature is secured. This means, among other things, that it must only be attributable to the signatory and be created by means under the sole control of the signatory. Second, the signature must be created through specific secured means, and the software generating the signature must obey Article 3.1 of the statutory instrument. It must ensure that the electronic signature can only be created once, that its confidentiality is preserved, that it cannot be found by deduction or be forged, and that it can be protected from third party use. Third, the signature must be verified through the use of a qualified electronic certificate. A qualified electronic certificate is delivered by a certified provider, and includes the identity of the provider, the state in which the provider is established, and the name of the signatory.

10.6.3
In Brazil,[3] on 29 June 2001 on enactment of provisional Executive Act 2,200 (MP 2200/01), re-enacted on 29 June 2001 (MP 2200/01), electronic documents gained legal validity. Through the Act the government instituted the Brazilian Public Key Infrastructure (ICP) in order to: one, guarantee the authenticity, integrity and legal validity of electronic documents, supporting applications and authorized applications that use digital certificates; and two, ensure the security of electronic transactions. The ICP will comprise a management committee (for which regulation is in

process), a structure of certification authorities formed by the National Information Technology Institute of the Science and Technology Ministry, appointed to perform the activities of the Root Certification Authority, and certification and registration authorities. The latter are licensed by the management committee and may be public agencies and entities or private legal entities.

10.6.4

In the UK the Electronic Communications Act 2000 (enacted 25 May 2000) ('the ECA'), supports e-commerce by making electronic signatures legal and providing for licensed cryptography services. The ECA did not implement all of the provisions of the 1999/93/EC directive as the problems of data protection and the liability of trusted service providers could not be resolved. The DTI Security Policy Unit anticipated that a statutory instrument would be implemented by August 2001, finally bringing in all of the provisions of the directive. The directive seeks to set a community-wide framework for digital signatures and related 'certificates'. It distinguishes between a 'certificate' and a 'qualified certificate', which meets certain requirements and is provided by a 'certification service provider' (a 'trusted service provider' under the Act). There is no mandatory requirement for a 'certificate' to be 'qualified'.

10.6.4.1

Section 8 permits ministers to make changes to other laws requiring signatures to be in a particular form on a piecemeal basis. The Consumer Credit Act 1974 requires contracts to be handwritten and will need to be amended. An example of secondary legislation implementing section 8 is the Companies Act 1985 (Electronic Communications) Order 2000 (see below). However, there is no rebuttable presumption of legal recognition for electronic signatures. It will be for the courts to decide in a particular case whether an electronic signature has been correctly used, so watch this space. The courts will also determine what weight should be given to any signature, for example in relation to the authenticity or integrity of a message, against other evidence. Certificates will be admissible in evidence.

10.6.4.2

The Companies Act 1985 (Electronic Communications) Order 2000 came into force on 22 December 2000. With the approval of your individual shareholders you can now distribute annual reports, accounts and other information on your Web site or by e-mail, and allow shareholders to appoint and give proxies voting instructions by e-mail. In addition you will soon be able to incorporate a company electronically.

10.6.5

The Secretary of State will establish and maintain a register of approved providers of cryptography support services. The Act also specifies the information that is to be contained in the register, how the public will gain access to the register and how any changes in the register will be published. It sets out the conditions that the Secretary of State must be satisfied with before granting approval. It also provides for handling complaints and disputes and modifying or withdrawing approval. The Office of Telecommunications (Oftel) has been delegated responsibility for such matters. Service providers for public key infrastructures do not have to be trusted service providers and many have already been set up where this is not the case.

10.6.6

A typical system for a public key infrastructure is an asymmetric cryptosystem. This cryptographic system uses a 'public key' to authenticate documents you sign. The public key 'decrypts' the digital signature created by your 'private key' and verifies the authenticity of the documents created with it. Your private key is embedded in your PC or lodged on a smart card, and identifies a message as coming from you. These public and private keys are software developed by various encryption companies. Cryptography acts as a support to e-commerce as it means that transactions can be carried out more quickly, without the need for lengthy processes to verify the authenticity of a message or document.

10.6.6.1

See Figure 10.1 for a diagram of the contractual relationship. Certificate authorities will provide an important support for your e-commerce business. In order to obtain the digital signature you must first sign up with a certificate authority and apply for the digital identity certificate that makes your signature unique. Most certificate authorities also provide the software and guide users through the process of using a digital signature. From a contractual point of view you will probably deal directly with the certificate authority if you are an individual or a single business. They will give you a form to complete and you will provide proof of identity before you are issued with a private key. The software will integrate seamlessly into most e-mail. You attach a digital signature to an ongoing e-mail message in much the same way as you would attach a file. A digitally signed e-mail message addressed to you will appear in your in-box marked with a red and yellow rosette icon, on which you double click to view and check the sender's signature. If you are using a digital signature for the first time, you will be prompted to install a public key from the sender's certificate authority, a simple software download. Your computer will automatically store the signature details and tell you whether it is authentic. Once two parties have exchanged a digitally signed message, they create a confidential channel via which they can correspond in complete privacy. Businesses can make bulk applications for staff. Certificate authorities include British Telecom (Trustwise) and consultants PricewaterhouseCoopers (be TRUSTed) in the UK. In France there is La

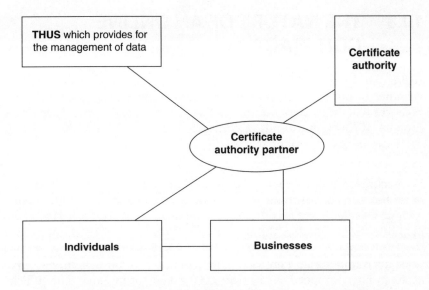

Figure 10.1 *Contractual relationships in the public key infrastructure*

Poste (Certinomis), in Germany there is Commerzbank, Deutsch Bank, and in Spain ACE (Agencia de Certficacion Electronica). Where an infrastructure is being set up for, say, several banks, as there are large volumes of data you may get a separate company managing the data, for example THUS. In this scenario the businesses do not contract with the certificate authority but with a partner of the certificate authority.

10.7 UNCITRAL MODEL LAW 1996

10.7.1
The UNCITRAL Model Law 1996 on E-commerce was adopted in 1998 by the international community including the United States, Singapore, Bermuda, Australia and Russia. The code is available in Arabic, Chinese, English, French, Russian and Spanish. It sets out to progress the harmonization and unification of the law in international trade. It does not override any rule of law intended for the protection of consumers such as the Unfair Contract Terms Act 1977. The code applies to commercial contracts carried out on the Internet, including but not limited to a contract for the sale or purchase of goods and services. It recognizes contracts carried out on the Internet as valid, that an offer and acceptance of that offer can be made over the Internet. It recognizes electronic data as being in writing for the purposes of national laws and accepts electronic signatures for authentication and authorization purposes.

10.8 THE NATURE OF AN ONLINE CONTRACT

10.8.1

Whether or not you have entered into a binding contract through your Web site will firstly depend on whether the content on your Web site is capable of forming a binding contract. To form a valid contract, it is necessary to have a proper agreement.

10.8.1.1

To reach agreement there is always an offer and acceptance. The offer must be clear, and intended to create a contract if accepted. Merely inviting an offer is not an offer. For example, in *Harvey* v. *Facey* [1893], the plaintiffs telegraphed to the defendants, 'Will you sell us Bumper Hall Pen? Telegraph lowest cash price'. The defendants replied, 'Lowest cash price for Bumper Hall Pen £900'. The defendants then telegraphed, 'We agree to buy Bumper Hall Pen for £900 asked for by you'. The judicial committee of the Privy Council held that the defendants' telegram was not an offer but merely a statement as to price; the plaintiff's second telegram was in fact an offer to buy, but as this had not been accepted by the defendants, there was no contract. A general offer, then, can be accepted by anyone, but a particular one can only be accepted by the particular person to whom it is made. The acceptance must be unqualified, or else it is not valid and may be interpreted as a counter-offer (which rejects the initial one). Of course the counter-offer may itself be accepted, in which case the parties proceed on the basis of those new terms. If the essentials have been decided (subject matter, price and so on) a contract is still valid even if not all the terms are agreed, so long as the terms remaining to be decided can be reasonably ascertained. If you wish to make an offer on your Web site then this needs to be made clear by your content. Clear unambiguous wording is needed to give effect to your intentions.

10.8.1.2

You may wish to expressly exclude any intention to create legal relations on your Web site. Recently the major retailer Argos made a serious slip-up when it advertised a television set on its Web site at £3, instead of the actual price of £300. Under English law Argos was merely inviting an offer at £3 and did not have to sell the TV for £3. However, if Argos accepted the customer's order, which formed the actual offer, at £3, then this could have been construed as a valid contract. The customer gave Argos his credit card number and received a unique order code that was proof of a contract. Although Argos said all items were 'subject to availability', on the facts the courts could have upheld that there was a contract. However, the courts can also declare a contract void if the seller has made a genuine mistake. Further, Part III of the Consumer Protection Act makes it a criminal offence to give consumers a misleading price indication. Shopkeepers can be fined up to £5,000 in the magistrates court each time a consumer is misled. Although a shopkeeper could claim he or she acted diligently and took all reasonable steps to avoid giving the consumer a misleading indication, a company must show it has reliable systems in place designed to prevent this sort of thing happening. The displaying of prices on the Internet makes no difference. Accordingly, you will need an express term on your Web site excluding any intention to create legal relations as well as diligently ensuring that all pricing is accurate. You should also remember that the intention to create legal relations can be inferred by the circumstance, despite a later denial by you, as in the case *Carlil* v. *Carbolic Smoke Ball Co* [1893].

10.8.2
The Electronic Commerce Directive June 2000 and the Consumer Protection (Distance Selling) Regulations 2000 were put in place to encourage consumer confidence in e-commerce. Transparency forms the cornerstone of this encouragement.

10.9   THE ELECTRONIC COMMERCE DIRECTIVE JUNE 2000 ('THE ECD')

10.9.1
The ECD is relevant to business to consumer and business to business Web sites. As with the Consumer Protection (Distance Selling) Regulations 2000 which are discussed in paragraph 10.15, the ECD seeks to support e-commerce by providing for transparency on the Internet. It does this by requiring business to consumer and business to business Web sites to comply with a number of information requirements and quality of service in terms of their form and the formalities of the way they do business. The directive was adopted in June 2000 and only applies to service providers within the EU. It is to be implemented in UK law early in 2002. The information requirements are as follows.

10.9.1.1
Identity: you must make available to users and authorities details, including your activities, name, address, e-mail address, company number, professional authorization number, membership of professional bodies (where applicable), and VAT number. Your Web site's places of business are your registered office and the premises from which you carry on business.

10.9.1.2
Terms and conditions: according to the ECD, if you are a service provider your liability for intermediary activities in respect of site users using your

chat rooms or e-mail facilities for illegal activities is either excluded or limited so long as you are in no way involved with the information transmitted, do not knowingly aid the site user to carry out an illegal act, and act quickly to disable or remove access to the illegal act, once it is notified or you become aware of its existence. The directive suggests that a code of conduct should be set up by service providers to deal with intermediary activities, and there have been several cases related to this subject matter. In *Laurence Godfrey* v. *Demon Internet*, [2000], Demon, the UK Internet service provider, settled out of court a libel suit by a UK scientist who sued them for failing to remove allegedly defamatory statements from a newsgroup they hosted. In the High Court, Mr Justice Moreland threw out Demon's defence of innocent distribution, and Demon failed to appeal. It was significant that Demon failed to respond to Laurence Godfrey's complaint, even after they were aware of it. It is my view that if they had responded sooner and were seen to be actively preventing their facilities from being used for illegal acts, they would not have been found liable. In the case of *Totalise plc* v. *Motley Fool Ltd and another* [2001], Mr Justice Owen ordered the defendants Motley Fool and Interactive Investor Ltd to disclose the identity of an anonymous contributor who had made defamatory postings on a discussion board. The claimant, Totalise, is an Internet service provider. The two defendants, Motley Fool and Interactive Investments, operate Web sites offering discussion boards on which members of the public can post material. One anonymous contributor, Z Dust, made numerous indisputably defamatory comments about Totalise. Although both Motley Fool and Interactive Investments removed the defamatory material and revoked Z Dust's right of access, they refused to disclose Z Dust's identity, citing their terms and conditions and the Data Protection Act 1998. The defendants agreed that there is jurisdiction to disclose Z Dust's identity under the principles confirmed by the House of Lords in *Norwich Pharmaceutical Co* v. *Customs and Excise Commissioners* [1974], but argued that the judge had discretion to grant the relief only where the claimant intended to take legal proceedings against the wrongdoer. They relied on the judgement in *Handmade Films* v. *Express Newspapers* [1986], which interprets section 10 of the Contempt of Court Act 1981 (CCA). Mr Justice Owen accepted Totalise's arguments that the House of Lords decision in *X Ltd* v. *Morgan Grampian* [1991] superseded the Handmade Films decision. In that case it was held that:

> to confine justice in section 10 of the Act of 1981 to the technical sense of administration of justice in the course of legal proceedings was too narrow. It is in the interests of justice, in the sense in which the phrase is used in section 10, that persons should be enabled to exercise important legal rights and to protect themselves from

serious legal wrongs, whether or not resort to legal proceedings, in a court of law would be necessary to attain these objectives.

Both these cases are in the spirit of the ECD which will become law in the UK early in 2002. It appears that not only should an intermediary take steps to ensure that its service is not being used as a platform for wrongful acts, it may also be required to take steps to assist those who are wronged. I would suggest that you set up a code of conduct to deal with intermediary activity that at least complies with the ECD.

10.9.1.3
Procedural arrangements: as mentioned above, you should think about how the contract is formed and the opportunities to correct a mistaken purchase. There is the issue of the timing of the contract. Should it be formed before acceptance, or during the performance of an obligation? What form should the contract take? The ECD states that it has to be in a 'durable medium', 'easily accessible' and in a 'permanent manner'. The consumer should be given some information on storing and reproducing terms and conditions. Your contract must be presented in a certain form, and there must be some sort of back-up.

10.9.1.4
Unsolicited communications: Article 7 permits unsolicited e-mail, but such e-mail shall be identifiable clearly and unambiguously as soon as it is received by the recipient. There is as yet no method of identification in the UK. In California, Tennessee and Nevada, 'spam' is identified with 'ADV' as an e-mail subject prefix.

10.9.2
The government's consultative document on the e-commerce directive covered the local laws that will apply in cross-border transactions, transparency issues including information provided to consumers, liability for intermediate activity, and unsolicited e-mails. The directive was to be implemented in the UK by 16 January 2002. You can view the consultative document at www.dti.gov.uk/cii/ecommerce/europeanpolicy/ecommerce_directive.shtml.

10.10 THE LAW APPLICABLE TO INTERNET CONTRACTS

10.10.1
Consumer protection law continues to be disharmonious. Article 46 of the Treaty of Rome gives the freedom to provide services in Europe: a resident of one European member state can supply cross-border goods or services.

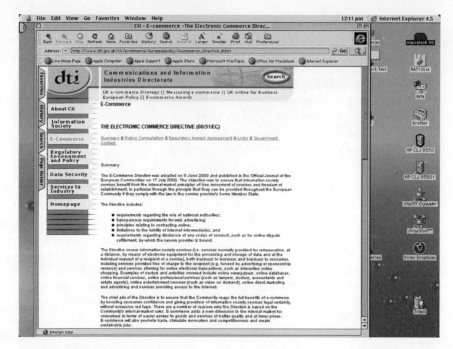

Figure 10.2   *Consultation on the EC E-commerce Directive on the DTI Web site*

The problem is that different countries have different ways of dealing with commercial and other issues. Leading on from this is the issue of jurisdiction.

10.10.2
Since 1999, Internet lawyers have been seething about proposals by the Brussels eurocrats that could give consumers the right to sue companies from other European countries offering services in their own courts, using their own laws. There have been consultations on jurisdiction over contracts completed over the Internet. The enforcement of judgements in foreign jurisdiction is still determined by the Brussels Convention 1968. The provisions differ whether contracts are business to consumer transactions or business to business. In broad terms, you are a business if you are acting as part of your normal trade or business, and you are a consumer if you are not.

10.10.3
Business to business: except where a contract contains a contrary jurisdiction clause or where a party is sued in the courts where the obligation is to be performed, the seller can only sue the other party in the courts of the country in which the other party is domiciled.

10.10.4
Business to consumer: the current situation is as follows:

- The consumer can choose to sue the seller either in his or her domicile or in the seller's domicile.
- The seller can only sue the consumer in his or her domicile.
- The seller cannot contract out of jurisdiction as it can in a business to business contract.

10.10.5
The seminal source of law governing the contractual choice of law within the EU is the Rome Convention on the Law Applicable to Contractual Obligations of 1980. All contracts should have a choice of law clause. The main points are as follows.

10.10.5.1
If there is a choice of law clause, in business to business transactions the entity suing is free to choose the contractual applicable law, except that where all the relevant factors are linked to another country, then the mandatory national rules of that country will apply. Mandatory rules include laws such as the Unfair Contract Terms Act 1977 (a UK law to stop the contracting out of obligations such as liability for death and personal injury caused by negligence). This is only rarely likely to apply to e-commerce since Internet transactions will involve more than one country and relevant factors will not connect to any one country.

10.10.5.2
If there is a choice of law clause, then in a business to consumer transaction the seller cannot deprive the consumer of the mandatory rules given to him or her by his/her country of habitual residence through use of that clause.

10.10.5.3
If there is no choice of law clause, then in a business to consumer transaction the applicable law is that of the consumer's habitual residence, and for business to business transactions it is the law of the country with which the contract is most closely associated. There is a presumption that the contract is most closely associated with the place where the obligation is performed for which the payment is due.

10.10.6
The Hague Conference on Private International Law is an intergovernmental organization, the purpose of which is 'to work for the progressive unification of rules of private international law'. It met from 6–22 June 2001 in The Hague to carry out negotiations towards a new convention on jurisdiction and foreign judgments in civil and commercial matters. This meeting proved inconclusive and a further meeting is scheduled for early 2002.

10.11 JURISDICTION OUTSIDE THE EEA

10.11.1
A good example of the implications of extraterritorial jurisdiction issues in
the context of Internet activities is the recent case concerning the well-
known Internet company Yahoo!.[4] In April 2000 the Ligue Internationale
Contre le Racisme et I'Antisemitisme (LICRA) and L'Union des Etudiants
Juifs de France (UEJF), organizations established in France, requested that
Yahoo!, a corporation incorporated under Delaware laws with its principal
place of business in California, adhere to French law and cease presenting
Nazi objects for sale on its US-based Web site. Le Nouveau Code Penal
(645–2) prohibits the public display of Nazi-related uniforms, insignia or
emblems in France. When Yahoo! did not comply, the defendants filed
civil complaints against Yahoo! and used the US Marshals Office to serve
them on Yahoo! in California. A French court then ordered Yahoo! to
reconfigure its Web site to stop users in France from bidding on Nazi
memorabilia, and imposed a daily fine for non-compliance. The court had
effectively entered a global injunction against Yahoo!. Yahoo! countered
by filing for the injunction to be set aside in the Northern District of
California, giving as reasons that: its French subsidiary did not permit Nazi
memorabilia auctions; that it was technically infeasible to distinguish the
geographic location of visitors; and the decision violated its First
Amendment right to free expression. The French defendants argued that
personal jurisdiction did not exist over them in the United States. On 7
June 2001, the US District Court for the Northern District of California
ruled in favour of Yahoo!, therefore exercising jurisdiction over the two
French defendants. In summary Justice Jeremy Fogel stated that it was
necessary to weigh France's interests against concerns of the United States
and California. The fundamental right to free expression had to be
accorded to its citizens. Clearly it is not obvious what happens when there
are conflicts of laws and regulations in different jurisdictions, and whether
a judgment in one jurisdiction will stand in another one.

10.12 OTHER LAWS

10.12.1
The EU draft explanatory memo on interactive against passive Web sites
states that passive Web sites do not constitute direct services. The issue of
guidelines on vertical restraints (OJ C291, 13/10/2000) considered passive
sales.

10.13 GOVERNMENT REGIME

10.13.1
OECD Ministers stated in 1998 that the principle for indirect sales tax should be that of the country of consumption. This rule changed because of the equitable regime. In June 2000 the draft regulation 'on certain services by electronic means' was met with controversy. The tax status and location of the recipient determines the application of VAT. This is difficult to apply since VAT registration numbers are not yet in place in many member states. There is not enough guidance to the identification status of customers and suppliers. The suggestions are online verification by VAT registration number, and verifiable indicators as proxy for place of consumption, for example a credit card billing address.

10.14 HOW A CONSUMER BRINGS A CLAIM AGAINST A SUPPLIER

10.14.1
The biggest problem for the consumer is cost. The average cost of cross-border litigation is about £2,000. However, EC Member States have independent bodies with power to obtain injunctions on behalf of consumers (see the Distance Selling Regulations Article 11 on the right of action, eg consumer association, and the Injunctions Directive (1998/27/EC), ECD, Article 17 on out-of-court dispute settlement). There is a parliamentary proposal for a Commission-accredited 'extrajudicial dispute resolution system'. Finally, labelling schemes may be set up to grade certain companies, for example Web trader trusted shops, to give consumers assurance that transactions are going to be carried out properly.

10.15 THE CONSUMER PROTECTION (DISTANCE SELLING) REGULATIONS 2000 ('THE CPDSR')

10.15.1
These UK regulations are relevant only to business to consumer transactions. The problem with distance selling is that the seller and buyer are in different environments. A distance contract is a contract for goods or services between a supplier and consumer under an organized distance sales or service provision scheme through the exclusive use of distance communication. The CPDSR's origins are in the Distance Selling Directive

(1997/7/EC). They try to encourage e-commerce through transparency. If you are carrying on regular business to consumer transactions through your Web site then you need to account for these regulations.

10.15.2
Certain 'excepted contracts' – real property sales, financial services, vending machines, payphones and auctions – do not fall within the regulations. Timeshare agreements, package holidays, goods for everyday consumption delivered by 'roundsmen' and contracts for accommodation, transport, catering or leisure services to be provided at a specific time are partially exempted.

10.15.3
The obligations imposed by the CPDSR can be divided into prior information, additional information and right to cancel. Generally suppliers cannot contract out of these rules.

10.15.4
The 'prior information' obligations comprise the following:

■ There has to be a clear description of the goods or services.
■ The seller's identity has to be clear: he, she or it must indicate a name and postal address.
■ The seller must clearly indicate all prices including taxes, and the duration of the price or offer.
■ The seller must make any extra costs such as delivery costs clear.
■ The method of payment for the goods or services must be clear. Offline the consumer is generally liable for the first £50 on a credit card payment in the event of fraud. In the event of online fraud the consumer is not liable for any of the credit card payment.
■ There must be a confirmation immediately following the purchase.
■ Delivery arrangements must be clearly stated. The seller must perform its side of the bargain within 30 days.

In addition:

■ The right of the consumer to cancel must be clear.
■ The costs of communication must be clear.
■ The duration of the offer period must be stated.
■ The minimum period of the contract's duration must be stated.
■ Any substitute goods must be made clear.

And the following written and additional information must be provided by the seller:

- How to cancel the contract and the cost of returning goods.
- A complaints procedure.
- After-sales and guarantee policies must be clearly stated.

10.15.5
As has been stated, the seller must set out clearly the formalities for cancelling a contract. The effect is that the contract never happened; and the rules set out in regulation 8 formalizing the user-turned-consumer's right to cancel for goods are slightly different from those for services (see exceptions below). In respect of goods, the consumer has a minimum cooling-off period of seven clear working days, excluding the day of delivery, to cancel the order. If the order is delayed, then the consumer has a period of seven clear working days, excluding the day of delivery, from whenever the goods are delivered. If there is a default in the delivery then the consumer has three clear months, excluding the day of delivery, and an additional seven working days, to cancel the order. If the supplier manages to deliver the goods within that three months then cancellation reverts back to a period of seven clear working days. However, there is a duty on the consumer to take care of returned goods. In respect of services, the rules are identical except for the first exception.

10.15.6
The exceptions to the cancellation provisions are as follows:

- If you are providing services, once you begin performance, the customer's rights to cancellation end.
- If goods and services are dependent on financial fluctuations, the consumer has no right of cancellation.
- There is no right of cancellation after the consumer opens a music or film recording or computer game (this applies to CDs and videos).
- Newspaper periodicals and magazines are excepted.
- Gaming, betting and lotteries are excepted.

There are criminal sanctions for inertia selling. However, generally you as supplier will not face criminal charges for failing to comply with these rules. Nevertheless not complying could be very costly as you will lose certain rights for failing to comply. In addition there are new powers for local Trading Standards Departments and the Office of Fair Trading, who have the right to obtain injunctions against Web sites that do not comply with the regulations.

10.15.7
Generally there is harmonization of laws across Europe in respect of distance selling regulations. There are some variations in some countries, however, and the following are some examples. In Germany the cooling

off period is 14 days. Failure to tell users of cancellation rights extends the cooling off period by four months. If goods are returned, the supplier may deduct 'rental' in relation to the period for which the customer had possession of the goods. If your Web site is accessible in Germany then German law will apply. In Sweden if you fail to inform a customer of cancellation rights the cooling off period is extended by a year. In France, refunds must be paid to the consumer within 15 days rather than 30.

10.16 SUMMARY

10.16.1
We have seen the hyped-up upside, and now we are witnessing the hyped-up downside of Internet business. E-commerce may be going through a virtual standstill; however, the Internet has not only been about just dot.coms. Business to Business (B2B) and Mobile to Commerce (M2C) are still attracting investment capital. In respect of e-business, companies can use the Internet to reduce costs, improve their services to the customers and increase distribution. So if you are using the Internet as part of your business plan to achieve growth, then you will need some understanding of the contractual principles that underlie e-commerce. Understanding the issues I have discussed in this chapter is a good place to start. It is clearly difficult to comply with all the above regulations. The idea is to minimize or manage the risks.

Action checklist
- Always remember that the Internet is not borderless or unregulated and that there may be legal issues involved before you launch a project.
- Make sure you identify whether the customer is a consumer or a business.
- Make sure you comply with the data protection principles.
- Check your Web site design to make sure that you are not implying anything you do not wish to imply.
- Check the content of your Web site and make sure there is no ambiguity in the information you provide to your users.
- Make sure your terms and conditions cover contractual issues including the international perspective. If you are concerned about something, include it in your terms and conditions.
- Identify and monitor your sales carefully.
- Make sure you are insured.
- Be as transparent as you can with information about your company on your Web site.

NOTES

1 Double Click Inc, a New York Internet advertising company, also created software that geographically directs banner advertisements on Web sites.

2 *Electronic Business Law,* May 2001, vol 3 no 4.

3 International Law Office *Legal Newsletter* [Online] www.international lawoffice.com

4 As reported in the International Law Office *Legal Newsletter* [Online] www.internationallawoffice.com

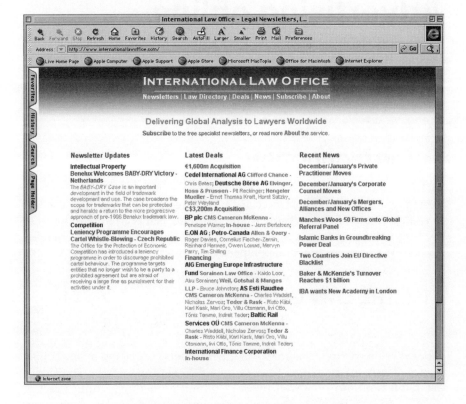

Figure 10.3   *International Law Office Web site*

11

Advertising online

11.1 INTRODUCTION

11.1.1
You may want to carry commercial advertising on your Web site. The fact is you cannot avoid advertising in the Internet, as it is an inherent part of the Internet. First I set out the law relating to online advertising generally, then I set out a more practical perspective.

11.2 THE LAW GENERALLY

11.2.1
Advertising and sales promotion (giving temporary gifts to make goods more attractive to the consumer) on the Internet is regulated by the British Codes of Advertising and Sales Promotion 1999 ('the Codes'). The Codes are published and reviewed by the Committee of Advertising Practice (CAP). CAP was set up by the advertising industry to regulate itself. Later the Advertising Standards Authority was set up as an independent self-regulatory body to administer the Codes.

11.3 SELF-REGULATION

11.3.1
Essentially the principles of the Codes are that advertising and sales promotion must:

- be decent, honest and truthful;
- be prepared with a sense of responsibility to the consumer and society in general;
- be in line with the principles of fair competition generally accepted in business; and
- not bring advertising into disrepute.

11.3.2
If an individual has a complaint he or she will contact the authority. If there is a case to answer it goes to adjudication, and the advertisement could be amended or removed. In addition the Internet is also self-regulated by the Internet Watch Foundation. This organization was launched in September 1996 to address the problem of illegal material on the Internet.

11.4 OTHER LAWS

11.4.1
You must not give false descriptions of the goods and services that you provide as part of your trade. To do so could be very costly under several different laws, all essentially addressing false descriptions of goods and services in advertisements. These laws were made before the commercial existence of the Internet, and it is arguable that they do not apply to the Internet medium; however, the Directive on Misleading Advertising as amended by the Directive on Comparative Advertising 1997 finally addressed advertisements on the Internet. First is the Trade Descriptions Act 1968 ('the 1968 Act'). There are several defences to the 1968 Act. The most popular is the innocent publication defence, which is available to you if you can prove that your business is to publish or arrange for the publication of advertisements. A service provider could realistically put in such a defence since it provides message boards and e-mail services, which are used for advertisements. The second piece of legislation is the Control of Misleading Advertisements Regulations 1988. This law means you could have the Office of Fair Trading after you as well if your advertisements are false. Thirdly, Part III of the Consumer Protection Act 1987 makes it very costly for you to give a consumer a false price indication about goods or services, accommodation or facilities.

11.5 INTERNET-RELATED LAW

11.5.1
The EC Directive on Misleading Advertising, 1984/450/EEC, as amended by the Comparative Advertising Directive, 1997/55/EC, includes in its scope

false adverts and comparative advertising on the Internet. At the time of writing it had not been implemented in UK law. Comparative advertising or 'knocking copy' is advertising which explicitly or by implication identifies a competitor, or the goods or services of a competitor. The Directive makes illegal any advertising which misleads, or is likely to mislead, its audience, and which is likely to harm competitors as a result of its misleading nature. Basically if your advertisements show false or deceptive words or pictures, regardless of whether its effect deceives or misleads, then they could be very costly for you. The Directive also covers advertising disguised as information, especially where it is directed at children.

11.6 ADVERTISING IN PRACTICE

11.6.1
An advertisement may unwittingly give rise to a contract. Where an offer is made by one party and it is unequivocally accepted by the other party (subject to some other elements being present), this could give rise to a binding contract. You need to ensure that adverts are invitations to treat, not offers, otherwise customers decide when to enter into the agreement. The danger with the Internet is the speed at which things happen. The case of the Argos £3 televisions (see page 108) illustrates well the importance of who makes the offer: in the Argos case the advertisement worked to the detriment of Argos. The display of goods is generally an invitation to treat, not an offer. The design of the Web site should be checked to ensure that it is consistent with what you are trying to achieve. You should also make sure that the terms of the contract are incorporated and that statements that are made are not incorrect.

11.7 SPECIFIC SECTORS

11.7.1
Section 21 of the Financial Services and Markets Act 2000 concerns financial promotions, which include in their 'invitations' or 'inducements' to engage in investment activity (see Chapter 6, page 57). Section 21 applies if information has an effect in the UK. Law enforcers think about the risk to investors, other infringements, whether the promotion is directed at the UK, the positive steps to avoid material being made available or receivable in the UK, and the registrable requirements for making such information available in the UK. Also, see Appendix 6.

11.7.2
You may take advantage of the Financial Promotions (Exemptions) Order

2001, as it provides a safe harbour for non-UK advertisements. There are, however, qualifications to this. Firstly:

- There has to be an indication that the advertisements are not addressed to UK persons; or
- There has to be an indication that UK persons should not rely on the information; or
- The information must not be retrievable from or directly accessible from UK aired communications.

Secondly, there must be procedures to prevent UK persons investing.

11.7.3
If you plan to give customers credit you should be aware of the law regarding credit transactions. The provision of credit is not to be confused with banking. Credit is an amount or sum placed by the creditor at the disposal of the debtor. A definition of banking could be a deposit taking business within the meaning of the Banking Act 1987 authorized by the Bank of England. A bank may offer a number of different products and services including the provision of credit to individuals and companies. Consumer credit might be defined as credit granted to an individual especially to finance the purchase of consumer goods or to defray personal expenses. With a few exceptions, anyone whose business involves offering credit or lending money to individuals, whether directly or as a broker, must be licensed by the Director General of the Office of Fair Trading (OFT), to carry on a consumer credit business under section 21 of the Consumer Credit Act 1974 (CCA). The OFT also monitors advertisements for the provision of credit to individuals. If an advertisement does not comply then you can be tried either in a magistrates court or the Crown Court. If you are found guilty in the former you can be fined up to £2,000. The maximum sentence in the Crown Court is two years imprisonment or a fine or both. Even if you are not yourself going to offer credit or hire and you want to introduce your customer to someone who will (that is, to carry out credit broking), you will require a licence under section 147 of the CCA. If a credit brokerage is unlicensed then this might affect the enforceability of the agreement against the debtor or hirer, made on the credit broker's introduction (s 149, CCA). With a few exceptions, the form and content of the consumer credit agreement is set out by the Secretary of State and must contain certain specific provisions (s 60,CCA). The agreement must also be signed in writing to be enforceable (s 61).

11.7.4
Gambling on the Internet is booming. Millions of dollars have already been transacted over the Internet through gambling. Golden Palace online casino has a jackpot going up to US$400,000. According to Christiansen Capital Advisors, the total market value for Internet gambling for the year

2001 in the United Sates exceeded US$3 billion. The total is expected to rise to US$4.5 billion in 2002 and US$6.3 billion in 2003. Currently there are two types of Web site in respect of gambling on the Internet: Web sites which advertise gambling, giving details of gambling opportunities and companies or results of races and lotteries, and sites where you can actually gamble and win (or lose) money. The vast majority of sites on the Internet that are gambling-related are information only. I class these as advertising Web sites and address advertising online in paragraph **11.7.6**. However, Web sites that offer the opportunity to win money are growing exponentially. As is becoming a characteristic of online business, the law is struggling to keep up. Under the current UK law, the same out-of-date law applies to both offline and online gambling. It is hardly surprising the laws do not work very well, as some of them date back to the 1960s when the Internet was a military and academic tool under the auspices of the Advanced Research Policy Agency Network (ARPANET). The regulatory regime in the UK currently comprises the Betting and Gaming and Lotteries Act 1963 ('the 1963 Act'), the Gaming Act 1968 ('the 1968 Act'), the Lotteries and Amusements Act 1976 ('the 1976 Act') and the Betting and Gaming Duties Act 1981. However, the Home Office are undertaking a review of online gambling. The Gaming Board of Great Britain Gambling Review Body produced a *Gambling Review Report* on Internet gambling in July 2001, which is available on www.gbgb.org.uk. If the recommendations of the report are enacted there will be some revolutionary changes in UK gambling laws. The recommendations include having one regulation for all types of gambling and incorporating the current Gaming Board of Great Britain into a Gambling Commission.

11.7.5
The ways to set up gambling include betting, gaming and lotteries.

11.7.5.1
Betting: under the 1963 Act, if you are already set up offline to arrange betting then you may do so online. A licensed bookmaker has been able to accept telephone bets from clients with credit accounts, so naturally it can also accept e-mail bids. This also applies to football pools, since entries have always been accepted by post. If you intend to set up an Internet betting service in the UK you must hold a bookmaking permit from the local licensing magistrates. Also, if you wish to locate your betting business offshore for tax reasons, you may do so without falling foul of any legislation.

11.7.5.2
Gaming is covered by the 1968 Act. In the United States gaming is big business. Many online gaming sites have evolved offering an array of games. There are the usual games like poker, blackjack, roulette and keno, and there are also several different slot machines. According to *Euro*

Business magazine, Golden Palace Online Casino had 2,000 players during its first year of trading. By January 2002 it has over 102,000 players with US$2.7 billion already wagered through its Web site. It is a different story in the UK. According to section 2 of the 1968 Act, gaming can only be conducted on licensed and registered premises. Persons taking part in gaming must be on the premises at the time when the gaming takes place. Users cannot participate in gaming by proxy or by post, so the use of e-mail would be prohibited (s 12). You cannot arrange gaming in a public place to which the public have access. This is meant as a preventative measure to stop under-age gambling (s 5) (gambling under the age of 18 is prohibited). So you cannot arrange gaming online in the UK; in fact to do so would be illegal and you could be liable to prosecution by the Gaming Board. Incidentally, you would be liable as the operator of the Web site. Users would not be liable as it is not illegal for a UK resident to take part in online gaming. Users are free to take part in online gaming anywhere else in the world, the Golden Palace Online Casino for example.

11.7.5.3
Lotteries are covered by the 1976 Act. You may run an online lottery provided it is registered with the appropriate local authority or the Gaming Board. Since lotteries can be run by phone or post, it would appear possible to participate in a lottery by e-mail. However, under the Act you cannot run a lottery entirely by machine. As lawmakers regard the Internet as a machine, this means you cannot sell lottery tickets by the Internet. The Gaming Board has permitted two Lottery Managing Companies to arrange lotteries over the Internet. However, this is limited to being able to use the Internet as a means of communication, connecting buyers and sellers of lottery tickets. The selling of tickets is done offline.

11.7.6
Advertising gambling.

11.7.6.1
Betting: in respect of the information-only Web sites discussed above, the legal position is slightly different. Although it is legal to have online betting, it is an offence to advertise offshore bookmakers and you cannot advertise gambling to persons under 18. In *Victor Chandler International* v. *Customs and Excise Commissioners and another* [2000], the Court of Appeal held that an overseas bookmaker placing advertisements on teletext amounts to circulating or distributing an advertisement in the UK, which is prohibited under section 9(1)(b) of the Betting and Gaming Duties Act 1981.

11.7.6.2
Gaming: section 42 of the 1968 Act places restrictions on advertisements relating to gaming. The Gaming Board published guidelines for gaming advertising on 16 January 2002. According to the guidelines, a passive Web

site (ie information only) because it is based on a 'pull' rather than 'push' principle, based in the UK or abroad, whose sole principal purpose is to provide information about gaming, including individual casinos, will not be taken as constituting advertising for the purposes of section 42 of the 1968 Act. You can also avoid the advertising restrictions if you are advertising to your existing members, for example, inviting them to subscribe for money. So you should convert your users into customers or members first. Then once they are customers you may invite them to subscribe for money.

11.7.6.3

Lotteries: as I mentioned above it is in the most part illegal to run an online lottery in the UK. You may give information about a UK lottery online but you would not be able to advertise or sell a lottery ticket online. It is also illegal to promote a foreign lottery in the UK, so it is therefore illegal to advertise a foreign Internet lottery.

11.8 SUMMARY

11.8.1

There are several different opportunities for advertising on the Internet. As well as banner advertisements, there are sponsorship, microsites, pop-ups, alliances and affiliate programs, direct e-marketing and many others. Along with all these advertising opportunities come the risks of running an inappropriate or illegal advertisement.

Action checklist

If you are an advertiser:
- Make sure the form of advertising is allowed.
- Check that any provider of advertising space complies with the applicable laws.
- Consider the scope of the advertisement.

If you are a site owner:
- Seek a warranty of compliance.
- Reserve wide rights to take down offensive material.
- Consider making your investigations as soon as you are aware of the possibility of an offence.
- Approach relevant regulators.

Part IV

Taxation

12

Online taxation

12.1 INTRODUCTION

12.1.1

An in-depth analysis of taxation is outside the scope of this chapter; I merely highlight some of the issues relating to taxation and e-commerce. Clearly the globalization effect of the Internet means that new questions must be addressed on how to adapt existing tax legislation, procedures and practices to overcome any deficiencies that emerge, as distance and geographical borders become increasingly blurred in the delivery of products and services. Tax authorities must provide a fiscal environment in which e-commerce can flourish, while preventing the use of e-commerce as a tool for tax evasion. The OECD has been active in developing framework conditions for the taxation of e-commerce, in close cooperation with the European Union, the World Customs Organization and the business community. Some of the complexities faced by policy makers are set out as follows.

12.1.2

The current assets of a typical bricks and mortar business are made up largely of tangibles, and the existing systems are designed to apply to them. A typical Internet company's current assets (other than shareholder funds) consist largely of intangibles such as their domain names, trade marks and patents. Broadly the tax treatments applied to different categories of intellectual property are different. The growth of e-commerce emphasizes the possible inadequacies of the taxation of intellectual property.

12.1.3

The systems for the taxation of e-commerce need to be more flexible and dynamic than the existing rigid tax systems, under which organizations are taxed according to fixed categories. The way a business is taxed depends on the type of business activity: for example whether it supplies goods or services, or is an investment business, and on the type of legal entity, that is, whether it is a sole trader, partnership or limited company. As an Internet company, constantly ensuring that you keep pace with the technological and commercial developments in the industry, you may focus on and then discontinue any or all types of business activity within weeks. Also, in a traditional commercial environment, tax administrations rely on being able to identify taxpayers, verify their financial information and collect the tax due. The anonymity and globalization of the Internet means it is difficult to identify businesses or their geographical locations. Unless you can identify taxpayers, it is difficult to levy taxes on them. The main method of identifying a business engaged in e-commerce is by its domain name, and the effectiveness of this is tenuous at best. Therefore unless your business is based entirely in the UK, with employees, equipment, customers, distributors and suppliers all from the UK, you will need to consider international tax systems. In cases where it is possible to identify taxpayers but not to pin them down to a single geographical location, issues arise regarding double taxation. At the time of writing there are no laws in place which extend double tax treaties to cover Web-based activities, and it is difficult to be clear about the situation regarding, for example, Web servers which are permanently established in a different jurisdiction from the organizations making use of them.

12.1.4

Value Added Tax (VAT) laws will depend on whether you are involved in business-to-business or business-to-consumers e-commerce, as they require a business to identify whether a customer is VAT registered (as most businesses will be) or not VAT registered (as most, but not necessarily all, individuals will be). The anonymity of the Internet makes it harder to distinguish one type of customer from another. This makes the Internet a potential loop-hole for tax evasion or money laundering. If your customer is VAT registered in, say, Norway, you should not charge VAT in the UK, otherwise there is a double charge to VAT. To avoid this you should obtain the VAT number of your customer and enter it onto your invoice. This will mean that VAT is zero rated. If your customers are not registered for VAT in another EC country, they pay VAT in the UK as normal.

12.2 VAT AND E-COMMERCE

12.2.1
In Europe there is a common framework for VAT, with a standardized assessment basis. VAT is levied on the following in the UK:

- the supply of goods or services;
- the acquisition of goods from other Member States;
- the importation of goods from places outside the Member States.

The wide scope of the tax means that VAT is as applicable to e-commerce as it is to other forms of commerce.

12.3 TAXATION OF TRADING PROFITS

12.3.1
These can be divided into the taxation of individuals and of companies. Whether you are trading as an individual or a company, the key issues to consider are, first, are you a tax resident, and second, if you are a non-resident, are you carrying on trade within the UK?

12.3.2
Taxation of resident individuals. Both employed and self-employed individuals are liable to income tax. A self-employed individual can be defined as 'an individual carrying on business with substantial control over the service or product he or she provides, supplying his or her own heavy or expensive equipment or tools and assuming a degree of personal financial risk. A self-employed individual may employ others to carry out work.' Income tax is charged under schedule D on the annual profits of any self-employed person residing in the UK from any trade carried on in the UK or elsewhere. under section 18(1) of the Income and Corporation Taxes Act 1988 (ICTA). An employed individual is charged under schedule E (see below). If you are a UK tax resident it will not usually serve any useful purpose to argue that your trade is conducted outside the UK on the Internet. Also a tax resident individual's trading profits will fall to be taxed under Schedule D wherever they arise.

12.3.3
Taxation of non-resident individuals. Income tax is charged on the profits of any person, although not resident in the UK, from any trade exercised within the UK, under Schedule D (s 18 (1), ICTA). If you are a non-domiciled individual who is resident in the UK you can benefit from the remittance basis of taxation. That is, any income arising from non-UK sources is only taxed when the profits are brought into the UK. In the case of a non-

resident, e-commerce does offer scope to avoid a UK tax charge on trading profits, even though your customer may be based in the UK. Even if a tax charge arises under domestic law, you may be able to claim the protection of a double tax treaty. Whether or not you are non-resident is a question of fact.

12.3.4
Taxation of resident companies. If you are a UK tax resident company carrying on trade you will pay corporation tax on your worldwide profits, not income tax.

12.3.5
Taxation of non-resident companies. The profits of a non-resident company conducting trade within the UK will be subject to UK corporation tax although the charge will depend on whether it is operating in the UK through a branch or agency (in which case you will pay corporation tax) or operating directly from its country of residency into the UK (in which case it will pay income tax at the basic rate). As with individuals, a non-resident company may benefit from the protection of a double tax treaty.

12.4 PAYE

12.4.1
UK income tax is charged under Schedule E on the emoluments from any office or employment, under section 19 of the ICTA. The Pay As You Earn (PAYE) system imposes a duty on an employer to account to the Inland Revenue once a month or quarterly for certain employees, for tax that the employer has (or ought to have) deducted from payments to employees (s 203, ICTA). The PAYE system also imposes requirements on an employer in respect of reporting benefits in kind. The PAYE system is also used to collect national insurance contributions.

12.4.2
There is often a preference on the part of some individuals to be classified as self-employed rather than employed, because of cash flow advantage and the greater scope to claim expenses as tax-deductible, although in practice the difference may be less worthwhile than anticipated. In some cases, it may be advantageous to be an employee. Nevertheless, technology now permits many work arrangements to be structured as instances of self-employment, rather than employment. There is no single test to establish whether or not someone is an employee. The full circumstances are considered.

12.4.3
Whatever the payment arrangements, someone will be responsible for PAYE for the employee. An employer with sufficient taxable presence in

the UK must operate PAYE. What volume of operations give rise to a sufficient taxable presence is a question of fact. Even if you are an overseas company with a UK branch you may satisfy this requirement. Even if the employer is outside the PAYE regulations it can still be made to operate PAYE for employees within the PAYE regulations under section 203 of the Income and Corporation Taxes Act 1988.

12.5 BUSINESS RATES

12.5.1
The UK has a system of business rates (non-domestic rating). In broad terms, occupiers of property used for business purposes pay amounts annually to the relevant local authority based on the rateable value of the property. The amount paid does not increase if the property is used to operate a 24-hour business (such as worldwide Internet trading).

12.6 CUSTOM DUTIES

12.6.1
Import duties are, like VAT, EC-regulated. Duty is paid at the point of entry of goods into the EC according to the duties applicable under the HM Customs and Excise Integrated Tariff. The World Trade Organization has ruled that it will not impose customs duties on electronic transmissions.[1] Customs duties do however apply to goods, and if goods are ordered electronically and delivered physically from outside the EC then customs duties will continue to apply at the appropriate rate for the product. However, 'goods' supplied electronically from outside the EC (for example, computer programs in electronic form) will be treated as services and therefore be free of import duties. At the time of writing there are no plans to introduce additional import duties to electronic transmissions.

12.7 SUMMARY

12.7.1
Implementing harmonization of tax regimes will be a difficult task for policymakers, as governments will be reluctant to give up their right to set their own local tax systems. The prime issue is how national fiscal boundaries can be reconciled with a borderless Internet. However the policymakers manage or resolve this problem, it is important that you keep watch for any new guidelines from the OECD.

> ### *Action checklist*
>
> - ■ Check to see if you qualify for the protection of a double tax treaty.
> - ■ Identify your customers. Are they private or business customers?

NOTE

1 World Trade Organization, 'Declaration on Global Electronic Commerce' (Adopted on 20 May 1998) [online] www.jus.ulo.no/lm/wta.electronic.commerce.1998/doc.html

13

Taxation opportunities

13.1 INITIAL ALLOWANCES

13.1.1
In some circumstances both existing businesses and new businesses can get 100 per cent initial capital allowances. These allowances are usually available for capital expenditure in enterprise zones such as large factories or hotels. You may also qualify for an enhanced allowance in the first year of trading of about 40 per cent for certain expenditure.

13.2 PRE-TRADING EXPENDITURE

13.2.1
Trading expenditure incurred within seven years before a trade begins can be deducted as pre-trading expenditure when the trade begins, under section 401 of the Income and Corporation Taxes Act 1988 (ICTA). You should make sure that you are incurring the expenditure and starting the trading. Pre-trading capital allowances are dealt with in a similar way to trading expenditure. The deduction is calculated at the time when trading commences (section 83(2), Capital Allowances Act 1990). Capital goods which are originally purchased for personal use then passed to the business are treated as having been acquired at the market value at the time of handover. You may recover any VAT incurred six months before registration for the purposes of the business for services offered. You may

also recover any VAT incurred on goods still retained by the business by the business at the date of registration.

13.3 TRADING LOSSES

13.3.1

It is possible for you to set a trading loss in a tax year against chargeable gains realized in that year (section 72, Finance Act 1991). Loss may be carried forward and set against future profits, if relief cannot be given under these provisions. As a general rule if the trade discontinues then relief from losses is lost. It is important that the trade is carried on a commercial basis with a view to making a profit. If not, the loss will not be accepted as a trading loss for these purposes (section 384(1), ICTA). A company can offset trading losses against profits (including capital gains) in the same accounting period and preceding three years (section 393A, ICTA). It may also carry forward the loss and set it against trading income of the same trade in succeeding accounting periods (section 393, ICTA).

13.4 THE ENTERPRISE INVESTMENT SCHEME

13.4.1

The Enterprise Investment Scheme (EIS) was devised for small high-risk-investment unlisted private companies, such as Internet companies, that meet certain conditions (see below). The idea is to incentivize investment in new shares. To qualify the shares must be held throughout a period of three years, beginning with the date on which they were issued. Only 'eligible shares' can qualify for EIS relief under section 289 of the ICTA. (See paragraph 13.4.6 for the six main conditions for 'eligible shares'.) The incentives for the investment are the range of tax reliefs available for the investors. Further, although the funds raised from the scheme must be used in the UK, a company does not have to be incorporated or resident in the UK to qualify for the scheme. This section provides a basic outline of the scheme. However, this is a complex area of law and you are advised to obtain specialist legal advice if you plan to use the scheme.

13.4.2

The reliefs available are income tax, deferral relief, capital gains exemption and loss relief.

13.4.3

Income tax reduction is available to investors on the amount invested. However, investors who are connected with the company at the time of buying the shares (such as paid directors) are not eligible for income tax relief (section 291, ICTA).

13.4.4
Individuals subscribing for shares in your company may be able to postpone the charge to capital gains tax on gains arising on the disposal of other assets around the time they make their investments. Investors who do not qualify for income tax relief because they are connected may qualify for deferral relief.

13.4.5
Investors who obtain income tax relief may also be eligible for either capital gains tax or loss relief when they sell their shares. Provided the disposal takes place three years after they have bought the shares, they may not have to pay tax on any gain. If investors make a loss on the sale of their shares, then regardless of when they sold they may be able to write off the loss against their income tax liability, less any income tax relief they obtained from the purchase. The availability of this relief does not stop investors from writing off the loss, less the income tax relief, against their chargeable gains.

13.4.6
There are six main conditions for eligible shares:

■ Shares must not be issued for tax avoidance.
■ The money from the shares must be for an eligible company.
■ The money raised must be used within 24 months.
■ If the money is used by a subsidiary company then it must be at least 90 per cent owned.
■ The company's asset value must not exceed £15 million before the issue and £16 million immediately afterwards.
■ At the time of the issue of the shares the company must be unquoted.

13.4.7
There are three steps in processing EIS:
■ You write to the Small Company Enterprise Centre, Tidotyglass, Llanishen, CF4 52G with your EIS1 form. They act as the central processing unit for the EIS. They then send it on to the appropriate revenue office.
■ Once the EIS1 form is approved, the Inland Revenue send you EIS2 and EIS3 forms (you should allow three to four weeks for receipt).
■ You then partly complete the EIS 3 forms and send them to investors who submit them to the Inland Revenue in the usual way.

13.4.8
Clearly the EIS is very helpful to investors and if you are running, or planning to set up, an eligible company, you should look into setting up an EIS. It does however mean that your company will have to qualify throughout the three-year period from the issue of shares. This may restrict your long-term strategy for a share flotation.

13.5 OTHER RELIEFS

13.5.1
A loss on the disposal of unquoted shares in a trading company or holding company of a trading group can be set off against income if various conditions are met (sections 573 et seq, ICTA).

13.6 NON-DOMICILED ENTREPRENEURS

13.6.1
'Domicile' for income tax and capital tax purposes is a general law matter. Domicile is not the same as nationality or residence. Generally the Inland Revenue is interested in where individuals have their permanent home. Someone born outside the UK can live in the UK for a considerable time without becoming a UK domicile.

13.6.1.1
A non-UK domiciled individual who is resident in the UK benefits from the remittance basis of taxation. Broadly, capital gains arising on non-UK assets are not subject to UK tax until all proceeds are remitted to the UK (section 12, Taxation and Chargeable Gains Act 1992). Similarly income arising from non-UK sources is taxed on a remittance basis. In the case of a UK-resident individual owning a business overseas it is, however, difficult to establish such a business as a non-UK source of income, because the 'head and brains' of the organization will normally be in the UK. From an inheritance tax point of view, a non-UK domiciled individual is only subject to inheritance tax on UK assets. There is, however, a different test of domicile for inheritance tax purposes (section 267, Inheritance Tax Act 1984). If you are a non-UK domicile you may prefer to conduct your business through non-UK incorporated companies. The shares in such companies will be non-UK assets for capital gains tax and inheritance tax purposes. Such a company could be a UK tax resident under the central management and control test, and pay corporation tax on its worldwide profits. However, if the company is operated so as to be a non-UK resident and no part of its business is conducted in the UK, then profits can arise

free of UK tax (and, possibly, free of any tax if the company operates from a 'tax haven' such as the Turks and Caicos Islands). Careful! If you give shares to an employee they may be taxable as an emolument.

13.7 SUMMARY

13.7.1
For all types of business and commerce, taxation is a cost that has to be considered. Being aware of the various tax opportunities can help to reduce your tax bill considerably and provide incentives for potential investors to invest in your business.

> ### *Action checklist*
> - Check your allowances and reliefs.
> - Is your company eligible for EIS? Do your shareholders regard EIS relief as a condition in making their investment decision?
> - Make sure your share register is well managed.

Appendices

Appendix I

Mutual non-disclosure agreement

Date   2001

[   ] (1)

and

[   ] (2)

Mutual Non-Disclosure Agreement

Peter Adediran

tomorrow's law online service ©
Advice Engineered for the Future

MUTUAL NON-DISCLOSURE AGREEMENT

This mutual non-disclosure agreement is entered into on [*Date*].

Between

(1)   [*company name*], of [*Address*] company number [*company number*];

and

(2)   [*company name*], of [*Address*] company number [*company number*]

hereinafter known as 'the Parties'.

Recitals:

(a) It is the mutual wish of the Parties to disclose certain Confidential Information to each other; and

(b) The Parties both recognize that careful protection and non-disclosure by the party receiving (the 'Receiving Party') Confidential Information from the party disclosing (the 'Disclosing Party') such Confidential Information is of vital importance to the prosperity of the Parties.

(c) In consideration of the promises made below, the Parties agree to disclose and receive certain Confidential Information under the terms and conditions set out below.

It is agreed as follows:

1.   Definition and Purpose

1.1   The purpose of the disclosure of Confidential Information is to enable the Parties to advance their efforts in the current or potential business of marketing connectivity service and software products, as well as any other business undertaken by [*name of either party*]. The Receiving Party shall use the Confidential Information for this purpose only. Either [*name of one party*] or [*name of another party*] may be a Receiving Party and/or a Disclosing Party under the terms of this Agreement.

1.2   Confidential Information shall mean any information and data of a confidential or proprietary nature which is disclosed by the Disclosing Party to the Receiving Party, including but not limited to, proprietary technical, financial, personnel, marketing, pricing, sales and/or commercial information with respect to computer networking, data communications and computing services, development, operation, performance, cost, know-how, business, process and marketing of computer software and other technology relating to computer networking, data communications and computing services as well as ideas, concepts, designs and inventions, computer source and object code and computer programming techniques; and all record bearing media containing or disclosing such information and techniques which are disclosed pursuant to this Agreement.

1.3   The Confidential Information shall be considered trade secrets, owned by the Disclosing Party. The Disclosing Party retains all right, title and interest in the Confidential Information. No licence to the Receiving Party, under any trade mark, patent or copyright, or applications for same which are now or may thereafter be obtained by such Receiving Party, is either granted or implied by the conveying of Confidential Information to the Receiving Party. The Receiving Party may only use the Confidential Information for the purposes stated above.

1.4   No licence to the Receiving Party, except as explicitly provided in the [*insert any underlying agreement here*], under any trade mark, patent or copyright, or applications for the same which are now or may thereafter be obtained by such Receiving Party, is either granted or implied by the conveying of Confidential Information to the Receiving Party.

2.   Non Disclosure

2.1   The Receiving Party agrees that the Confidential Information is regarded by the Disclosing Party as valuable trade secrets and agrees to use it only for the above purpose. The Receiving Party recognizes that this Agreement imposes an affirmative duty to hold such information in confidence and protect it from dissemination to and use by unauthorized persons. In the absence of the Disclosing Party's prior written consent, the Receiving Party shall not reproduce nor disclose the Confidential Information to any third party.

2.2   The Receiving Party agrees to use the same degree of care to protect the confidentiality of the Confidential Information as it would exercise to protect its own trade secrets, but in no case less than a reasonable degree of care. Receiving Party will grant access to the Confidential Information only to its employees or consultants who have a clear need to know for purposes of this Agreement and shall advise those employees or consultants of the existence and terms of this Agreement and of the obligations of confidentiality herein. Each Party shall be responsible for the breach of the terms of this Agreement by such Party, or its employees or consultants.

3.   Duration

3.1   The Receiving Party shall maintain the Confidential Information in confidence in accordance with the terms of this Agreement for a period of [*three (3) years*] from the date of receipt of the Confidential Information, excepting, however, that any Receiving Party receiving confidential product source code shall hold this code in strict confidence in perpetuity. Upon the expiration or earlier termination of this Agreement, or upon request by the Disclosing Party, the Receiving Party will cease to use the Confidential Information and will deliver to the Disclosing Party all documents, papers, drawings, tabulations, reports documentation and other record bearing media obtained in the course of this Agreement.

4.   Price Sensitive Information

4.1   If the information disclosed under this Agreement is material non-public price sensitive information about the Disclosing Party, then the Receiving Party agrees not to trade in the shares of the Disclosing Party or in the shares of any appropriate and relevant third party until such time as there will not be a violation of the applicable securities laws resulting from such trading in the shares of the Disclosing Party.

5.   Remedies

5.1   The Receiving Party agrees that unauthorized disclosure of the Confidential Information may irreparably damage the Disclosing Party. Such damages cannot be fully compensated by money damages. Therefore, the Parties agree that relief for such disclosure may be sought in equity, for which no bond will be required.

6.   Exceptions

6.1   No information shall be considered Confidential Information if such information: (a) was in the Receiving Party's possession before execution of this Agreement, as established by Receiving Party's records; (b) is or becomes a matter of public knowledge through no fault or without violation of any duty of confidentiality of the Receiving Party; or (c) is rightfully received by the Receiving Party from a third party without a duty of confidentiality. Neither Party shall be liable for disclosure of Confidential Information if disclosure was in response to a valid order of a court or authorized government department; provided that prior written notice first be given to the Disclosing Party so that a protective order or other relief, if appropriate, may be sought by the Disclosing Party.

7.   General Provisions

7.1   The Disclosing Party assumes no responsibility for any loss or damages to the Receiving Party, its customers or any third parties caused by or arising from the Confidential Information. The Disclosing Party makes no warranties of any kind, whether expressed or implied, including but not limited to any implied warranty of merchantability of the Confidential Information or fitness of the Confidential Information for a particular purpose.

7.2   Each of the Parties represents and warrants that its actions with respect to this Agreement do not conflict with any prior obligations to any third party. The Parties further agree not to disclose or to use on behalf of the other Party any Confidential Information belonging to any third party unless sufficient written authorization from the third party is provided.

7.3   Either party may terminate this Agreement upon written notice to the other. Duties of non-disclosure as set out above will survive any termination of the Agreement.

7.4   During the term of this Agreement and for a period of two (2) years thereafter, each Party agrees not to hire, solicit, nor attempt to solicit the services, of any employee or subcontractor of the other Party, its parent or affiliate companies, without the prior written consent of the other Party; provided, however, that each Party is not prevented from employing such person who contacts that Party on his or her own initiative and without any direct or indirect solicitation by that Party. Violation of this provision shall, in addition to other relief, entitle the offended Party or its parent company to assert liquidated damages[1] against the offending Party equal to [*one hundred fifty (150) per cent*] of the solicited person's annual compensation.

7.5   Neither Party may sell, transfer, or assign this Agreement, except to entities completely controlling or controlled by that Party or to entities acquiring all or substantially all of its assets, without the prior written consent of the other which consent shall not be unreasonably withheld. Any act in derogation of the foregoing shall be null and void; provided, however, that any such assignment shall not relieve the assigning Party of its obligations under this Agreement. Both parties shall require written notice, however, in the event of any assignment. This Agreement shall be binding upon and inure to the benefit of the Parties and their rightful successors and assigns.

7.6   The waiver or failure of either Party to exercise in any respect any right provided for in this Agreement shall not be deemed a waiver of any further right under this Agreement.

7.7   If any provision of this Agreement is held by a court of competent jurisdiction to be contrary to law, it shall be enforced to the extent legally permissible, and as necessary to reflect the intent of the Parties and shall not affect the remaining provisions of this Agreement, which shall remain in full force and effect.

7.8   This Agreement may only be amended by a writing executed by both Parties. This Agreement is binding upon each Party and their respective affiliates.

7.9   This Agreement shall be deemed to be a contract made under the laws of the United Kingdom and shall be governed by the laws thereof as if between residents of the United Kingdom.

7.10   This Agreement represents the entire agreement between the Parties with respect to the subject matter herein.

SIGNED by a Director
duly authorized for and on
Behalf of [   ]:-

A Director duly authorized for and on
Behalf of [   ]:-

NOTES

1 Unless liquidated damages are a genuine pre-estimate of loss suffered, they may be unenforceable as a penalty. Also, the damages must flow from a breach of the subject matter of the contract, not some additional punishment (Dunlop Pneumatic Tyre Co Ltd [1915]). Further, as damages are agreed beforehand, a party cannot then claim more for that breach at trial, even if the actual damages suffered are much greater than the agreed liquidated sum.

Appendix 2

Master Web site development and promotion agreement

(This Agreement is written in favour of the Web site owner. Clauses in square brackets may be deleted as required, as they favour the Web site developer)

Date	2001
[	] (1)
and	
[	] (2)]

Master Web Site Development and Promotion Agreement

Peter Adediran

tomorrow's law online service©
Advice Engineered for the Future

MASTER WEB SITE DEVELOPMENT AGREEMENT

This master Web site development agreement is made on [*Date*].

Between

(1)   [*company name*] of [*Address*], company number [*company number*]
('   ');

and

(2)   [*company name*] of [*Address*], company number [*company number*]
('Client')

together known as the Parties.[1]

It is agreed as follows:

1.   Recitals

1.1   [*Name of Agency*] is in the business of providing integrated consultancy, advice, design, enhancement, technical, development, implementation and promotion, marketing and advertising services in connection with interactive media including Internet Web sites.

1.2   The Client desires to engage [   ], and [   ] desires to be engaged by the Client, to provide consulting, advisory, design, enhancement, technical, development and implementation services with respect to the Client's Web Site upon the terms and conditions set forth in this Agreement.

1.3   The Client desires to engage [   ], and [   ] desires to be engaged by the Client, to provide promotion, marketing and advertising services with respect to the Client's Web Site upon the terms and conditions of the Advertising Agency Agreement set forth in Schedule 1 to this Agreement.

1.4   The Client enters into this Agreement effective from the Commencement Date. An individual SOW will be produced by [   ] and submitted to the Client for advance approval for each Project under consideration by the Client and shall be agreed as schedules to this Agreement and be subject to the terms and conditions of this Agreement.

2.   Definitions

2.1   'Client Content' shall mean all pictorial, graphic, editorial, textual and other content and materials provided by or originated from the Client or its other contractors hereunder for incorporation or use in connection with the Client Web Site and/or the Services. Client Content shall also include the names, logos, and related trade marks and service marks of the Client.

2.2   'Client Web site' shall mean the World Wide Web site(s), or other Internet protocol addressable material, identified in an applicable SOW and through which Client Content and certain of the Work Product and [   ] Tools will appear and be made available to End Users.

2.3   'Confidential Information' shall mean, subject to Clause 17.4 below, all proprietary information (either oral, written, or digital) provided to the Receiving Party by the Disclosing Party in connection with this Agreement, including but not limited to: (a) any data, trade secrets, process, know-how, technique, diagram, program, source code, invention, and/or work in process; (b) any financial, supplier, technical, customer, employee, investor or business information; and (c) the terms and conditions of this Agreement.

2.4   'Creative Work' shall be such work carried out by [   ] orally, written or otherwise, whether preliminary or during the Project relating to the alteration, improvement, enhancement or other service arising out of this Agreement.

2.5   'Work Product' shall mean video images, sounds, computer software, or other materials and information and any modifications, improvements or enhancements to it or derivative works from it developed by [   ] and Third Party Providers further to this Agreement and delivered to the Client, except that Work Product shall not include [   ] Tools, Client Content, [   ] Software or Third Party Software.

2.6   'Disclosing Party' shall mean the Party in this Agreement that is disclosing its Confidential Information.

2.7   'End User' shall mean any person or entity accessing or having access to the Client Web Site through the Internet.

2.8   '[   ] Business Methods' shall mean that part of the Creative Work which relates to the creative development process, Internet operability, Web site development, data display, data transfer, data tracking, data gathering, Web site operation, Web site implementation and Web site integration arising out of this Agreement.

2.9   '[   ] Software' shall mean algorithms, concepts, system architectures, embedded scripts, functions, procedures, objects, components, packages, applets, programs, source code (not including HTML text), and object code, developed or owned by [   ] either prior to this Agreement or after the date of this Agreement which is delivered to the Client as part of the Services. Except that all rights and property in any alteration, improvement, enhancement or other modification to the Client Web Site, by [   ] as part of the Services shall belong to the Client.

2.10   '[   ] Tools' shall mean all methodologies, know-how, processes, technologies, software (including source code, object code and documentation relating thereto), tools, devices, computer system designs, documentation, ideas, trade secrets, data, discoveries or inventions (whether or not patentable), products, user interfaces, and other materials and information delivered to the Client under this Agreement. Except that all rights and property in any alteration, improvement, enhancement or other modification to the Client Web Site, by [   ], as part of the Services shall belong to the Client.

2.11   'Project' shall mean the services, as part of a project, to be rendered by [   ] to the Client under this Agreement as expressly described in an applicable SOW.

2.12   'Receiving Party' shall mean the Party in this Agreement that is receiving the other Party's Confidential Information.

2.13   'SOW' shall mean any [   ] statement of work submitted to the Client which shall, at a minimum, describe the services to be rendered by [   ] to the Client to effect a Project and the Work Product, if any to be delivered by [   ] to the Client in connection with such Project.

3.   The Services

3.1   [   ] Services. [   ] shall provide services as may be mutually agreed on between the Parties in any duly executed SOW included in each Project. The services provided by [   ] will consist of consulting, advisory, design, enhancement, technical, development and implementation services with respect to the Client Web Site which are subject to the terms and conditions set out in this Agreement and/or promotion, marketing and advertising services with respect to the

Client Web Site which are subject to the terms and conditions of the Advertising Agency Agreement set out in Schedule 1 to this Agreement ('[   ] Services'). All [   ] Services contained in each SOW are hereby made a part of this Agreement by this reference provided it is executed by an authorized representative of both parties, except where services relate to the Advertising Agency Agreement in Schedule 1 to this Agreement. The Client hereby acknowledges and agrees that [   ] shall have no obligation whatsoever to provide any services that are not expressly described in a duly executed SOW. To the extent there is any conflict between the terms and conditions of any SOW and the terms and conditions of this Agreement, the terms and conditions of this Agreement shall control. The Parties acknowledge that, unless otherwise agreed in writing, this Agreement shall govern any engagement for similar services as covered hereunder that may be entered into by and between parents or majority-owned subsidiaries of the Parties and that any such engagement for services shall be further to a SOW under this Agreement. [   ] may have the Projects performed by its subsidiaries, subject to the written consent of the Client, such consent not to be unreasonably withheld, in which case such subsidiary shall be considered [   ] for the purposes of this Agreement.

3.1.1   [   ] shall perform all [   ] Services included in each Project to the satisfaction of the Client.

3.1.2   The Client will arrange regular meetings and receive monthly reports from [   ] to monitor the process of any Project.

3.2   Changes to the Parties' respective obligations under a SOW shall be made as set forth in this Clause 3.2 and [   ] shall not be obligated to undertake any change to any SOW requested by the Client other than in accordance with this Clause 3.2. The Client may request changes to a SOW by providing [   ] with a written request for changes (a 'Change Request') that specifies the desired change with at least the same degree of specificity as that contained in the original SOW.

3.2.1   If [   ] agrees to make the requested changes, [   ] shall submit to the Client a written response which will outline the tasks to be performed by each Party and the cost of the changes, and any other items applicable to the Change Request (a 'Change Order'). Unless specified otherwise in writing, [   ] will charge the Client on a time and material basis, at the then-current time and material rates, for the time spent by [   ] in analysing the Client's Change Request and preparing a Change Order. If, within [five (5) working days] after [   ] delivery of such Change Order to the Client, the Client provides [   ] with written notice of acceptance of the Change Order, the Change Order will amend and become a part of, the applicable SOW. In the event of a conflict among the terms and conditions of the Change Order and the applicable SOW, the terms and conditions of the Change Order shall control. If the Client fails to provide [   ] with written notice of acceptance of the Change Order within said [five (5) working day period], the Change Order will be deemed rejected by the Client and the original SOW shall remain in full force and effect.

3.2.2   [   ] shall have the right to decline to make the Change Request if the Change Request materially affects the scope, staffing requirements, timing or cost of the SOW at issue. In such a case the Client shall have the right to terminate the SOW. In the case of termination of such a SOW, the parties shall have the rights and obligations set forth in Clause 10.5 of this Agreement.

3.3   Each Party recognizes that each SOW may include assumptions regarding the software, hardware or related systems. [   ] shall not be responsible for the performance of Services under a SOW if the relevant software, hardware or related system environment has been substantially changed by the Client or a third party without [   ] prior written approval.

4.   Approvals and Authority

4.1   Any reference in this Agreement to the Client's 'written approval' shall mean written approval by directors or employees of the Client authorized to approve [   ]'s work and/or expenditure and whose names are set out below or are set forth in the SOW as having authority to provide approval for Services provided under that SOW:

'Authorized Person'
Name [   ]   Title [   ]
Name [   ]   Title [   ]
[   ] will notify the Client in writing of any change to the Authorized Persons during the continuance of this Agreement.

4.2   For the purposes of this Agreement, written approval shall include approval given by:

4.2.1   any fax, letter or purchase order on the Client's notepaper bearing the signature of an Authorized Person; or

4.2.2   e-mail emanating from the personal e-mail address of an Authorized Person;

4.2.3   estimates or quotations of the cost of the various items of Work Product and other services covered by this Agreement together with terms of payment, which shall be set forth in a SOW.

5.   Fees and Payment

5.1   Each month [   ] shall invoice the Client in accordance with the fee and payment schedule set forth in the applicable SOW. If the SOW does not designate the fees and/or payment schedule [   ] will invoice the Client on a monthly basis in accordance with the time and material rates in effect when the Services were performed by [   ]. If the applicable SOW does not specify payment instructions, the Client shall pay [   ] no later than [thirty (30) days] after the date of [   ] invoice. Any amount due under this Agreement which is not paid within [thirty (30) days] after the payment due date shall bear interest from the payment due date to the date of payment at the rate of [3]% above the base lending rate of [insert name of [   ] bank]. If the Client fails to pay, when due, any amount payable under this Agreement or fails to fully perform its obligations under this Agreement, the Client agrees to pay, in addition to any amount past due, plus interest accrued thereon, all reasonable expenses incurred by [   ] in their enforcing this Agreement, including without limitation all expenses of any legal proceeding related thereto and all reasonable attorneys' fees incurred in connection with this Agreement, provided that [   ] shall and shall be seen to mitigate any losses direct or consequential that they may have incurred as a result of a default of this Agreement by the Client.

5.2   Both parties shall be responsible for their respective tax liabilities in accordance with the terms of the applicable tax regulations.

6.   Client's Responsibilities

6.1   The Client shall undertake and perform each and every task and obligation identified in a SOW in a timely manner (collectively, 'Client Obligations'). The Client shall fully cooperate with [   ], including without limitation by:

a)   providing [   ] with all information, Client Content and materials as may be reasonably required by [   ]; and

b)   making available to [   ] at least one employee or consultant of the Client, reasonably acceptable to [   ], who shall have substantial relevant knowledge and experience to act as a project manager in connection with the rendering of the Services. The name of the Client's project manager should be set forth in any applicable SOW. The Client acknowledges and agrees that the Client's failure to timely perform one or more of the Client's Obligations may negatively affect [   ]'s ability to perform the Services under this Agreement. To the extent the Client fails to perform timely the Client Obligations, resulting delays in performance of the Services will be excused and applicable schedules for performance of Services shall be likewise extended. [   ] will advise the Client in writing of such extended dates.

6.2   The Client shall procure, at its own expense, all necessary rights, licences, permissions, waivers, releases and all other agreements and documentation to permit use of Client Content as contemplated and required hereunder.

6.3   The Client shall review, proof and ensure the accuracy and completeness of all content on the Client Web Site, including Client Content, [   ] Tools and Work Product, prior to publication of such content on the Client Web Site or in any other media expressly permitted under this agreement. [   ] shall also review the Work. If [   ] determines that according to its reasonable judgement that certain Work Product should not be used, [   ] shall inform the Client of the same and the basis for such belief. If the Client wishes to use such Work Product, then such Work Product shall be considered Client Content for the purposes of the warranties and indemnifications below.

6.4   The Client shall not tamper with, remove or modify the trade mark, copyright or other proprietary notices of [   ] from any [   ] Tools. If there is a modification or distortion of the [   ] Tools, at [   ]'s request, the Client shall remove [   ] name from such Web site containing such content.

7.   [   ] Responsibilities

7.1   [   ] shall:

7.1.1   provide its consulting, advisory, design, enhancement, technical, development, and implementation knowledge and experience in relation to the Client Web Site exclusively for the Client, (for the avoidance of doubt, [   ] may engage with other clients using its general knowledge and experience, this genuine knowledge and experience shall not include, knowledge specific to the Client), and not permit any third party access to or use of the algorithms, concepts, system architectures, embedded scripts, functions, procedures, objects, components, packages, applets, programs, source code (not including HTML text), and object code, relating to the Client Web Site in any way whatever.

7.1.2   effect and maintain adequate security measures to safeguard the algorithms, concepts, system architectures, embedded scripts, functions, procedures, objects, components, packages, applets, programs, source code (not including HTML text), and object code, relating to the Client Web Site from access or use by any unauthorized person.

7.1.3   make no copies of the Client Web Site except incidental to normal use of the Client Web Site for the purposes of this agreement.

8.   Timescales

8.1   Notwithstanding paragraph 7.1 above, [   ] shall use its best endeavours to ensure that any Project is performed and completed in accordance with the timescales set out in each individual SOW. Time is of the essence in this Agreement.

8.2   [   ] undertakes that it will use its best endeavours to ensure that any project is completed within the timescales and achieves the results defined in each individual SOW.

9.   Intellectual Property Rights

9.1   Copyright and all other intellectual property rights in the Client Web Site and any content on the Web Site provided by [   ] for the Client, shall remain at all times the property of the Client and [   ] shall acquire no rights in any such material. Copyright and/or other intellectual property rights belonging to the Client further to this Agreement shall survive termination of this Agreement set out in Clause 10.

9.2   [   ] has no right to have access to the algorithms, concepts, system architectures, embedded scripts, functions, procedures, objects, components, packages, applets, programs, source code (not including HTML text), and object code relating to the Client Web Site except as expressly set out in this Agreement.

9.3   If, despite not being permitted by the Client, [   ] makes any alteration, improvement, enhancement or other modification to the Client Web Site, all rights and property in such modification shall belong to the Client and [   ] shall promptly provide the Client with full details of such modifications, and shall take such other steps as the Client may reasonably require, at the expense of [   ], to perfect the vesting of rights and property in such modification in the Client.

9.4   [   ] shall indemnify the Client against all actions, claims, demands, costs, charges and expenses finally awarded as a result of the infringement of copyright in respect of the design of the Client Web Site (unless such infringement is caused or significantly contributed to by the Client).

9.5   [   ] shall give prompt notice to the Client if [   ] becomes aware of any unauthorized use or exploitation of the whole or any part of the Client Web Site by any person or body.

10.   Term and Termination

10.1   This Agreement shall commence on the Effective Date and shall remain in effect until the later of:

a)   termination, as set out in this clause 10; or
b)   the expiration or termination of all outstanding Statements of Work.

10.2   Either Party may terminate this Agreement without cause on [ninety (90) days] prior written notice to the other Party. In such case within a reasonable period of time after delivery of a written notice of termination, [   ] shall provide the Client with a transition plan detailing each Party's respective responsibilities in winding down each engagement under this Agreement, including scheduling and resource commitments. The Client shall provide all cooperation and assistance reasonably necessary to execute the transition as efficiently as possible. [   ] shall provide all reasonably necessary services, at the Client's expense, to wind down each engagement under this Agreement.

10.3   If either Party is in material breach of this Agreement and/or any SOW, the non-breaching Party may provide a written notice to the breaching Party specifying the nature of the breach. The breaching Party shall have [thirty (30) days] from receipt of such written notice to cure the material breach. If the breaching Party does not cure the breach within such period, the non-breaching Party may terminate this Agreement. The non-breaching Party shall terminate this Agreement by a [thirty (30) day] written notice. Such written notice shall include the date on which the notice was given. The date on which the notice is given shall be no earlier than the first day following the expiration of the [thirty (30) day] cure period. The rights and obligations of the Client and [   ] shall continue in full force and effect during the [thirty (30) day] cure period and up through and including the date of termination of this Agreement.

10.4   Either Party may terminate this Agreement and/or any or all outstanding SOW upon 48 hours written notice to the other Party following the occurrence of any of the following events with respect to the other Party:

a)   a receiver is appointed for such Party or its material assets;
b)   such Party becomes insolvent, generally unable to pay its debts as they become due, or makes an assignment for the benefit of its creditors or seeks relief under any bankruptcy, insolvency or equivalent law;
c)   if proceedings are commenced against the other Party, under any bankruptcy, insolvency or equivalent law, and such proceedings have not been vacated or set aside within [sixty (60) days] after the date of commencement of such proceedings; or
d)   if such Party is liquidated, dissolved or ceases operations.

10.5   In the event that this Agreement or any SOW(s) are terminated by Party the Client shall pay [   ]:

a)   any amounts owing for Services provided under any outstanding SOW;
b)   any reasonable out of pocket expenses incurred by [   ], as a result of an existing non-cancellable contract or commitment made pursuant to a SOW or with the Client's written authorization, up to and including the effective date of termination of this Agreement or any SOW;
c)   for any materials or services [   ] has committed to purchase for the Client, or any uncompleted work previously approved by the Client either specifically or as part of a plan and any other applicable compensation as outlined herein and/or in the applicable SOW; or
d)   if termination is for other than for material breach by [   ], on a time and material basis for any and all Services it performs through the effective date of the termination. The Client shall have no right to use or exploit in any manner, the Work Product or [   ] Tools provided under such SOW unless the Client has paid the full fees related thereto.

10.6   In the event of any termination of this Agreement, the Parties agree that Clause 2 (Certain Definitions), Clause 5 (Fees and Payment), Clause 10.5 (Rights upon Termination), Clause 10.6 (Survival), Clause 11 (Agreements with Third Parties), Clause 12.1 (Work Product), Clause 12.3 (Ownership of [   ] Tools), Clause 12.4 (Licence to Client), Clause 12.5 (Residual Knowledge), Clause 14 (Limitation of Liability),

Clause 15 (Indemnification), Clause 17 (Confidentiality), Clause 18 (Non-Solicitation) and Clause 22 (General) shall survive such termination.

11.   Agreements with Third Parties

11.1   [   ] shall have the right, but not the obligation, to engage third parties in connection with the provision of the Services here-under, including contracts for the development of a Work Product and [   ] Tools ('Third Party Providers'). [   ] shall use commercially reasonable efforts to select only Third Party Providers that perform services of the same quality and at the same professional services level as [   ]. If such Third Party Provider does not provide at least the same level of warranties, indemnification or assignment of rights as those set forth herein by [   ] to the Client, [   ] shall obtain approval from the Client for the use of such Third Party Provider, which approval shall be deemed an acceptance by the Client of such lesser rights for those particular Services. Unless otherwise specified in a SOW, the costs of any Third Party Providers shall be reflected in the SOW and shall be part of the fees and expenses paid to [   ] as reflected in the invoices to the Client. The Client acknowledges that in conjunction with rendering the Services, the Client may receive certain services originating from one or more Third Party Providers (collectively, the 'Third Party Services').

11.2   If the Client directs [   ] to cancel or terminate any contract or commitment made by [   ] to a third party in performance of the Services, [   ] shall take proper steps to carry out the Client's directions. In turn, the Client agrees to assume [   ] liability for cancellation or termination of all such contracts or commitments, to reimburse [   ] for all expenses incurred; and except for events of [   ] gross negligence to hold harmless and indemnify [   ] for all claims and actions by third parties for damages and expenses that result from carrying out the Client's directions. However, before [   ] makes any contract or commitment made to a third party on behalf of the Client or in performance of [   ]'s Services that is non-cancellable without the payment of additional fees and/or the assumption of additional liabil-ities, [   ] must advise the Client of such non-cancellable provisions and such commitments will be set forth in the relevant SOW. If such non-cancellable commitment is still in effect at the termination of this Agreement or a SOW, [   ], upon its own election, may carry such commitment to completion, and shall be paid by the Client in accor-dance with the provisions of this Agreement.

11.3   The Client acknowledges that from time to time [   ] may act as its agent to purchase media on behalf of the Client and to bind the Client with respect to such purchases which have been authorized in writing by the Client in a media buy authorization or similar document. The Client shall bear the costs of any such media buying, [   ] shall invoice the Client for such costs and the Client shall reimburse [   ] for such costs within [thirty (30) days] of the invoice date.

11.4   The Client understands and acknowledges that the development and operation of the Client Web Site may require the Client to obtain certain software, technology and other products provided by third parties other than Third Party Providers, including without limitation dynamic content engine(s), content management software, ad server software, mapping software, operating systems, server hardware and other Software described in an applicable SOW ('Third Party Software'). The Client shall be solely responsible for obtaining licences to, and otherwise acquiring, such Third Party Software, including the right to incorporate such Third Party Software into the Client Web Site.

12.   Ownership and License

12.1   On the Client's request at the end of the term for each SOW, [   ] shall assign to the Client with full title guarantee, such of the copyright in the Work Product as may be owned by [   ] and capable of assignment together with the right to sue for damages for past infringement provided all obligations of the Client arising from this Agreement have been met (including but not limited to those relating to the period of notice). Notwithstanding anything to the contrary herein, in the event that Work Product or portions thereof is created, developed, made or written by Third Party Providers as permitted by Clause 11.1, the Client shall have only those rights in such Work Product as are granted to [   ] in agreements with such Third Party Providers or third parties and which are sub-licensable or assignable to the Client.

12.2   The Client hereby grants to [   ] an irrevocable, perpetual, royalty-free, worldwide, non-exclusive licence to use, reproduce, distribute, publish, sublicense, and display the [   ] Business Methods and to create, use, reproduce, distribute and display derivative works derived from the [   ] Business Methods in any media now known or hereafter developed and, which licence [   ] may not be used for any purpose that is directly competitive with the Client. Except all [   ] Business Methods arising out of this Agreement shall belong to the Client.

12.3   All [   ] Tools and [   ] Software (collectively '[   ] Objects') are and shall remain the sole and exclusive property of [   ] and all right, title and interest therein or related thereto, including, without limitation, copyrights, trade marks, trade secrets, patents, and other intellectual property or proprietary rights, are hereby exclusively reserved by [   ]. [   ] reserves all right, title and interest in the[   ] Tools and no right, title or interest in the [   ] Objects is or shall be transferred to the Client under this Agreement except for the limited use licence expressly set forth in Clause 12.4.

12.4   On payment in full of all applicable fees and provided that the Client is not in material breach of this Agreement, [   ] grants to the Client a worldwide, non-exclusive, non-transferable, perpetual licence to use the [   ] Objects solely for the purpose of making the Client Web Site available to End Users through use of their browsers and/or for such other purposes, if any, expressly set forth in an applicable SOW. The Client shall not have the right to license, sublicense, or otherwise transfer to others this licence to use the [   ] Tools. The Client may create derivative works from the [   ] Tools, but such derivatives may only be used for the purpose of making the Client Web Site available to End Users and may not be licensed or transferred to third parties. The Client shall not permit: (a) the unauthorized copying or disclosure of the source code forms of the [   ] Tools; or (b) the decompiling, reverse engineering, disassembling or otherwise reducing the object code forms of the [   ] Tools to human perceivable form.

12.5   Nothing in this Agreement shall be construed to prevent or in any way limit [   ] from using general knowledge, skill and expertise acquired in the performance of this Agreement, save where such general knowledge or skill and expertise should cause the Client any commercial prejudice, in any current or subsequent endeavours.

13.   Warranties

13.1   [   ] Warrants and undertakes to the Client:

13.1.1   Subject to Clause 15 of this Agreement, [   ] hereby represents and warrants to the Client that:

a)   [   ] is the owner or licensee of the Work Product and [   ] Objects and each element thereof delivered to the Client, and [   ] has secured all necessary licences, consents, permissions and releases for the Client's use of the Work Product and [   ] Objects and each element thereof, provided that such warranty shall not apply to the names, logos and related trade marks and service marks created for the Client by [   ] pursuant to this Agreement;

b)   the use of the Work Product and [   ] Objects shall not infringe the copyright or trade mark right of any person, constitute a defamation, invasion of privacy, or violation of any right of publicity or to the best of [   ]'s knowledge and belief, infringe the patent of any person;

c)   the Work Product and [   ] Objects are not obscene and do not otherwise violate any law in any applicable jurisdiction which may have a material impact on the Client or its Web Site;

d)   there is currently no actual or threatened suit by any third party based on an alleged violation of any patents, trade marks, trade secrets or other intellectual property rights by [   ];

e)   the Services will be performed in a commercially reasonable manner in accordance with the standards generally prevailing in the industry for similar services;

f)   [   ] will comply with its own obligations under the Data Protection Act 1998;

g)   [   ] has full corporate power and authority to execute and deliver this Agreement and perform its obligations under this Agreement; and

h)   all Deliverables (as defined in the SOW) shall meet any specifications set forth in that SOW.

13.2   [   ] will use its best endeavours to provide continuity of resources of people skilled in the algorithms, concepts, system architectures, embedded scripts, functions, procedures, objects, components, packages, applets, programs, source code (not including HTML text), and object code relating to the Client Web Site and will seek the client's agreement by prior discussion to any removal of key individuals from any Project.

13.3   [   ] warrants to the Client that it will carry out any Project with reasonable care and skill.

13.4   The Parties understand that the Client's Web Site may include certain software or other products provided by third parties other than Third Party Providers, including without limitation certain software set forth in the applicable SOW ('Third Party Software'). The Client shall be solely responsible for obtaining licences to, and otherwise acquiring, such Third Party Software, including the right to incorporate such Third Party Software into the Client Web Site. The Client shall look solely to the warranties and remedies, if any, provided by the respective Third Party Providers of Third Party Software. Third parties with whom the Client contracts directly to provide Third Party Software, including without limitation Product Suppliers, shall not be considered Third Party Providers, regardless of the extent to which such Third Party Software relates to, or interacts with, [   ]'s Services under this Agreement.

[   ] hereby disclaims and waives any and all warranties, express or implied, with respect to Third Party Software, including, without limitation, implied warranties of satisfactory quality and fitness for a particular purpose.

13.5   [Further to Clause 11, the Client acknowledges that in conjunction with rendering the Services, the Client may receive certain Third Party Services where [   ] is unable to fully secure the warranties set forth in Clause 11. In such a case, the Client agrees to look solely to the warranties and remedies, if any, provided by the Third Party Provider for those particular Services.]

13.6   [Except as expressly set forth in Clause 15, all Services, Work Product, [   ] Tools, Third Party Software, Third Party Services, Content and other products provided under this Agreement by [   ] or third parties are provided on an 'as is' basis and [   ] hereby expressly disclaims and the Client hereby expressly waives any and all warranties, whether express or implied, including without limitation any warranty of satisfactory quality or fitness for a particular purpose.]

13.7   The Client hereby represents and warrants to [   ] that: the Client is the owner or licensee of the Client Content and each element thereof, and the Client has secured all necessary licences, consents, permissions and releases for [   ]'s use of the Client Content in its performance of the Services and each element thereof, including without limitation all trade marks, logos, names and likenesses contained therein; the use of the Client Content shall not i) infringe the copyright or trade mark right of any person, ii) constitute a defamation, invasion of privacy, or violation of any right of publicity or iii) to the best of the Client's knowledge and belief, infringe the patent of any person; the Client has complied with, and will continue to comply with at all times, all applicable laws, ordinances, regulations and codes to the extent that they would have a material impact on [   ]; the Client Content is not obscene or otherwise in violation of any law of any applicable jurisdiction; the Client Content is and will remain accurate and correct in all material respects; and the Client will comply with its own obligations under the Data Protection Act 1998; and has full corporate power and authority to execute and deliver this Agreement and perform its obligations under this Agreement.

14.   Limitation of Liability

14.1   In no event shall the Client be liable to [   ] or to any third party for any indirect, incidental, special, consequential, exemplary or punitive damages or reliance, loss, damage or expense, including without limitation lost profits or loss of use or revenues, or expense of procurement of substitute goods or services, arising out of or in connection with any act or omission relating to the subject matter of this Agreement.

14.2   The maximum aggregate liability of the Client for any reason or upon any cause of action or claim shall be limited to GB£10,000.

14.3   No action arising out of breach of this agreement or transactions related to this agreement may be brought by one Party against the other more than [one (1) year] after the client has become aware of the cause of action.[2]

14.4   Nothing in this Agreement shall limit or exclude either Party's liability for fraud, fraudulent misrepresentation, or for death or personal injury caused by its negligence.

15.   Indemnification

15.1   Subject to Clause 13 of this Agreement, [   ] shall defend, indemnify and hold harmless the Client from and against any and all third party actual or threatened claims suits, proceedings, actions, damages, liabilities, losses, costs and expenses, including without limitation reasonable attorneys' fees and expenses ('Loss') which arise out of or as the result of third party claims brought or threatened against the Client and arising out of [   ]'s breach of its express warranties set forth in Clause 13. [With respect to any [   ] Objects or such Work Product that is the subject of an actual or threatened claim of infringement or misappropriation, [   ] may elect, at [   ]'s expense, to:

a)   obtain for the Client a licence to continue using the [   ] Objects or Work Product;
b)   replace or modify the [   ] Object or Work Product to be non-infringing; or
c)   if neither (a) or (b) is available on commercially reasonable terms, at the request of [   ], the Client shall discontinue use and return the [   ] Objects or Work Product and [   ] will provide the Client with a refund of all fees, retainers, expenses and consequential economic loss suffered by the Client flowing from the portion of the [   ] Objects or Work Product.

[Notwithstanding the foregoing, [   ] shall have no indemnification obligation for any Loss: (a) asserted by a parent, subsidiary or Affiliate of the Client; (b) arising directly out of the Client Content, (c) arising out of the Third Party Software.]

15.1.1 [[   ] shall have no indemnification obligation for losses arising out of or related to Third Party Providers, to the extent the Client agreed to proceed with such a Provider that provided indemnities or warranties that were not substantially in conformance with the express indemnities or warranties of [   ] herein with respect to the Services. In such case the Client agrees to look solely to the warranties and remedies, if any, provided by the Third Party Provider for those Services. If [   ] did not satisfy its obligations under this Clause 15.1, [   ] shall give the indemnity obligations of Third Party Services as [   ] Tools under this Clause 15.1.]

15.2[3] [Subject to Clause 15.3 hereof, the Client shall defend, indemnify and hold harmless [   ] from and against any Loss which arise out of or as the result of third party claims brought or threatened against the Client except where such claims arise from any claims from any relationship between the third party and [   ], and the Client's breach of its express warranties set forth in Clause 13; the Client Content; the placement in any media of the Client Content or any other material prepared by the Client or anyone acting on the Client's behalf; any content uploaded to, contributed to, or altered on Client Web Site by anyone other than [   ] [   ] 's compliance with the Client's specific instructions; or any Web site hyperlinked with the Client Web Site, including without limitation Product Supplier Web sites. Notwithstanding the foregoing, the Client shall have no indemnification obligation to the extent such Loss arises out of or relates to any of the circumstances set forth in the first paragraph Clause 15.1 above.]

15.3 [Upon the assertion of any claim or the commencement of any suit or proceeding against an indemnified Party by any third party that may give rise to liability of an indemnifying Party under this Clause 15, the indemnified Party shall promptly notify in writing the indemnifying Party of the existence of such claim, suit or proceeding and shall give the indemnifying Party a reasonable opportunity to defend and/or settle the claim at its own expense and with counsel of its own selection. The indemnified Party shall make available to the indemnifying Party all books and records relating to the claim and the Parties agree to render to each other such assistance as may reasonably be requested in order to ensure a proper and adequate defence. The indemnified Party shall have the right to participate in such defence at its own cost and expense. An indemnifying Party shall not make any settlement of any claims that might give rise to liability of an indemnified Party hereunder without the prior written consent of the indemnifying Party, which consent shall not be unreasonably withheld.]

16.   Insurance

16.1   Without prejudice to either Party's obligations under this Agreement, each Party shall effect and maintain with reputable insurers such policy or policies of insurance as may be necessary to cover their respective obligations and liabilities under this Agreement. Each Party shall produce on request evidence of the insurance coverage, typically a certificate of insurance.

17.   Confidentiality

17.1   Prior, during and at any time after this Agreement [   ] agrees to treat the Client's Confidential Information as strictly confidential. Any information oral, written or otherwise arising from this agreement is to be treated as Confidential Information.

17.2   The disclosing of Confidential Information shall not be an implied licence to the Client's intellectual property.

17.3   The Receiving Party agrees to treat the other Party's Confidential Information as strictly confidential and shall not, directly or indirectly:

a)   use such Confidential Information for any purpose other than the performance of its obligations under this Agreement;
b)   copy or modify such Confidential Information without the prior written consent of the Disclosing Party; or
c)   distribute or disclose such Confidential Information to any third party other than to the Receiving Party's Affiliates, employees, directors, agents and independent contractors (collectively, 'Representatives') who have a specific need to know the Confidential Information and who are obligated to maintain the Confidential Information in confidence under similar terms and conditions as set forth herein.

The Receiving Party agrees, at its sole expense, to take all reasonable measures to prevent its Representatives from breaching this Agreement and the Receiving Party agrees that it shall be responsible for any breach or threatened breach of this Agreement by any of its Representatives. The Receiving Party agrees not to sell, transfer, lease, or license the Confidential Information of the Disclosing Party in any manner whatsoever.

17.4   The Receiving Party shall not be required to treat as Confidential Information any information or material that the Receiving Party can demonstrate by written documentation:

a)   is or has entered the public domain through no fault of the Receiving Party or its Representatives;

b)   is or was independently developed by or for the Receiving Party without use, directly or indirectly, of the Confidential Information;

c)   is or was received by the Receiving Party from a third party on a non-confidential basis, provided that the Receiving Party did not know or should have known that the source of such Confidential Information was not bound by an obligation of confidentiality with respect to such information; or

d)   is approved for release by the prior written authorization of the Disclosing Party.

17.5   In the event that the Receiving Party or any of its Representatives receive a request or demand to disclose all or part of the Confidential Information pursuant to a court order, operation of law, subpoena, requirement of a governmental authority, or otherwise, the Receiving Party agrees to:

a)   promptly notify the Disclosing Party of the terms and surrounding circumstances of such request or demand so that the Disclosing Party may seek a protective order, or other appropriate relief and/or waive compliance with the provisions of this Agreement;

b)   promptly consult with the Disclosing Party on the advisability of taking steps to resist or narrow such request or demand;

c)   in the absence of a protective order or other remedy or the receipt of a waiver from the Disclosing Party and only after the Receiving Party's compliance with (a) and (b) above, minimize the disclosure of the Confidential Information ultimately required to be disclosed to only that Confidential Information which is reasonably necessary to meet the express requirements of the request or demand; and

d)   subject to the mutual agreement of the Parties concerning costs and expenses, cooperate with the Disclosing Party to obtain an order or other reliable assurance that confidential treatment will be accorded to any Confidential Information ultimately required to be disclosed after the Receiving Party's compliance with (a) and (b) above.

17.6   Upon any termination of this Agreement, or within [ten (10) days] after the Receiving Party's receipt of the Disclosing Party's written request, the Receiving Party shall return to the Disclosing Party all tangible materials containing or embodying the Confidential Information, and/or at the specific request of the Disclosing Party, destroy all documents (paper, electronic or otherwise) containing or embodying the Confidential Information unless the Confidential Information is the subject of an effective licence pursuant to Clause 12 of this Agreement. Notwithstanding the return and destruction of the Confidential Information, the

Receiving Party and its Representatives shall continue to be bound by the terms and conditions of this Clause 17.

17.7   Notwithstanding this Clause 17, within [thirty (30) days] after the Effective Date, and only upon approval in advance in writing by both Parties, [   ] and the Client shall issue at least one joint press release which shall include [   ]'s and the Client's names and announce the Parties' relationship pursuant to this Agreement. The Parties may mutually consent to issue other press releases, and consent shall not be unreasonably withheld with respect to the same. Each Party may disclose the fact that they are provider/purchaser of the Services respectively, including, but not limited to, listing such information on their Web sites.

17.8   The Receiving Party agrees that the breach or threatened breach of any of the terms or conditions of this Clause 17 will cause the Disclosing Party and/or the owner of such Confidential Information irreparable injury for which the recovery of money damages would be inadequate. Therefore, the Disclosing Party or such other Party shall be entitled to obtain injunctive relief against the breach or threatened breach of this Agreement, in addition to any other remedies the Disclosing Party may have under applicable law and without the necessity of posting a bond, even if otherwise normally required.

18.   Non-solicitation

18.1   Each Party recognizes that the employees of the other constitute a valuable asset of that Party. Accordingly, during the period commencing on the Effective Date of this Agreement and ending [one (1) year] after any termination of this Agreement, each Party shall not, without the prior written approval of the other Party, directly or indirectly solicit, employ, offer to employ, or engage as a consultant any employee or former employee of the other Party; provided, however, that this restriction shall not apply with respect to employees who voluntarily or involuntarily terminated employment with the other Party at least [six (6) months] before the solicitation.

18.2   Each Party agrees that the duration, geographical scope, activity and subject matter of the non-solicitation terms and conditions set forth in this Clause 18 are fair, reasonable and not excessively broad and are necessary to protect the parties' goodwill and Confidential Information and that the parties would not have entered into this Agreement but for their agreement to comply with such terms and conditions.

18.3   Both parties agree that the breach or threatened breach of any of the terms or conditions of this Clause 18 could cause each Party irreparable injury for which the recovery of money damages would be inadequate. Therefore, the injured Party may be entitled to obtain injunctive relief against the breach or threatened breach of this Clause 18, in addition to any other remedies that Party may have under applicable law.

19.   Notices

19.1   Any notice required or permitted under this Agreement shall be in writing and shall be deemed given:

a)   if by hand delivery, upon receipt thereof;
b)   if mailed, [three (3) days] after postage or [seven (7) days] if outside the UK, postage prepaid, certified mail, return receipt requested;
c)   if by facsimile transmission, upon electronic confirmation thereof;
d)   if by next day delivery service, upon such delivery; or
e)   for notices for purposes of Clause 3 and the SOW, by e-mail with a confirmation by appropriate means. All notices shall be addressed as follows (or to such other address as either Party may in the future specify in writing to the other):

In the case of [   ]:   In the case of the Client:

Attn: _____   Attn: _____

Fax: _____   Fax: _____

20.   Force Majeure

20.1   [   ] shall not be deemed in default or otherwise liable for any delay in or failure of its performance under this Agreement or any SOW by reason of any Act of God, fire, natural disaster, accident, riot, act of government, restrictions of laws or regulations, strike or labour dispute, shortage of materials or supplies or of suppliers of goods or services, failure of transportation or communication, network or power failures or interruptions, mechanical or electrical breakdowns, or any other cause beyond the control of [   ].

21.   Assignment

21.1   Neither Party shall assign its rights, duties or obligations under this Agreement, in whole or in part, without the prior written consent of the other Party, such consent not to be unreasonably withheld, and any attempt to do so shall be deemed null and void and a material breach of this Agreement; provided, however, a change of control, merger or acquisition of either Party shall not be deemed an assignment under this Agreement.

22.   General Provisions

22.1   No delay or failure by either Party in exercising or enforcing any of its rights or remedies hereunder, in whole or in part, and no course of dealing or performance with respect thereto, shall constitute a waiver thereof in any other instance. In addition, the express waiver by a Party hereto of any right or remedy in a particular instance will not constitute a waiver thereof in any other instance. All rights and remedies shall be cumulative and not exclusive of any other rights or remedies available at law or in equity.

22.2   No change, deletion, modification, amendment, supplement to or waiver of this Agreement shall be binding upon a Party to this Agreement unless made in writing and signed by duly authorized representatives of both Parties.

22.3   This Agreement shall be governed by, construed and enforced in accordance with UK Law and proceedings arising from this Agreement shall be heard in UK Courts.

22.4   In the event that any provision of this Agreement shall for any reason be determined to be void, invalid, illegal or otherwise unenforceable in any respect by any court of competent jurisdiction, then, to the full extent permitted by law: (a) all other provisions of this Agreement will remain in full force and effect and will be liberally construed in order to carry out the intent of the Parties to this Agreement as nearly as may be possible; (b) such determination will not affect the remaining provisions of this Agreement; and (c) any court of competent jurisdiction will have the power to reform such provision to the extent necessary for such provision to be enforceable under applicable law.

22.5   The clause and other headings contained in this Agreement are intended solely for convenience of reference and are not intended to be part of or affect the meaning or interpretation of this Agreement. The Parties hereby acknowledge that this Agreement is the product of negotiation between the Parties and/or their respective solicitors and the Parties hereby agree that this Agreement shall not be construed against either Party on the basis that the Agreement was drafted by one Party or the other.

22.6   This Agreement, along with any and all Statements of Work, exhibits, and attachments to this Agreement or any SOW, constitutes the entire agreement between [   ] and the Client relating the subject matter hereof and supersedes all prior or contemporaneous agreements, proposals, understandings and representations, written or oral, between the Parties with respect to the subject matter hereof. All terms and conditions of this Agreement shall govern and prevail over any additional or contrary terms and conditions contained in the Client's purchase orders, requests for quotations, payments or other writings, all of which are hereby rejected by [   ].

22.7   This Agreement may be executed in counterparts, each such counterpart shall be an original and altogether shall constitute but one and the same document.

SIGNED by a Director
duly authorized for and on
Behalf of [   ]:-

SIGNED by a Director
duly authorized for and on
Behalf of [   ]:-

NOTES

1 [References in this Agreement to [   ] shall include their Agents. Agents shall mean Third Party Providers and individual consultants employed, contracted, subcontracted or otherwise engaged by [   ] to carry out work further to this Agreement.]
2 In contract law the cause of action accrues when the damage is done. If an alternative date is intended the contract can specify that the cause of action is to accrue within a period of time from the making of the contract or from the date of knowledge.
3. This clause places on the client the complete obligation to ensure that the function of the work they are performing does not contravene any third party rights, without any of the limitations which they have reserved for themselves in clause 15.1.

Appendix 3

Advertising agreement

Schedule 1

THIS AGREEMENT is made on [*date of agreement*]

Between:

(1)   [   ] (UK) Limited, a company registered in [England and Wales] with company number [   ] whose registered office is at [   ] ('Agency'):

(2)   [   ], a company registered in [England and Wales] with company number [   ] whose registered office is at [   ] (the 'Client'), together known as the Parties.

Whereas

(a)   The Agency and the Client have entered into a Master Services Agreement, for the purposes of the Client engaging the Agency, to provide consulting, advisory, design, enhancement, technical, development and implementation services with respect to the Client Web Site; and

(b)   This Agreement sets out the terms and conditions governing the Client engaging the Agency, to provide promotion, marketing and advertising services with respect to the Client Web Site.

It is agreed as follows:

1.   Defined Terms

1.1   All words which appear in quotation marks and bold type will throughout this Advertising Agency agreement (the 'Agreement') have the meaning given to them when they first appear in that form.

2.   Engagement

2.1   The Agency agrees to render to the Client certain services in connection with advertising on the World Wide Web as specified in the Agency's form proposal(s) (the 'Proposal') agreed between the parties from time to time.

2.2   Each Proposal shall detail the individual assignment(s) to be performed by the Agency (the 'Assignment') and include a schedule of charges detailing the Agency's remuneration and the terms of payment for the Assignment (the 'Schedule of Charges').

2.3   Each Proposal agreed by the parties shall constitute a separate agreement and shall be governed by this Agreement. In the event of any conflict between the terms of any Proposal and the terms of this Agreement, the terms of this Agreement shall control.

2.4   From now on in this Agreement all work produced by the Agency for the Client under this Agreement shall be called the 'Advertising'.

3.   Agency Services

3.1   Generally the Agency's engagement shall relate to providing promotion, marketing and advertising services with respect to the Client Web Site. Specific details of the Advertising will be set out in the Proposal (the 'Services').

4.   Exclusivity

4.1   The Agency shall be a non-exclusive advertising agency in the UK for the Client with respect to the Client Web Site. The Client may arrange for another outside agency to provide any of the general services other than that for which the Agency has been engaged.

5.   Agency Status

5.1   The Agency acts in all its contracts as principal at law.

6. Cooperation

6.1   The Client will give the Agency clear briefings and ensure that all the facts given in relation to the Assignment are accurate, while the Agency will cooperate fully with the Client and use reasonable care and skill to make the advertising as successful as is expected from a competent advertising agency.

6.2   The Client will make available to the Agency in a timely and orderly fashion all relevant information, appropriate offices and facilities, access to the Client's staff and computer equipment and cooperate with the Agency in the prompt provision of approvals and authorities.

7.   Term of Appointment

7.1   Any services set out in any Proposal agreed by the Parties shall be subject to termination by either Party giving [ninety (90) days] notice in writing. The Parties decide on the duration of Advertising in each Proposal. The period from the commencement to the end of all individual Assignments within a proposal is the ('Term').

8.   Remuneration

8.1   The Agency shall receive a fixed fee calculated on the time and materials required to perform the Services in accordance with the Agency's rates for time and materials applicable at the time the Services are performed, excluding any incidental expenses or applicable duties and taxes. The Agency shall pay its own incidental expenses, applicable duties and taxes in accordance with the terms of the applicable regulation.

8.2   The Agency will receive 33.3 per cent of the fixed fee at commencement of the Term, 33.3 per cent during the Term and 33.3 per cent at the end of the Term. If during the Term either Party gives notice to terminate as set out in clause 7.1 above, then the third payment will be made at the end of the notice period. No amount will be added to the fixed fee for packing, shipping, express, postage, telephone, telex, fax, travel expenses and other out of pocket expenses of Agency personnel.

8.3   Except in the case of paragraph 12 below, other than the Fixed Fee the Client shall not be responsible to the Agency or any third party in respect of any additional costs of whatever nature relating to the Proposal.

9.   Billing

9.1   The Agency will invoice the Client in respect of Agency fees and production costs in accordance with the Schedule of Charges. Payment of invoices shall fall due immediately upon presentation and invoices shall be forwarded to the Client as and when the Proposal is agreed and signed.

9.2   The Agency reserves the right to charge interest on all invoices presented to the Client which are not paid within [thirty (30) days] of presentation at the rate of 4 per cent above the base rate from time to time of Barclays Bank plc compounded on a weekly basis. The Agency may also (without limitation) suspend any further work on the Assignment by service of written notice on the Client.

10.   Approvals and Authorities

10.1   Any reference in this agreement to the Client's written approval shall mean written approval by directors or employees of the Client authorized to approve the Agency's work and whose names are set out below:

'Authorized Person'

Name[......................]   Title [...........................]

Name[......................]   Title [...........................]

Any change to the Authorized Persons during the Term will be notified in writing by the Client to the Agency.

10.2   For the purposes of this Agreement 'written approval' shall include approval signified by fax, letter, telex or e-mail where such e-mail emanates from the e-mail server and address of the Authorized Person.

10.3   The Agency shall submit to the Client for its specific written approval the format, copy, design and layout of the Advertising.

10.4   The Client's written approval of the format, copy, design and layout of the Advertising will be the Agency's authority to prepare the coding of the Advertising in machine readable form.

10.5   The Agency will advise the Client immediately of any changes in the estimated cost of items of Advertising or any changes in plans, schedules or work in progress previously approved in writing by the Client.

11.   Contact Reports

11.1   Contact reports will be issued by the Agency dealing with matters of substance discussed at meetings or in telephone conversations between the client and the Agency within [three (3) working days] or before of the deadline for implementation of the subject matter of the meetings or telephone conversation. If the subject matter of a contact report is not questioned by the Client within [three (3) working days] of its receipt, it will be taken to be a correct record of the meeting or telephone conversation to which it refers. Notwithstanding this, the Agency must allow the Client a minimum of [fourteen (14) working days] to consider any matters of substance arising from meetings or in telephone conversations with the Client, prior to issuing a contact report.

12.   Amendments

12.1   In the event of any amendment the Client will reimburse the Agency for any reasonable charges or expenses incurred by the Agency to which the Agency is committed and also pay the Agency's remuneration covering these items.

13.   Copyright and Other Intellectual Property Rights

13.1   From now on in this Agreement, 'Rights' means any copyright, extended or revived copyright, design right, registered design right, patent, performer's property right, trade mark, database right or any similar right exercisable in any part of the world, including any application for registration of any patent, trade mark, registered design or similar registrable rights in any part of the world; 'Existing Material' means any photograph, design, specification, instruction, software, information, data or any other material protected by Rights, created by a third party and in existence at the time it is desired to make use of it for the purposes of the Advertising; 'Agency Material' means any artwork, copy, design, specification, instruction, software, information, data and all other material created for the Advertising by directors or employees of the Agency, provided that it is approved by the Client and incorporated into Advertising during the Term; 'Commissioned Material' means any artwork, copy, design, specification, instruction, software, information, data and all other material the creation of which is commissioned from third parties during the Term by the Agency for the Advertising; and 'Moral Rights' means all rights described in Part 1, Chapter IV of the Copyright Designs and Patents Act 1988 and any similar rights of authors anywhere in the world.

13.2   The Rights in all Agency Material vest in the Agency unless different arrangements are made in writing.

13.3   The Agency shall obtain all usage rights in Existing Material and Commissioned Material as are deemed necessary by the Agency at the time such material is selected or obtained.

13.4   If the Client so requests and provided all obligations of the Client arising from this Agreement (including those relating to the period of notice) have been met, the Agency shall assign to the Client, after the Term, with full title guarantee, such of the Rights in the Agency Material, Commissioned Material and Existing Material as may be owned by the Agency and capable of assignment together with the right to sue for damages for past infringement. Such Assignment shall be subject to sub-clauses 13.5 to 13.7 below.

13.5   The Agency shall hold all source code and object code for all application programming which is incorporated in the Advertising as agents for the Client, and shall grant the Client a licence to use the object code of such application programs in the course of its use of the Advertising.

13.6   The Client warrants that it owns and/or controls all Rights in the Existing Materials and has secured the requisite permission to use any person's name, voice, likeness and performance incorporated into any such Existing Materials.

13.7   The Agency acknowledges that the Advertising may include certain Third Party Software programs and that the Agency will be solely responsible for obtaining licences to use such Third Party Software. The Agency make no warranties or representations whatsoever, express or implied, as to the quality, capabilities, performance or suitability of such Third Party Software.

13.8   Notwithstanding any of the above the Agency shall be able during and after the Term to use Advertising for the purpose of promoting its own business; and retain the copyright in any material contained in any presentation made in competition with any other agency in the event of the Agency's presentation being unsuccessful.

14.   Ownership and Custody of Material

14.1   The Agency will keep in its care materials entrusted to the Agency by the Client (the 'Property'). The Agency will mark or otherwise identify the Property as being the property of the Client and will be responsible for its safekeeping.

14.2   The Agency shall not be entitled to destroy Property without the Client's prior written consent, except that if after [twelve (12) months] from the Property coming into its possession the Agency shall be entitled to return the Property to the Client by delivery to the Client's offices at the address shown at clause 1.

15.   Insurance

15.1   Property and items such as negatives and software coming into existence for the purpose of producing the Advertising (the 'Items') retained by the Agency will at all times that they are in the Agency's possession be insured by the Agency against loss or damage even though the Items will have become the Client's property as a result of the Client paying the relevant production costs.

15.2   The Agency will insure Property and Items against loss or damage when in transit between the Agency and third parties for the purposes of production or publication and will ensure that such Property and Items are insured when in the possession of those third parties.

16.   Confidential Information

16.1   The parties acknowledge a duty not during or after the Term to disclose without the other's prior written permission any confidential information either concerning the other's business, its business plans, customers or associated companies or resulting from studies or surveys commissioned and paid for by the Client.

16.2   In particular during and after the Term the Agency acknowledges its responsibility to treat in complete confidence all the marketing and sales information and statistics relating to the Client's business with which the Client may supply the Agency in the course of any work for the Client.

16.3   From now on in this clause 16 'Information' will be used to describe the categories of information referred to in sub-clauses 16.1 and 16.2.

16.4   The Agency shall where so requested by the Client impose obligations in terms equivalent to those in sub-clauses 16.1 and 16.2 on its own personnel and obtain written assurances from any third parties to whom Information has to be disclosed in order to enable the Agency to carry out its obligations under this Agreement.

16.5   The Client acknowledges and agrees that any identifiable and original idea or concept presented by the Agency in relation to any promotion or advertising campaign invented or developed by the Agency shall be acknowledged as being available only for such promotion or campaign and shall not be used for any other purposes whatsoever without the Agency's express prior agreement given in writing. Even where no promotion or campaign is agreed, the ideas and concepts presented to the Client shall remain strictly confidential and shall not be used in any way, including communication to any third party, without the Agency's express prior written consent.

16.6   For the avoidance of doubt, the restrictions in this clause 16 shall not prevent:

16.6.1   the disclosure or use of Information in the proper performance of the Agency's duties;

16.6.2   the disclosure of Information if required by law;

16.6.3   the disclosure of Information which has come into the public domain otherwise than through unauthorized disclosure.

16.7   The Client acknowledges that nothing in this Agreement shall affect the Agency's right to use as it sees fit any general marketing or advertising intelligence gained by the Agency in the course of its appointment.

17.   Warranties and Indemnities

17.1   If there is an error in Advertising as published or publication is delayed or does not occur as planned, the Agency will not be liable unless this is caused by its default or neglect. Nothing in this Agreement shall exclude the Agency's liability to the Client for death or personal injury resulting from the Agency's negligence.

17.2   The Agency's total liability in contract, tort or otherwise arising out of or in connection with the performance or observance of the Agency's obligations or otherwise in respect of any Assignment shall be limited to [£5,000,000].

17.3   The Agency shall not be liable in any event for any indirect or consequential or economic loss suffered by the Client, including (without limitation) loss of business, use profits, future contracts or anticipated savings arising out of or in relation to the provision by the Agency of the Services.

17.4   The Client warrants that to the best of its knowledge information and belief all information supplied to the Agency before and during the Term will be accurate and not in any way contrary to English law.

17.5   The Agency warrants that all Advertising will be lawful. The Client accepts legal responsibility in respect of any Advertising approved by it for publication, relying on the warranty of the Agency.

18.   Termination

18.1   Either Party may terminate this Agreement forthwith by notice in writing to the other if the other Party :

18.1.1   is in material breach of any of the terms of this Agreement and, in the case of a breach capable of remedy, fails to remedy such breach within [thirty (30) days] of receipt of written notice giving full particulars of the breach and of the steps required to remedy it; or

18.1.2   (being a company) passes a resolution for winding up (otherwise than for the purposes of a solvent amalgamation or reconstruction) or a court makes an order to that effect; or

18.1.3   (being a partnership or other unincorporated association) is dissolved or (being a natural person) dies; or

18.1.4   becomes or is declared insolvent or convenes a meeting of or makes or proposes to make any arrangement or composition with its creditors; or

18.1.5   has a liquidator, receiver, administrator, administrative receiver, manager, trustee or similar officer appointed over any of its assets; or

18.1.6   ceases, or threatens to cease, to carry on business.

18.2   The parties' rights, duties and responsibilities shall continue in full force during the agreed period of notice and whether or not there is a period of notice, the Client shall pay all sums due in respect of work done and expenditure committed by the Agency until the end of the Term, such sums shall be limited to the fee payable pursuant to clause 9.1.

19.   Survival of Obligations of Termination

19.1   The following clauses shall survive the end of Term:

Clause 16   Copyright and other intellectual property rights
Clause 17   Ownership and custody of material
Clause 19   Confidential information
Clause 20   Warranties and indemnities
Clause 27   Non-solicitation
Clause 30   Notices
Clause 31   Applicable law.

20.   Advertising Standards

20.1   Both parties shall comply with the British Codes of Advertising and Sales Promotion and other relevant codes of advertising laid down whether on a statutory or self-regulatory basis. Both parties shall abide by the rulings of the Advertising Standards Authority and the Committee of Advertising Practice.

20.2   In order to satisfy the requirements of these codes or any statutory requirements the Client and the Agency will cooperate with each other in ensuring that suitable objective factual product and other information is available as required.

20.3   The Client shall inform the Agency without delay if the Client considers that any Advertising submitted to the Client by the Agency for approval is false or misleading or in any way contrary to law or to any applicable code. The Client does not in any way accept liability for breach by the Agency of its obligations either at law or in relation to any applicable code for false or misleading Advertising.

21.   Data Protection

21.1   Each Party shall ensure that any mailing list or customer database supplied to the other Party shall comply with the requirements of all legislation in force from time to time including, without limitation, the Data Protection Act 1998 and that each Party shall comply with the relevant obligations of the Data Protection Act 1998.

22.   Waiver

22.1   No whole or partial waiver of any breach of this Agreement shall be held to be a waiver of any other or any subsequent breach. The whole or partial failure of either Client or Agency to enforce at any time the provisions of this Agreement shall in no way be construed to be a waiver of such provisions nor in any way affect the validity of this Agreement or any part of it or the right of either Party to enforce subsequently each and every provision.

23.   Force Majeure

23.1   If due to war, strikes, industrial action short of a strike, import or export embargo, lockouts, accidents, fire, blockade, flood, natural catastrophes or other obstacles over which the Agency has no control, the Agency fails to perform any of its obligations under this Agreement, the Agency shall not be held responsible for any loss or damage which may be incurred as a result of such failure. Should the event of force majeure continue for longer than [one (1) month], the Party adversely affected shall have the option of terminating this Agreement immediately with further liability other than such liabilities as have already accrued when the Term ends.

24.   Non-solicitation

24.1   The Parties agree that neither of them will either on their own account or in partnership or association with any person, firm, company or organization or otherwise and whether directly or indirectly during or for a period of [twelve (12) months] from the end of the Term solicit or entice away or attempt to solicit or entice away (or authorize the taking of any such action by any other person) any employee of the other Party who has worked on the Advertising at any time during the last [twelve (12) months] of the Term without the prior written consent of the other Party.

25.   Severance

25.1   If any part of this Agreement is found by a court of competent jurisdiction or other competent authority to be invalid, unlawful or unenforceable then such part will be severed from the remainder of this Agreement, which will continue to be valid and enforceable to the fullest extent permitted by law. In the event of a holding invalidity so fundamental as to prevent the accomplishment of the purpose of the Agreement, the parties shall promptly commence good faith negotiations to remedy such invalidity.

26.   Notices

26.1   Any notice, invoice or other communication which either Party is required by this Agreement to serve on the other Party shall be sufficiently served if sent to the other Party at its specified address at clause 1 (or such other address as is notified to the other Party in writing) as follows:

26.1.1   by hand;

26.1.2   by registered or first class post or recorded delivery;

26.1.3   by facsimile transmission confirmed by registered or first class post or recorded delivery; or

26.1.4   by e-mail sent from the mail address of the authorized person.

Notices sent by registered post or recorded delivery shall be deemed to be served [three (3) working days] following the day of posting. Notices sent by facsimile transmission or e-mail shall be deemed to be served on the day of transmission if transmitted before 4 pm on a working day, but otherwise on the next following working day. In all other cases, notices are deemed to be served on the day when they are actually received.

27.   Applicable Law

27.1   This Agreement shall be construed in accordance with and governed by the law of England and Wales and both parties hereby irrevocably agree that the Courts of England and Wales shall have exclusive jurisdiction to resolve any controversy or claim of whatever nature arising out of or relating to this Agreement or any alleged breach of it.

SIGNED by a Director
duly authorized for and on

Behalf of [   ]:-

SIGNED by a Director duly authorized for and on

Behalf of [   ]:-

Appendix 4

Sample business plan

This document contains confidential information, which may only be disclosed for the purpose set out in it. Any party receiving this document recognizes that it must hold the information contained in it in confidence and protect it from unauthorized copying, dissemination and use by unauthorized persons. In the absence of FictionWeb's prior written consent, any party receiving this document shall not reproduce nor disclose its contents to any third party.

Peter Adediran

tomorrow's law online service ©
Advice Engineered for the Future

BUSINESS PLAN CONTENTS

1. Directors, Secretary and Advisors

2. Introduction

3. The Concept
    3.1 Aggressively Building the FictionWeb Branded Content
    3.2 Aggressive Marketing/Promotions
    3.3 Expand into a Distributor

4. Executive Summary
    4.1 Financial Projections
    4.2 Marketing – Marketing Communications
    4.3 Advertising
    4.4 Direct Mail
    4.5 Search Engines
    4.6 The Directors
    4.7 Financial Requirements

5. Detailed Report on FictionWeb Business
    5.1 Trading and Revenue
         5.1.1 Electronic Commerce
         5.1.2 Leasing Revenue
         5.1.3 Advertising Revenue
         5.1.4 Subscription Revenue
    5.2 cuckooconcept.com Experience
         5.2.1 Animation
         5.2.2 Macromedia Flash 5 Technology
         5.2.3 Product Channels
    5.3 Market Analysis
         5.3.1 Interactive Leisure Products Analysis
         5.3.2 General Analysis
    5.4 Competition
         5.4.1 Where does cuckooconcept.com fit in?
    5.5 Regulatory and Proprietary Rights
    5.6 Property

6. Management Team
    6.1 Professional Adviser
    6.2 Technical Staff
    6.3 Administrative Assistant

7. Operations – Financial Summary

1.   DIRECTORS, SECRETARY AND ADVISORS

Directors

Tom Bloggs (Founder & Creative/Animation Director)
Dick Bloggs (Financial Director)
Harry Bloggs (Director)

Secretary and Registered Office

Joe Solicitor
Law Firm
London
UK

Auditors

Joe Accountant
London
UK

Corporate Solicitor	Bankers
Peter Adediran	Retail Bank Plc
Company Solicitor	Ruin Road
tomorrow's law	London
	UK

2.   INTRODUCTION

This document constitutes the business plan to launch the Web site located at www.cuckooconcept.com. cuckooconcept.com is one of the online Web sites that is in the process of development by FictionWeb, a private limited company incorporated in England and Wales under the Companies Act 1985 on 1 March 2000 with registered number 00000000. This document will refer to FictionWeb and cuckooconcept.com. For the avoidance of doubt, FictionWeb is the Company and the online Web site, cuckooconcept.com is the concept for which FictionWeb is seeking funding. In this first round of funding, FictionWeb intends to raise [US$700,000 by way of a bank loan to finance expansion growth to the next stage of development in September 2003, with an initial public offering of cuckooconcept.com shares in 2004.]

3.   THE CONCEPT

cuckooconcept.com is a high quality animated Web site, created by macro-media flash 5 animation technology. Its target audience are between the ages of 5 and 18, providing interactive leisure products which vary in sophistication according to the user profile including edutainment, info-tainment and games. The Web site caters for the individual user by communicating. The site or parts of it will also eventually be reauthored and licensed to cuckooconcept.TV for broadband viewing. The product is designed around the user's characteristics. When users visit the Web site they are asked a series of questions to build up a brief user profile. The profile then results in a product recommendation. cuckooconcept.com is icon driven and operates via a full screen animated interface. cuck-ooconcept.com core product is the telling of stories from around the world, varying in sophistication, whether users are from the mid-western states of the United States or a small village in Peru.

The key components behind cuckooconcept.com strategy are content, strong branding and marketing and distribution capabilities.

3.1   Aggressively building the cuckooconcept.com branded content

The Directors believe that the Internet is in desperate need of branded content and compelling entertainment for the technology that exists at the time and not some broadband future. They see an immediate opportunity, because although the Internet is a high-tech infrastructure, at this point in their opinion it is low-tech in its ability to deliver any kind of compelling entertainment. They believe that the best low-tech entertainment that exists is panel-graphic comic books. The Directors believe that if FictionWeb could develop compelling animation around the genre of fantasy, it would be in the forefront of delivering global branded enter-tainment franchises.

3.2   Aggressive marketing/promotions

The Directors intend to establish a studio dedicated to the development of compelling original content created by globally recognized content creators, or in association with global entertainment franchises to pioneer the way that the Internet is developed as an independent entertainment and marketing medium distinct from any other medium. The Directors also intend to experiment with the ways in which global brand and content and marketing and promotion can be synergized with offline media. cuckooconcept.com is an umbrella to harness other global-branded entertainment groups to develop strategies that integrate the best use of the Internet with rich content to enhance offline promotions, marketing and activities.

3.3   Expand into a distributor

The Directors believe that by the year 2005 cuckooconcept.com will become the successor to Disney as a global lifestyle-brand content creator, producer, marketing and distribution company. This distribution capability will also be bolstered by its eventual availability through television.

4.   EXECUTIVE SUMMARY

The Directors believe that cuckooconcept.com's valuation before the completion of the first round of funding is US$2,800,000. This figure is based on the value of similar concepts to cuckooconcept.com, the value of the copyright in the concept and the initial investment by the founders to date. cuckooconcept.com will earn its first revenues during the 2001/02 financial year, by content enfranchisement, content leasing, subscription and advertising revenue. A comprehensive marketing campaign will be designed to increase the user base to up to 10,000,000 visitors and 1,000,000 subscribers by January 2003 and justify the addition of 70 new seven-minute animations to the Web site.

4.1   Financial Projections

Table A.1

Fiscal year	2000	2001	2002	2003	2004
Revenue (US$)	446,075	541,666	710,932	895,780	1,081,655
Cost of services	162,590	246,997	315,453	381,096	394,745
Operating expenses	208,617	189,986	211,381	234,211	256,303
Interest expense	13,199	59,367	55,537	44,131	33,291
Net profit	61,669	45,316	128,566	252,099	397,316
Profit margin (%)	3.0	8.4	18.1	28.1	36.8

4.2   Marketing – Marketing Communications

FictionWeb has budgeted US$105,000 for marketing expenses during its first year of operation and an increasing amount thereafter. FictionWeb's initial marketing resources will be devoted to capturing the European markets. Beginning in the second year of operation, FictionWeb intends to broaden its efforts to include international markets as well. FictionWeb will advertise on all the major offline sources used by consumers to find URLs for Internet products and in particular television. In late 1999, 34 per cent of all Web site visitors came directly from picking up addresses on television. This figure is expected to increase by more than 200 per cent in 2000. The bar chart below shows this year's offline sources to find URLs for product and service information.

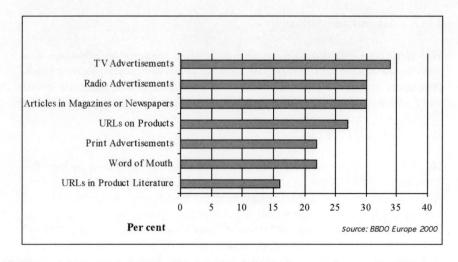

Figure A.1 *URLs in product literature*

4.3 Advertising

FictionWeb will advertise on children's cable television channels at a cost of approximately US$5,600 per advert, place brochures in bookshops, advertise on video games, enter into hypertextlink agreements with other children's sites and pay for listings in children's magazines (the cost of Web site affiliation is not expected to exceed US$5,000). All FictionWeb's print materials will show its Web site address and logo.

4.4 Direct Mail

FictionWeb will develop a high quality colour brochure for cuckooconcept.com designed to convey the personalization and exceptional quality of the Web site. All of FictionWeb's marketing materials, including its brochures, will be designed with a common look and will feature the cuckooconcept.com Internet address and logo. The cost of brochure design, layout, printing and postage is estimated to be US$28,500 during the first year. Brochures will be sent to prospective bookshops, libraries and possible partners accompanied by personalized letters from the CEO. These names will be identified from FictionWeb's client list and from mailing lists purchased from directory services at little cost.

4.5 Search Engines

FictionWeb will register keywords with various search engines.

4.6   The Directors

The creative director has had several years' experience as a writer/creative consultant in the media/entertainment industry. The financial director has served as chief executive officer of a public quoted property company. FictionWeb also benefits from an experienced non-executive director who will be advising on brand marketing.

4.7   Financial Requirements

FictionWeb intends to use the net proceeds from the US$700,000 raised to develop the ideas set out in this plan. These include primarily marketing/branding and content development. The current cost of a seven-minute animation is US$12,000. FictionWeb wishes to launch the site with 25 animations, which will cost approximately US$305,000. FictionWeb will also use funds raised to pay the rents on its existing premises, employ a Web master and pay for the professional services of Peter Adediran. These funds should take cuckooconcept.com to the next stage of funding in four years' time after which another fundraising will be needed. By 2004 FictionWeb intends to have 100 seven-minute animations.

5.   DETAILED REPORT ON THE CUCKOOCONCEPT.COM BUSINESS

5.1   Trading and Revenue

5.1.1   Electronic Commerce

E-commerce offerings will be found throughout the site and services such as books, T-shirts, posters, baseball caps, toys, games, puzzles, videos, DVD, CD ROMs and travel will be available for purchase. The Directors believe that substantial revenue can be made from the sale of books, as cuckooconcept.com is a natural environment for purchasing children's books. Publications will be by cuckooconcept.com and other children's publishers. The world's largest book retailer – www.amazon.com – is probably one of the most famous success stories on the Internet. The bookshop today has 3 million books, CDs and video titles on its 'cyber shelves'. Amazon.com's prices are estimated to be up to 40 per cent lower than those of an ordinary retailer, primarily because of the lower costs of distribution and marketing. Within its first year of trading FictionWeb will enter into e-commerce agreements with two of the world's largest publishing houses. Revenue from e-commerce can be earned in a variety of ways:

- Upfront and variable payments. In the case of upfront payments, cuckooconcept.com earns this by including third parties' e-commerce on its site or by providing a minimum number of page views or request for information from its site by a user; in the case of a variable payment, for delivering a number of page views in excess of the agreed number.
- Exclusivity fees: this represents fees paid for a third party's exclusive e-commerce rights on the cuckooconcept.com site.
- Bonus fee and commissions and revenue sharing: these represent where either there is a fixed per capita fee for an initial purchase on the third party's site or there is a percentage paid for ongoing purchases.

5.1.2   Leasing Revenue

Leasing the use of cuckooconcept.com content to other sites and to interactive television companies.

5.1.3   Advertising Revenue

cuckooconcept.com will derive revenue from banner advertising or pop-up windows. The Directors estimate that on average a visitor will spend 15 minutes on the cuckooconcept.com Web site, returning at least three times a year – a total of 45 minutes annually. This degree of stickiness is guaranteed since the fables are related in two or three separate chapters on a periodic basis, and the visitor must return to complete the fable. Compared with the average television exposure of five minutes, this is extremely high. As well as the big difference in the number of minutes exposed to the medium, a major difference is also that the consumer voluntarily participates on the cuckooconcept.com Web site. This high involvement is not available with television advertising. Viewers have lost patience with television and look to the Internet to establish a more permanent individual contact. According to an analysis carried out by BBDO, New York, in 1995, people in the United States watched on average 40.2 hours of television a week, while only 2.44 hours were spent in cyberspace. The relative amounts are changing quickly, however. Three years later, in 1998, 5.02 hours a week were spent in cyberspace. BBDO's analysis also shows that on average people surf the Internet for 30–40 minutes at a time. The average duration of a visit to a Web site is estimated to be three to four minutes. By way of comparison, viewers spend only between 30 and 40 seconds viewing a particular brand on television. The Internet is a serious competitor to television for advertising revenue.

5.1.4   Subscription Revenue

Access to the site is free. However, the Directors intend to charge US$1.50 per view of each animation. New animations will be released biweekly and the subscription fee will have to be paid for each new viewing; however, the user can repeat the last episode for free.

5.2 cuckooconcept.com experience

5.2.1 Animation

The animations forming the cuckooconcept.com experience will all be prepared following a rigorous process rarely seen in delivering entertainment on the Internet. First comes the story, plot, action or situational idea, which may be a written treatment with or without supporting sketches. It describes the continuity of what is proposed. Such a treatment, perhaps very brief, precedes any fuller scripting. This process is made easier as the ideas are largely based on already existing local fables. In order to get the maximum visual emphasis and sound emphasis, the ideas are immediately translated into pictures. A storyboard is created which provides the continuity of the action, and is worked out scene by scene simultaneously with the animation script. In the storyboard the story is told and to some extent graphically styled in a succession of key sketches with captions and fragments of dialogue. The creative/animation director will prepare model drawings for the principal characters and drawings establishing the backgrounds. The modelling drawings indicate the nature and temperament of the characters as well as their appearance when seen from a variety of angles and using a number of characteristic gestures. These will act as guides for the key animators, who with their assistants must bring the figures to dramatic life through the succession of final drawings created on the drawing board. Although animation needs to be choreographed, animation using Macromedia Flash 5 is quite limited in its mobility. Nevertheless, the key animators and their assistants will still ensure that the movements are exactly timed and so deployed through the right number of successive drawings. The movements of the characters will be synchronized with the words they appear to utter. Sound tracks, both dialogue and music, will be pre-recorded, so that the animators have an exact time scheme to follow. The creative/animation director will create a time chart to ensure that all sound and movements are properly synchronized. Once the preparation of the ideas is completed then the key, or senior, animators draw the highlights, or salients, of the movement, which will give the special edge of liveliness or characterization to the movements. The assistant animators close the gaps by completing any other intermediate drawings. The animation is eventually delivered using Macromedia Flash 5 technology. The preparation and execution of the technology will be based on the highly technically skilled and creative ideas of the creative/animation team, which will make cuckooconcept.com the most compelling producers of animation enter-tainment on the Internet.

5.2.2   Macromedia Flash 5 Technology

Macromedia Flash 5 fuses the precision and flexibility of vector graphics with bitmaps, audio, animation, and advanced interactivity to create brilliant and effective Web experiences which attract and engage visitors. In June 2000, NPD Research, the parent company of MediaMetrix, conducted a study to determine what percentage of Web browsers have Macromedia Flash preinstalled. The results show that 91.8 per cent of Web users can experience Macromedia Flash content without having to download and install a player. That means that more than 248 million people can view Macromedia Flash.

5.2.3   Product Channels

There are five product channels on the Web site:

5.2.3.1. World Map/Fables Channel

This is the core product category on the Web site and is based on inter-active branding. The world map is an interactive directory to the fables. The user chooses a continent, then clicks on the subsequent country. Once on a country the user will receive information on that region and then choose one of its fables. The fables are based on the original classic tales of morality passed down through the generations; however, they vary in sophistication and will vary in style according to user profile.

5.2.3.1.1 There will be 100 fully animated, narrated and text driven fables. Each chapter in a fable will be approximately 7.5 minutes, and there will be two or three chapters per fable. The characters in the fables will vary depending on the user.

5.2.3.1.2 Using users between the ages of three and nine as an example, their fables are hosted by Ollie the orang-utan, a lovable monkey who with his friends wants to share these great stories with the world. Ollie will introduce each story personally, dressed in the traditional costume of the fable's host nation. Ollie will also host his own show, entitled 'Olliewood'. Ollie has several friends who act out the stories. These cyber marionettes are:

- Charlie Chimplin;
- Lisa Gibbon;
- Robert de Baboono;
- Balthazaar Yeti;
- Alicia Silverback.

The style of animation will depend on the fable's location, as all stories will be told in the traditional storytelling form of the host nation. For example, the Chinese fable will be animated with the same effect as that of the ancient shadow theatre, where cut-outs of characters are placed in front of a candle and projected onto a wall. The French fable will have the look of the old string puppet theatre. Each fable will be accompanied by traditional music from its country.

5.2.3.2. Edutainment Channel

Through partnerships, FictionWeb will offer different edutainment sections within an edutainment channel such as:

5.2.3.2.1 History section
Ollie and his friends will act out different historic events. After each act Ollie will ask questions, and each time a correct answer is chosen Ollie gains a banana. For each one answered wrong, Ollie loses one. When they are all lost, you have to start again; however if Ollie fills his bag with bananas you get a password to enter the games/play room.

5.2.3.2.2 Maths section
Contains maths-related questions that refer to fables and numbers.

5.2.3.2.3 Games/playroom channel
This area is for virtual toys, puzzles and a number of interactive activities aimed at building up dialogue with young people.

5.2.3.2.4 Competition channel
There will be regular competitions surrounding the fables. The audience will have an opportunity to win a prize/toy from our sponsor/s.

5.2.3.2.5 Picture gallery channel
The gallery contains pictures from all over the world.

5.3 Market Analysis

5.3.1 Interactive Leisure Products Analysis
One of the most appropriate product categories for exposure on the Internet is products based on interactivity. Exposure in the traditional media is difficult as, for example, a game looks neither particularly exciting nor involving in an advertisement or on a poster. The Internet can present extracts from the game (for example, one level) which the user can try out, and can enable the user to download the whole game in return for

payment. Often the price for downloading will be cheaper than the price users would pay for the same product offline as on the Internet there are no costs such as packaging, retail trade distribution and advertising.

The latest methods also take care of automatic updating of new versions of software through the net.

Walt Disney's Disney Blast is an excellent example of how the Internet can be used as an entertainment medium. Disney Blast, the digital Donald Duck comic, is updated daily and 20 to 25 new games and stories are added each week.

According to Forrester Research, 19 per cent of Web sites with positive incomes belong to the entertainment industry.

5.3.2 General Analysis

From Iceland to India the Internet is transforming the world. The table below shows the current number of Internet users per 1,000 people in 50 different countries worldwide published by the American Electronics Association this year.

Table A.2 *Internet users per 1,000 people*

Rank	Country	Internet users
1	Iceland	492.7
2	United States	485.6
3	Finland	485.0
4	Sweden	478.7
5	Norway	475.1
6	Australia	434.2
7	Canada	422.3
8	Denmark	354.6
9	Singapore	349.3
10	Switzerland	345.7
11	New Zealand	317.0
12	United Kingdom	287.6
13	Netherlands	266.7
14	Germany	265.3
15	Israel	263.2
16	Hong Kong	238.1
17	Belgium	230.8
18	Taiwan	204.3
19	Austria	193.3
20	Ireland	177.5
21	Japan	163.2
22	France	147.1
23	Spain	133.3
24	Italy	132.3

25	Portugal	93.4
26	South Korea	76.0
27	Czech Republic	73.9
28	Hungary	73.7
29	Slovakia	71.1
30	Greece	57.2
31	Poland	47.0
32	South Africa	46.0
33	Malaysia	40.4
34	Chile	39.6
35	Argentina	32.5
36	Russia	25.1
37	Brazil	24.6
38	Bulgaria	23.6
39	Mexico	22.1
40	Romania	17.4
41	Venezuela	15.3
42	Colombia	14.2
43	Thailand	13.5
44	Turkey	12.6
45	Saudi Arabia	8.8
46	Ukraine	8.3
47	Philippines	7.4
48	Peru	6.6
49	China	4.0
50	India	2.0

The Internet continues to grow rapidly, enabling millions of people all over the world to share information, communicate, be entertained and conduct business. International Data Corporation (IDC), a market research firm, estimates in its report *Internet Usage and Commerce in Western Europe 1997–2002,* published in 1998, that Web users worldwide will grow from approximately 142.2 million at the end of 1998 to approximately 398.6 million by the end of 2002. IDC estimates that Web users in Western Europe will grow from approximately 41 million in 1998 to approximately 136 million by the end of 2002, representing an increase from 11 per cent to 35 per cent of the entire population.

5.4   Competition

cuckooconcept.com operates in the younger generation's edutainment market. The market for entertainment online is relatively new and rapidly evolving. cuckooconcept.com's main competitors include www.libresse.dk, www.libragirl.com, www.disneyblast.com, Stan Lee Media,   www.dreamweaver.studios.com,   www.ninjaturtles.com,

www.inetcomics.com, www.asterix.okukbooks.com, www.dccomics.com
and www.biocomics.com.

Competition is intense; however, cuckooconcept.com is based on global
branded content. The Directors believe that with 2 million channels of
different technologies that deliver content, an emerging global audience
will be overwhelmed by the variety of media that present themselves on a
minute-by-minute basis in their lives, and they will retreat to the comfort
of things that they recognize, like localized fables. The Directors believe
that cuckooconcept.com will be in the forefront of all the new media entertainment companies which recognize the immediacy of a global audience
and the need to design content that is interesting and compelling to a
global audience of multicultural users.

5.4.1   Where does cuckooconcept.com fit in?

cuckooconcept.com is unique in that in order for a brand to be successful
worldwide it needs a different brand profile for every country. Great variations in a brand's profile are necessary due to historical factors, cultural
differences or locally developed marketing strategies which over time
have established an independent 'local' brand profile. cuckooconcept.com
naturally fits the global yet localized individual Web sites comfortably, as
the concept already encompasses the historical and cultural differences of
nations.

5.5   Regulatory and Proprietary Rights

The Directors of FictionWeb will ensure that cuckooconcept.com is fully
compliant with the Data Protection Act 1984, Children Online Privacy
Protection Act 1998 and meets the Federal Trade Commission and EU
standards on privacy online.

FictionWeb will ensure that sufficient protection is afforded to it and to
its users through comprehensive terms and conditions of use of the Web
site.

cuckooconcept.com has registered the domain names cuckoo
concept.com, cuckooconcept.co.uk, cuckooconcept.net and cuckoocon
cept.org.

FictionWeb will also apply for the cuckooconcept.com trade mark to be
registered in the EU and United States.

The Directors are aware of the proposals by the Independent Television
Commission, Internet Watch Foundation and the Advertising Standards
Authority and cuckooconcept.com will be actively involved in the devel-
opment of the legal and regulatory status of interactive services.

5.6   Property

FictionWeb Limited has taken a one-year lease on small draughty offices for US$40,000 payable in four instalments.

6.   MANAGEMENT TEAM

Tom Bloggs, Founder and Creative Director, Age 34
Mr Bloggs currently serves as creative director for FictionWeb Limited. Tom has considerable knowledge of the worldwide Internet, entertainment and media industries. He has worked as a consultant at Exciting Pictures on an animated project for Steven Spielberg and at Hanna Carrera for the Jungle Cartoon Network, and has written several screenplays. He also founded Medusa Limited, an advertising company, which was one of the first to sell advertising space on software. He will begin drawing a US$40,000 annual salary beginning [   ].

Dick Bloggs, Financial Director, Age 38
[   ] He will begin drawing a [   ] annual salary beginning [   ].

Harry Bloggs, Non Executive Director, Age 36
[   ] He will begin drawing a [   ] annual salary beginning [   ].

6.1   Professional Adviser

In return for preparing the business plan and advising in the raising of the first round of funding Peter Adediran will receive [US$].

6.2   Technical Staff

During its first year of trading, FictionWeb will employ one key animator and an assistant animator, both of whom will be trained in using Macromedia Flash 5 applications. They will receive salaries of [US$] and [US$] respectively.

6.3   Administrative Assistant

FictionWeb will employ an administrative assistant beginning [   ] at an annual salary of US$25,000. The assistant's duties will include answering the phone and performing general administrative tasks.

7.   OPERATIONS – FINANCIAL SUMMARY[1]

Exhibit 1 displays FictionWeb's projected revenue, net income and profit margin over time.

Exhibit 2 summarizes the projected financial performance of FictionWeb over the five-year period ending in September 2004.
Exhibit 3 summarizes the projected cash flow performance of FictionWeb over the five-year period ending in September 2004.
Exhibit 4 provides an overview of FictionWeb's use of the proceeds of its first round of financing.

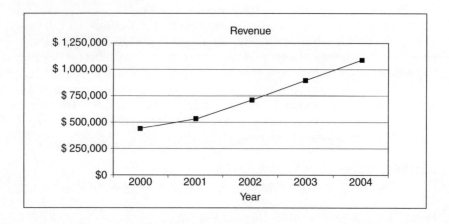

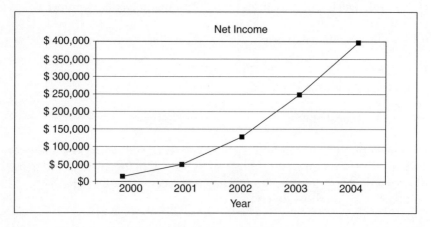

Figure A.2   *Exhibit 1*

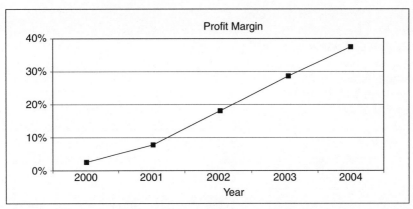

Figure A.2   *Exhibit 1 (continued)*

Exhibit 2
Profit and loss: 5-year projection

FictionWeb Limited
Income Statement
For the year ending September 30

(Amounts in US$)	2000	2001	2002	2003	2004
Revenue	446,075	541,666	710,937	895,780	1,081,655
Cost of services	162,590	246,997	315,453	365,339	394,745
Gross margin	283,485	294,669	395,484	530,441	686,910
% of revenue	64%	54%	56%	59%	64%
Operating expenses	208,617	189,986	211,381	234,211	256,303
% of revenue	47%	35%	30%	26%	24%
Interest expense	61,669	59,367	55,537	44,131	33,291
Net income/(loss)	13,199	45,316	128,566	252,099	397,316
Net profit as % of revenue	3.0%	8.4%	18.1%	28.1%	36.7%

Balance sheet: 5-year projection

FictionWeb Limited
Balance Sheet
September 30

(Amounts in US$)	*2000*	*2001*	*2002*	*2003*	*2004*
Current assets					
Cash	192,655	185,702	163,176	222,401	371,924
Accounts receivable	16,828	20,280	26,618	33,539	40,498
Total current assets	209,483	205,982	189,794	255,940	412,422
Intangible assets					
Goodwill/non-compete	195,000	195,000	195,000	195,000	195,000
Organization costs	13,000	13,000	13,000	13,000	13,000
Accumulated amortization	13,961	29,561	45,161	60,761	75,494
Net intangible assets	194,039	178,439	162,839	147,239	132,506
Fixed assets	395,457	428,165	582,550	647,558	710,066
Accumulated depreciation	29,137	101,722	190,816	274,971	331,553
Net fixed assets	366,320	326,443	391,734	372,587	378,513
Total assets	769,841	710,865	744,367	775,766	923,441
Liabilities					
Total current liabilities	18,642	20,921	23,484	26,231	28,750
Loan liability	551,484	493,669	430,272	360,757	284,532
Capital lease liability	102,422	71,793	88,988	35,897	18,889
Total liabilities	672,548	586,383	542,745	422,884	332,170
Total assets less liabilities	97,294	124,481	201,622	352,882	591,270

Exhibit 3
Cash flow forecasts – 5-year projection

FictionWeb Limited
Statement of cash flows
For the year ending September 30

(Amounts in US$)	2000	2001	2002	2003	2004
Cash flows from operating activities:					
Net income/(loss)	13,199	45,316	128,566	252,099	397,316
Adj. to reconcile net income/(loss) to cash					
Depreciation and amortization	87,682	88,185	104,694	99,755	71,315
Changes in operating assets and liabilities:					
(Increase)/decrease in accounts receivable	(16,828)	(3,453)	(6,338)	(6,921)	(6,959)
Increase/(decrease) in accounts payable	16,356	2,279	2,563	2,747	2,519
Net cash provided/(used) by operating activities	100,409	132,326	229,486	347,681	464,191
Cash flows from investing activities:					
Purchase of fixed assets	(310,457)	(32,708)	(89,385)	(65,008)	(62,508)
Other investing activities	(175,000)	-	-	-	-
Net cash provided/(used) by investing activities	(485,457)	(32,708)	(89,385)	(65,008)	(62,508)
Cash flows from financing activities:					
Principal payments	(76,094)	(88,444)	(111,201)	(122,607)	(93,233)
Contributions	700,000	-	-	-	-
Distributions	-	(18,126)	(51,426)	(100,840)	(158,926)
Net cash provided/(used) by financing activities	623,906	(106,570)	(162,627)	(223,447)	(252,159)
Net cash provided/(used) by financing activities	238,858	(6,952)	(22,527)	59,226	149,523
Cash – beginning of period	40,000	278,858	271,906	249,379	308,605
Cash – end of period	278,858	271,906	249,379	308,605	458,128

Exhibit 4

Use of Proceeds

FictionWeb intends using the proceeds of the first round of financing (US$700,000) as follows:

US$305,000 (approximately one-half of the proceeds) will be used by FictionWeb to purchase 30 animations. As more fully described in the business plan, this transaction will provide FictionWeb with its initial branded content to launch the cuckooconcept.com Web site.

US$250,000 will be used by FictionWeb for other capital expenditures, including, but not limited to:

- recruitment of personnel;
- development of technology;
- fixed assets;
- hardware lease;
- payment of commission fee for business/legal adviser.

US$145,000 (approximately one-quarter of the proceeds) will be used by FictionWeb for working capital. These funds will be roughly allocated as follows:

- marketing expenditures (budgeted at approximately US$105,000);
- office lease (approximately US$40,000).

NOTES

1 Whilst the figures given in these financial forecasts show realistic growth rates, investors may require you to produce a set of management accounts for, say, 2000.

Appendix 5

Subscription and shareholder agreement

[This Agreement is written from the perspective of the venture capitalist firm]

Date

[   ] (1)

and

[   ] (2)]

Subscription and Shareholder Agreement

Peter Adediran
tomorrow's law online service ©
Advice Engineered for the Future

This Agreement is made on [   ] between:

(1) [   ] of [   ] (2) [   ] whose registered office is at [   ] (the 'Company'); and

(3) [   ] whose registered office is at [   ] ('the Investor').

Recitals:

(a)   The Company was incorporated in [   ] on [   ].

(b)   The Founders and the Investor (the 'Initial Shareholders') have agreed to subscribe for Ordinary Shares on the terms and conditions of this Agreement.

It is agreed as follows:

1.   Interpretation

In this Agreement (including the Recitals):

1.1   Definitions

'Agreed form' means a document in the form agreed between the parties and signed for identification by or on behalf of the parties;

'Articles' means the Articles of Association of the Company and those Articles as amended from time to time;

'Associated Company' means, in relation to a party, any holding company, subsidiary, subsidiary undertaking or fellow subsidiary or subsidiary undertaking or any other subsidiaries or subsidiary undertakings of any such holding company;

'Audited Accounts' mean the audited accounts of the Company to be prepared for the financial period ending on [   ];

'Board' means the Board of Directors of the Company or an authorized committee of the Board;

'Budget' means the annual budget for the Company approved from time to time by the Directors;

'Business' means the business of [   ];

'Business Day' means a day which is not a Saturday or Sunday or a bank or public holiday in England and Wales;

'Business Plan' means the business plan for the Company in the agreed form as set out in [Schedule], prepared annually in respect of the forth-coming [12 month period] setting out details of the Company's strategic planning in respect of customers (including market development and capacity growth), capital expenditure, financing, tax, competitors and contingency planning;

'Completion' means completion of this Agreement in accordance with Clause 3;

'Deed of Adherence' means a deed in the form set out in Schedule 3;

'Directors' means the Directors of the Company and 'Director' means any one of them;

'Founders' means [   ] and [   ];

'Intellectual Property Rights' means all existing and future copyright, patents, trade marks, know-how, trade or business names, rights to extract information from databases, design rights, trade secrets, rights of confidence and associated goodwill, and all rights or forms of protection of a similar nature or having an equivalent effect to any of them which may subsist anywhere in the world whether or not any of them are registered and including applications for registration of any of them;

'IPR Assignment' means the IPR Assignment dated [   ] in the agreed form to be entered into between the Founders and the Company;

'LIBOR' means the British Bankers Association Interest Settlement Rate displayed on the appropriate Reuters screen as of 10 am on the date hereof (and each subsequent anniversary) for the offering of six-month deposits in Sterling;

'Listing' means the listing of the Shares on the Official List of the London Stock Exchange Limited or the admission of Shares to the Alternative Investment Market or the listing or admission of Shares on NASDAQ or any other Recognized Investment Exchange and 'Listed' shall be construed accordingly;

'Losses' means all losses, liabilities, damages, costs (including, without limitation, legal costs and experts' and consultants' fees), charges, expenses, actions, proceedings, claims and demands;

'Name' means [   ] and/or any other name under which the Company carries on the Business;

'Option Agreement' means the Investor Option Agreement in the agreed form between the Founders and the Investor;

'Ordinary Shares' means the A-Shares of [*eg* £1] each and the B-Shares of [*eg* £1] each in the capital of the Company;

'Recognized Investment Exchange' means a recognized investment exchange as defined by Section 285 of the Financial Services and Markets Act 2000;

'Resolutions' means the resolutions of the Directors and the Company in the agreed form;

'Retail Prices Index' means the General Index of Retail Prices (All Items) which is published in the United Kingdom in the monthly *Digest of Statistics* by the Office for National Statistics;

'Service Agreements' means the service agreements in the agreed form to be entered into between the Founders and the Company on Completion;

'Shareholders' means the holders of the Shares;

'Shares' mean the Ordinary Shares and (1) any shares issued in exchange for those shares or by way of conversion or reclassification and (2) any shares representing or deriving from those shares as a result of an increase in, reorganization or variation of the capital of the Company;

['Venture Capitalist Firm' means];

'Warranty' means a warranty set out in Clause 4 and 'Warranties' means all those warranties.

1.2   Clauses, Schedules etc

References to this Agreement include any Recitals and Schedules to it and this Agreement as from time to time amended and references to Clauses and Schedules are to Clauses of and Schedules to this Agreement.

1.3   Headings

Headings shall be ignored in construing this Agreement.

1.4 Joint and Several Liability

Any provision of this Agreement which is expressed to bind more than one person shall, save where inconsistent with the context, bind them jointly and each of them severally.

1.5 Time of Day

References to time of day are to London time unless otherwise stated.

1.6 Winding-up

References to the winding-up of a person include the amalgamation, reconstruction, reorganization, administration, dissolution, liquidation, merger or consolidation of such person and any equivalent or analogous procedure under the law of any jurisdiction in which that person is incorporated, domiciled or resident or carries on business or has assets.

1.7 Information

Any reference to books, records or other information means books, records or other information in any form including paper, electronically stored data, magnetic media, film and microfilm.

1.8 Definitions in Articles

Words and expressions defined in the Articles have the same meanings in this Agreement unless the context otherwise requires.

2. Conditions

2.1 Conditions Precedent

Completion of this Agreement is conditional on fulfilment or waiver of the following conditions:

2.1.1 the passing of the Resolutions at the Board Meeting and the Extraordinary General Meeting of the Company to be held on Completion;
2.1.2 the execution and completion subject only to Completion of the Option Agreement by all the parties to it;
2.1.3 the execution and completion of the IPR Assignment by all the parties to it;
2.1.4 the Company and the Founders entering into the Service Agreements; and
2.1.5 the subscription of the Shares on the terms of this Agreement.

2.2 Responsibility of the Parties

The Founders, the Investor and the Company shall use their best endeavours to ensure that the conditions in Clause 2.1 are satisfied as soon as reasonably practicable.

2.3 Non-satisfaction

The parties to this Agreement may waive all or any of the conditions in Clause 2.1 by agreement amongst them all. If any condition in Clause 2.1 is not satisfied or waived on or before Completion or such other date as the parties agree this Agreement shall lapse and no party shall have any claim against any other under it, except that:

2.3.1   Clause 10.5 and 11 shall continue to apply; and
2.3.2   the parties' accrued rights and obligations shall not be affected.

3.   Completion and Subscription

3.1   Completion

Subject to Clause 2, Completion shall take place at the offices of the Investor, [   ] as soon as reasonably practicable following execution of this Agreement on a Business Day agreed between the parties and if not so agreed prior to [   ] in any event on [   ].

3.2   Subscription etc

At Completion:

3.2.1   the Founders and the Investor (or its then holding company, or its then holding company's subsidiary, as nominated by it in writing to the Company) shall subscribe and pay for the number of Ordinary Shares set out against their names in Schedule 1 and the consideration for such subscription being the payment of [   ] to be paid within [30 days] from the full registration of the Company;
3.2.2   the Company shall, and each of the Initial Shareholders shall procure that the Company shall, allot and issue to each of the Founders and the Investor (or as they may direct) the Shares subscribed by it under Clause 3.2.1 and register those shares in the relevant names and issue share certificates in respect of them;
3.2.3   the Budget and the Business Plan shall be adopted by the Company;
3.2.4   the Company shall appoint one person notified to it by the Investor as a Director;

3.2.5   the Option Agreement shall be entered into by the Founders and the Investor;

3.2.6   the IPR Assignment shall be entered into by the Founders and the Company.

3.3   Simultaneous Subscription

No Shareholder shall be obliged to complete the subscription for any of the Shares unless the subscription of all such Shares is completed simultaneously.

4.   Founders' Warranties

The Founders warrant to the Investor as follows.

4.1   The Founders have the full power and authority to enter into and to perform their obligations under this Agreement which when executed will constitute valid and binding obligations on them in accordance with its terms.

4.2   The entry and delivery of, and the performance by the Founders of, this Agreement will not constitute a breach of any law or regulation to which the Founders are subject or by which they are bound nor result in any claim by any third party against the other Shareholders of the Company nor, where such Shareholder is a corporation, result in any breach of any provision of its Memorandum, Articles of Association or constitutional bylaws.

4.3   The Founders are not aware of any fact which would prevent the Company from implementing the Business Plan. All the Intellectual Property Rights necessary to carry on the Business of the Company and its subsidiaries as set out in the Business Plan have been assigned by the Founders to the Company. There are no Intellectual Property Rights owned or used by the Company which have not been assigned to the Company by the Founders.

4.4   The particulars of the Company set out in Schedule 2 of this Agreement are correct.

4.5   No person has the right (whether exercisable now or in the future and whether contingent or not) to call for the allotment, conversion, issue, sale or transfer of any share or loan capital or any other security giving rise to a right over the capital of the Company under any option or other Agreement (including conversion rights and rights of pre-emption) and there are no encumbrances on the shares of the Company or any arrangements or obligations to create any encumbrances.

4.6   The Company has never traded or carried on any business nor incurred any liabilities or obligations of any kind other than as provided in or contemplated by this Agreement, its paid up Shares, and those imposed on the Company by virtue if its incorporation and any changes in its officers and constitution since its incorporation.

4.7   The Founders are free to be or become an employee, director and shareholder of the Company and to devote the whole of their time and attention to the business and affairs of the Company and are not bound by any restriction, covenant or other obligation or commitment which would in any way impair their ability so to do.

4.8   The Founders have not ever been charged with or convicted of any criminal offence other than a road traffic offence nor have bankruptcy or any analogous proceedings been brought or threatened in respect of the Founders, and the Founders are not aware of any facts or matters which they believe might give rise to any such criminal or bankruptcy proceedings.

4.9   There is no agreement or arrangements under which the Founders or any connected person of the Founders is to receive from any person and, so far as the Founders are aware, no person is entitled to receive from the Company, any finders' or other fee, brokerage or commission in connection with this Agreement or any of the matters contemplated or referred to in those agreements.

4.10   All information which has been given by or on behalf of the Founders to the Investor or to the solicitors or agents of the Investor in the course of the negotiations leading to this Agreement was when given and is at the date of this Agreement true, accurate and not misleading in any respect.

4.11   The Founders have supplied to the Investor in writing all information concerning the Company which they reasonably consider to be material for an Investor to know when making a decision to invest in the Company on the terms of this Agreement.

5.   Investor's Warranty

5.1   The Investor warrants to the Founders that the Investor has the full power and authority to enter into and to perform its obligations under this Agreement which when executed will constitute valid and binding obligations on it in accordance with the terms of this Agreement.

6.   The Board

6.1   Directors

6.1.1   Unless the Investor gives prior consent to an increase in numbers, the Board shall comprise a maximum of five Directors.
6.1.2   Subject to the Articles, the Founders may appoint four Directors.
6.1.3   Subject to the Investor holding at least 20 per cent of the Shares, the Investor may appoint one Director.
6.1.4   The Shareholders may remove a Director in accordance with the Articles. The Shareholders can appoint another Director in his or her place.
6.1.5   Those removals shall take effect without any liabilities on the Company for compensation for loss of office or otherwise except to the extent that the liability arises in relation to a service contract with a Director who was acting in an executive capacity.
6.1.6   The Shareholders may appoint or remove a Director by giving written notice to the Company.
6.1.7   If:
(i) with the prior consent of the Investor, the number of Directors on the Board exceeds five; and
(ii) the Investor holds 30 per cent or more of the Shares in issue at the relevant time;
the Investor may appoint two Directors.

6.2   Support from the Investor

The Investor hereby agrees that it shall provide the Company with access to the advice, support and, as relevant, sharing of technology know-how of the Investor. The Investor shall provide general advice and support in relation to the following:

6.2.1   advice on a worldwide market plan and how to best market the [Business] in each market;
6.2.2   allow the Company to utilize the Investor in marketing and selling and use the Investor as a general reference;
6.2.3   utilize all feasible and effective contacts to market the Company and its products;
6.2.4   open the global network of the Investor's subsidiary undertakings, partners and contacts for the Company wherever suitable and help in establishing a global network of partners for the Company; and
6.2.5   market, promote and support the development of the Company and take an active part in expanding and promoting the Company towards Listing.

7.   Board Meetings and Committees of Directors

7.1   Board Meetings

7.1.1   Board meetings shall be held at least four times a year and at not more than three monthly intervals. At least two clear days' written notice shall be given to each of the Directors of all Board meetings (except if there are exceptional circumstances or the majority of the Directors agree to shorter notice).
7.1.2   Each notice of meeting shall:
   (i)   specify a reasonably detailed agenda;
   (ii)   be accompanied by any relevant papers, including the most recently prepared monthly management accounts; and
   (iii) be sent by courier or facsimile transmission if sent to an address outside the United Kingdom.

7.2   Committees of Directors

7.2.1   The Board may constitute committees of Directors.
7.2.2   The voting and quorum for Board committee meetings shall be the same as for Board meetings.

7.3   Subject to the provisions hereof, a meeting of Directors or of a committee of Directors may be validly held notwithstanding that such Directors may not be in the same place provided that:

7.3.1   They are in constant communication with each other throughout by telephone, television or some other form of communication.
7.3.2   A majority of the Directors participating in the meeting are physically present in [country]; and all Directors in attendance so agree.

8.   Further Financing and Steps to Listing

8.1   The parties agree that in the event that the Board resolves to raise further financing for the Company, whether by way of loan or equity or any other method whatsoever, the Board shall immediately notify the Investor and the Investor or any other person nominated by the Investor shall have the right but not the obligation to seek, arrange or instruct any person to advise and arrange such further financing exclusively on behalf of the Company.

8.2   The parties shall use their reasonable endeavours to ensure that all actions necessary to achieve the Listing are taken as soon as reasonably practicable and financially prudent, including taking the following steps:

8.2.1　reorganizing the share capital structure of the Company and determining the number of shares to be issued;

8.2.2　changing the composition of the Board;

8.2.3　amending the Memorandum and Articles of Association of the Company as appropriate;

8.2.4　instructing a suitable investment bank and reporting accountants (such instruction to be made by the Investor);

8.2.5　meeting the financial reporting requirements of the investment exchange to which the application for Listing is made (for example as to trading history, extracts from audited accounts of prior years, cash flow and profit forecasts, working capital report and indebtedness statement);

8.2.6　establishing or amending employee/executive share option schemes if necessary and obtaining Inland Revenue clearance as appropriate;

8.2.7　setting the issue price;

8.2.8　carrying out verification of the prospectus and other documents pertinent to the Listing in respect of which verification is required;

8.2.9　procuring (so far as it is able) that its appointees to the Board accept responsibility for the listing particulars or prospectus to be issued by the Company;

8.2.10　procuring that their appointees to the Board provide any other confirmations or consents which are either reasonably necessary to secure the Listing;

8.2.11　agreeing to any indemnities and/or warranties which are required to be given; and

8.2.12　entering into an undertaking not to sell by way of a public offering by the Company's sponsoring banker any Shares not sold on listing for such specified period as may be reasonably required in order to maintain an orderly market in the Shares following Listing.

9.　Reserved Matters

9.1　Matters Requiring Consent

Each of the Shareholders shall procure, as far as they can, that no action is taken or resolution passed by the Company in respect of the following matters ('Reserved Matters'), without the prior written consent of the Investor:

9.1.1　any change to its Memorandum and Articles;

9.1.2　any change of name;

9.1.3　the appointment and removal of the Auditors;

9.1.4　the adoption of the Audited Accounts;

9.1.5　any change to the accounting reference date or accounting policies;

9.1.6   the presentation of any petition for winding-up;

9.1.7   any change in the share capital or the creation, allotment or issue of any shares or of any other security or the grant of any option or rights to subscribe for or to convert any instrument into such shares or securities;

9.1.8   any reduction of the share capital or variation of the rights attaching to any class of shares or any redemption, purchase or other acquisition of any shares or other securities of that company;

9.1.9   the adoption of any bonus or profit-sharing scheme, any share option or share incentive scheme or employee share trust or share ownership plan or retirement benefit scheme;

9.1.10   the entry into of any joint venture, partnership consortium or other similar arrangement;

9.1.11   the sale of the Company or any consolidation or amalgamation with any other company;

9.1.12   the acquisition or disposal (including the lease to a third party) in any financial year of:

(i)   a significant asset;

(ii)   the whole or a significant part of its undertaking; or

(iii)   a subsidiary undertaking,

the proceeds or net book value of which represent more than £25,000 (such figure to be increased on 30 June in each year by the percentage variation in the Retail Prices Index for the preceding 12 month period);

9.1.13   capital expenditure of greater than £25,000 (such figure to be increased on 30 June in each year by the percentage variation in the Retail Prices Index for the preceding 12 month period) which is not provided for in the Budget;

9.1.14   the entering into of any lease, licence or similar obligation under which the rental and all other payments exceed £25,000 a year (such figure to be increased on 30 June in each year by the percentage variation in the Retail Prices Index for the preceding 12 month period) which is not provided for in the Budget;

9.1.15   the adoption of and material amendment to any Business Plan;

9.1.16   the adoption of and material amendment to any Budget;

9.1.17   the entry into of any contract or commitment not provided for in the Budget under which the Company may incur costs of £25,000 or more or which may not be fulfilled or completed within one year;

9.1.18   any material transaction with a party to this Agreement or any of its Associated Companies not in the ordinary course of business or not on arm's length commercial terms;

9.1.19   the borrowing of amounts (or indebtedness in the nature of borrowings) other than in the ordinary course of trading or the creation of any charge or other security over any of its assets or property other than in the ordinary course of trading;

9.1.20   the giving of any guarantee or indemnity other than in the ordinary course of trading;

9.1.21 the making of any loan or advance to any person, firm, body corporate or other business otherwise than in the normal course of business and on an arm's length basis;

9.1.22 the payment or declaration of any dividend or other distribution on account of shares in its capital;

9.1.23 the commencement or settlement of any litigation, arbitration or other proceedings which are material in the context of its business;

9.1.24 the granting of any power of attorney or other delegation of directors' powers;

9.1.25 the incorporation of a new subsidiary undertaking or the acquisition of any share capital or other securities of any body corporate; and

9.1.26 the making of any political or charitable contribution exceeding in aggregate £25,000 per annum.

9.2 Related transactions

A series of related transactions shall be construed as a single transaction, and any amounts involved in the related transactions shall be aggregated, to determine whether a matter is a Reserved Matter.

10. Budgets and Information

10.1 Financial Information

The Company shall prepare and submit to the Investor the following information as soon as possible and no later than the dates/times set out below:

10.1.1 a draft Business Plan for the Company for the following 12 month period within 30 days of the date of this Agreement;

10.1.2 a detailed draft Budget for the Company for the following financial year (including estimated major items of revenue and capital expenditure). The Budget shall be broken down on a monthly basis, shall contain a cash flow forecast and a balance sheet showing the projected position of the Company as at the end of the following financial year within 60 days of the date of this Agreement;

10.1.3 such further financial or management information as the Investor may reasonably require from time to time relating to the Company.

The Founders shall make every effort to procure full and prompt performance by the Company of its obligations under this Clause 10.1.

10.2 Approval of Budgets and Business Plans

The Initial Shareholders shall approve the draft Budget and Business Plan within 30 Business Days of receiving them, subject to such amendments as the Initial Shareholders agree are appropriate. The Initial Shareholders shall procure that the Board shall review the Budget regularly.

10.3 Failure to Provide Information

If the Company fails to provide any of the information provided for in this Clause 10 within the time period specified, the Initial Shareholders or any one of them shall be entitled to appoint a firm of accountants to produce such financial information at the Company's expense.

10.4 Rights to Information

The Investor and any person designated by it may at all reasonable times and at its own expense:

10.4.1 discuss the affairs, finances and accounts of the Company with its officers and principal executives; and
10.4.2 inspect and make copies of all books, records, accounts, documents and vouchers relating to the business and the affairs of the Company.

10.5 Passing of Information by the Investor

10.5.1 The Investor may pass any information received from the Company to any adviser to, trustee or manager of, any fund managed by that Investor and to its other professional advisers. Except as permitted by the Board no person permitted to receive information under this Clause 10.5 shall use such information other than for the purposes of the Company or its business.
10.5.2 The Investor shall remain responsible for any breach of this Clause 10.5 by the person to whom that information is disclosed.
10.5.3 The provisions of Clause 10.5 shall survive the termination of this Agreement for whatever cause for a period of five years.

11. Confidentiality

11.1 Confidential Information

The parties shall use all reasonable endeavours to keep confidential and to ensure that their respective Associated Companies and their respective officers, employees, agents and professional and other advisers keep confidential any information (the 'Confidential Information'):

11.1.1 relating to the customers (including all data held by the Business in relation to any person who has accessed the Company's Web site), Business, Intellectual Property Rights, other assets or affairs of the Company which they may have or acquire through ownership of an interest in the Company;

11.1.2 relating to the customers (including all data held by the Business in relation to any person who has accessed the Company's Web site), Business, Intellectual Property Rights, other assets or affairs of the other Shareholders or any member of their groups which they may have or acquire through being a Shareholder or through the exercise of its rights or performance of its obligations under this Agreement.

11.2 Restrictions

11.2.1 No party has the individual power over or may use for its own business purposes or disclose to any third party any Confidential Information without the prior written consent of the Board.

11.2.2 This Clause does not apply to:

(i) information which is or becomes publicly available (otherwise than as a result of a breach of this Clause);

(ii) information which is independently developed by the relevant Shareholder or acquired from a third party, to the extent that it is acquired with the right to disclose it;

(iii) information which was lawfully in the possession of the relevant Shareholder free of any restriction on disclosure as can be shown by that Shareholder's written records or other reasonable evidence;

(iv) following disclosure under this Clause, information which becomes available to the relevant Shareholder (as can be shown by that Shareholder's written records or other reasonable evidence) from a source other than another party which is not bound by any obligation of confidentiality in relation to such information;

(v) the disclosure by a Shareholder of Confidential Information to its directors or employees or to those of its Associated Companies who need to know that Confidential Information in its reasonable opinion for purposes relating to this Agreement but those directors and employees shall not use that Confidential Information for any other purpose;

(vi) the disclosure of information to the extent required to be disclosed by law or any court of competent jurisdiction, any governmental official or regulatory authority (including the London Stock Exchange and the Panel on Takeovers and Mergers) or any binding judgement, order or requirement of any other competent authority;

(vii) the disclosure of information to any tax authority to the extent reasonably required for the purposes of the tax affairs of the Shareholder concerned or any member of its group;

(viii) the disclosure to a Shareholder's professional advisers of information reasonably required to be disclosed for purposes relating to this Agreement.

11.2.3 Each Shareholder shall inform any officer, employee or agent or any professional or other adviser advising it in relation to matters relating to this Agreement, or to whom it provides Confidential Information, that such information is confidential and shall instruct them:
(i) to keep it confidential; and
(ii) not to disclose it to any third party (other than those persons to whom it has already been or may be disclosed in accordance with the terms of this Clause).

11.3   Damages Not an Adequate Remedy

Without prejudice to any other rights or remedies which a Shareholder may have, the parties acknowledge and agree that damages would not be an adequate remedy for any breach of this Clause 11 and the remedies of injunction, specific performance and other equitable relief are appropriate for any threatened or actual breach of any such provision and no proof of special damages shall be necessary for the enforcement of the rights under this Clause 11.

11.4   Survival

11.4.1 The disclosing Shareholder shall remain responsible for any breach of this Clause by the person to whom that Confidential Information is disclosed.
11.4.2 The provisions of this Clause 11.4 shall survive the termination of this Agreement for whatever cause for a period of five years.

12.   Distribution Policy

12.1   Annual General Meeting

The annual general meeting of the Company at which Audited Accounts are laid before the Shareholders must be held not later than three months after the end of the relevant financial year.

12.2   Amount Available for Distribution

The Auditors shall be instructed to report (at the expense of the Company) the amount of the profits available for distribution by the Company at the same time as they sign their report on the Audited Accounts.

12.3   Amount to be Distributed

The Company shall distribute to the Shareholders such percentage as the Board determines of the Company's profits lawfully available for distribution in each financial year subject to the Board making reasonable provisions and transfers to reserves.

13.   Additional Finance for the Company

The Initial Shareholders acknowledge that, in addition to the share capital to be subscribed to under Clause 3, the Company will require further finance to fund its projected cash requirements under the Budget and the Business Plan. The Board is authorized to enter into any financial arrangements which it determines necessary to fund its projected cash requirements under the Budget and the Business Plan.

14.   Transfers of Shares

14.1   Transfers

In the event of the sale or other disposal of any Shares in the Company under this Agreement, the selling or disposing Shareholder shall procure that no person other than an existing Shareholder acquires any Shares unless such person enters into a Deed of Adherence as set out in Schedule 3 agreeing to be bound by this Agreement as a Shareholder and any other agreements in connection with the Business as a Shareholder.

14.2   Further Assurance

Each party shall do all things and carry out all acts which are reasonably necessary to effect the transfer of the shares in accordance with the terms of this Agreement in a timely fashion.

14.3   Return of documents, etc

On ceasing to be a Shareholder or an Associated Person, a Shareholder must hand over to the Company material correspondence, Budgets, Business Plans, agreements, reports, schedules, documents and records relating to the Business held by him or any third party which has acquired such matter through that Shareholder and shall not keep any copies thereof.

14.4   Transfer of Shares

The Investor may transfer all of its Shares to an Associated Company on giving prior written notice to the other Shareholders. An Associated Company must be under an obligation to retransfer its Shares to the Investor or another Associated Company of that Investor immediately if it ceases to be an Associated Company.

15.   Public Announcements

A Shareholder must not make any public announcement or issue any circular relating to the Company or this Agreement without the prior written approval of the Board. This does not affect any announcement or circular required by law or any regulatory body or the rules of any recognized stock exchange, but the party with an obligation to make an announcement or issue a circular shall consult with the other party/parties so far as is reasonably practicable before complying with such obligation.

16.   Intellectual Property Rights

Any Intellectual Property Rights (including, without limitation, patents, trade marks, service marks, registered designs, copyright, rights in designs, inventions and confidential information) which arise in the course of the Company's activities shall belong to the Company.

17.   Competition with the Business

17.1   Restrictions

17.1.1   Unless it has obtained the prior written consent of the Board, a Shareholder must not, either alone or jointly, with, through or on behalf of any person, directly or indirectly:
(i)   carry on or be engaged or concerned or interested in any activities which are in competition with the Business;
(ii) seek to, in competition with the Business (1) procure orders from, (2) do business with or (3) procure directly or indirectly any other person to procure orders from or do business with, any person who is or has been a customer of the Company at any time during the term of this Agreement; or
(iii) solicit or contact with a view to the engagement or employment by any person, any employee, officer or manager of the Company or any person who has been an employee, officer or manager of the Company within the previous two-year period, except for an employee who has been seconded to the Company.
17.1.2   Without limitation to Clause 17.1.1 the Founders must not either alone or jointly, with, through or on behalf of any person, during the period of four years from the date of this Agreement, carry on or be engaged or concerned or interested in any activities which are in competition with the Business whether directly or indirectly.
17.1.3   Each Shareholder agrees to procure that each of their Associated Companies shall comply with the provisions of this Clause as though it applied directly to them.

17.2 Invalidity

17.2.1 Each of these restrictions is an entirely separate and independent restriction on each Shareholder and the validity of one restriction shall not be affected by the validity or unenforceability of another.

17.2.2 Each Shareholder considers the restrictions in this Clause to be reasonable and necessary for the protection of the interests of the Company. If any such restriction shall be held to be void but would be valid if deleted in part or reduced in application, such restriction shall apply with such deletion or modification as may be necessary to make it valid and enforceable.

17.3 Duration

The covenants set out in this Clause shall continue to apply to a Shareholder for a period of twelve months from the date on which that Shareholder ceases to be a Shareholder. The covenants shall be construed during this period by reference to the Business, customers, employees, officers or managers or contracting parties of the Company or during the two-year period prior to the date on which the Shareholder ceased to be a Shareholder.

17.4 Exclusions

Nothing contained in this Clause precludes or restricts any Shareholder or any of its Associated Companies:

17.4.1 holding not more than 5 per cent of the issued voting share capital of any company whose shares are listed on a Recognized Investment Exchange;

17.4.2 acquiring any business or company, as an integral part of a larger transaction or acquisition of a business, company or group of companies, not predominantly engaged in a competing business PROVIDED THAT:

(i) it uses all reasonable endeavours to dispose of such business or company which competes with the Business within six months of the date of completion of the original transaction (or as soon as possible thereafter);

(ii) in making any such disposal, it must grant the Company a right of first refusal to acquire the business or company on bona fide arm's length terms; and

(iii) if the Company does not purchase the business or company within a reasonable period it may dispose of the business or company to a third party;

17.4.3 carrying on any activity carried on by it in the twelve months before the date of this Agreement; or

17.4.4   from carrying on and/or developing, whether organically or by acquisition, any of its existing activities which at the date of this Agreement are similar to the Business.

18.   Third Party Offers

18.1   Notice of Offers

Subject to Clause 18.6, if a Shareholder receives a bona fide offer in writing from a third party (the 'Offer') which it wishes to accept, it must immediately give written notice (the 'Transfer Notice') to the other Shareholders (the 'Remaining Shareholders') offering to sell those Shares which are the subject of the Offer to the Remaining Shareholders at the same cash price as set out in the Offer, and on the same terms as those contained in the Offer, save that the Remaining Shareholders shall be unable to claim under any warranties which are to be given by the selling Shareholder in relation to matters about which the Remaining Shareholders knew or ought to have known at the time of the transfer of the Shares which are the subject of the Offer. The Transfer Notice must also state:

18.1.1   the period within which the offer to sell the Shares to the Remaining Shareholders shall remain open to be accepted. This period must be at least 30 Business Days from the date of the Transfer Notice (the 'Acceptance Period'); and
18.1.2   the name of the third party making the Offer and full details of all other terms and conditions of the Offer.

18.2   Revocation of Transfer Notice

The Transfer Notice shall only be revocable with the consent in writing of the Remaining Shareholders and if it is revoked:
18.2.1   the selling Shareholder may not give a further Transfer Notice within three months after the date on which the Transfer Notice is revoked; and
18.2.2   the remaining provisions of Clauses 18.3 to 18.9 shall cease to apply in relation to the revoked Transfer Notice.

18.3   Options of Remaining Shareholders

Once the Remaining Shareholders have received a Transfer Notice it/they may either:

18.3.1   send a written notice to the selling Shareholder (an 'Acceptance Notice') within the Acceptance Period accepting the offer set out in the Transfer Notice; or

18.3.2   send a written notice to the selling Shareholder within the Acceptance Period declining the offer set out in the Transfer Notice; or

18.3.3   not reply to the Transfer Notice within the Acceptance Period. In this case, the Remaining Shareholders shall be deemed not to have accepted the offer set out in the Transfer Notice.

18.4   Consequences of Transfer Notice

18.4.1   If the offer set out in the Transfer Notice is accepted, the selling Shareholder must sell its Shares to the Remaining Shareholders at the price and on the terms set out in the Transfer Notice, save that the Remaining Shareholders shall be unable to claim under any warranties which are to be given by the selling Shareholder in relation to matters about which the Remaining Shareholders knew or ought to have known at the time of the transfer of the Shares which are the subject of the Offer, and the sale and purchase of the Shares shall be completed in accordance with Clauses 18.5, 18.8 and 18.9 at such time (not being less than 48 hours nor more than seven Business Days after the date of the acceptance) and place as shall be specified in the Acceptance Notice.

18.4.2   If the offer set out in the Transfer Notice is not accepted or is deemed not to have been accepted, the selling Shareholder may accept the Offer and sell its Shares to the third party making the Offer at the price and on the terms and conditions of the Offer and the sale and purchase of the Shares shall be completed within 20 days of the end of the Acceptance Period.

18.5   Completion of Transfer

Where the Remaining Shareholders have served an Acceptance Notice, the sale shall be made on the following terms:

18.5.1   the selling Shareholder must perform in respect of the Shares which it is selling, on or before the date specified for completion, the execution of the transfer of the Shares;

18.5.2   the Remaining Shareholders must pay the total consideration due for the Shares to the selling Shareholder, by telegraphic transfer to the bank account of the selling Shareholder notified to it for the purpose, on the date specified for completion;

18.5.3   completion of the sale of all the Shares of the selling Shareholder must take place simultaneously; and

18.5.4   completion of the sale must take place in accordance with Clauses 18.8 and 18.9.

18.6   Restriction on Founders

Each of the Founders is not permitted to any part of their shareholding in the Company during the period of four years from the date of entering into this Agreement.

18.7   General

18.7.1   The Shareholders shall keep the Company informed, at all times, of the issue and contents of any notice served pursuant to this Clause and any election or acceptance relating to those notices.
18.7.2   The Shareholders waive their pre-emption rights to the transfer of Shares contained in this agreement and the Articles to the extent necessary to give effect to this Clause.

18.8   Transfer Terms

Any sale and/or transfer of Shares pursuant to an Acceptance Notice shall be on terms that those Shares are transferred free from all claims, pledges, equities, liens, charges and encumbrances.

18.9   Further Assurance

The selling Shareholder pursuant to an Acceptance Notice shall do all things and carry out all acts which are reasonably necessary to effect any transfer of the Shares in accordance with the terms of this agreement in a timely fashion.

19.   Duration and Termination

19.1   Duration

Subject to the other provisions of this Agreement, this Agreement shall continue in full force and effect without limit in point of time until the earlier of:

19.1.1   Shareholders holding at least 75 per cent of the Shares agree in writing to terminate this Agreement;
19.1.2   the tenth anniversary of this Agreement;
19.1.3   the Board resolve to seek a listing of the Company's issued share capital on a Recognized Investment Exchange;
19.1.4   subject to the terms of this Agreement and the Articles, the Shareholders transfer the entirety of the issued Share capital in the Company to a purchaser in accordance with the Articles;
19.1.5   an effective resolution is passed or a binding order is made for the winding-up of the Company;
19.1.6   the Investor goes into liquidation;

19.1.7   the Investor disposes of an amount of Shares that reduces its remaining shareholding in the Company to below 20 per cent of the total amount of Shares at that time in issue;

provided that this Agreement shall cease to have effect as regards any Shareholder who ceases to hold any Shares, save for any of its provisions which are expressed to continue in force after termination (and without prejudice to any accrued rights or obligations relating to the period during which such Shareholder was a Shareholder).

19.2   Termination

Termination of this Agreement shall be without prejudice to any liability or obligation in respect of any matters, undertakings or conditions which shall not have been observed or performed by the relevant Shareholder prior to such termination.

20.   Notices

20.1   Addresses

Any notice, claim or demand in connection with this Agreement (each a 'Notice') shall be sufficiently given to the recipient at its fax number, telex number or address set out in Schedule 1 (or, as applicable, the relevant Deed of Adherence) or any other fax number, telex number or address previously notified from time to time to the Company by the recipient for the purposes of this Agreement.

20.2   Form

Any Notice shall be in writing and may be sent by messenger, telegram, telex, fax, electronic mail or prepaid post (first class in the case of service in the United Kingdom and airmail in the case of international service). Any Notice shall be deemed to have been received on the next working day in the place to which it is sent, if sent by telegram, telex, fax or electronic mail, or 60 hours from the time of posting, if sent by post.

21.   Share Option Scheme

21.1   The Shareholders acknowledge that the Company intends to put in place a Share Option Scheme to incentivize key employees and/or advisers, the effect of the exercise of any such options will mean that each of the Shareholders' shareholding will be diluted prorata.

21.2   The issue of new Shares and options under such a Share Option Scheme shall not exceed a value of 10 per cent of the total amount of Shares in the Company at any time before the termination of this Agreement in accordance with the provisions in Clause 19.

22.   General

22.1   Whole Agreement

This Agreement contains the whole agreement and understanding between the parties relating to the subject matter of this Agreement at the date hereof to the exclusion of any terms implied by law which may be excluded by contract and supersedes any previous written or oral agreement and/or arrangements between the parties in relation to the matters dealt with in this Agreement (including (and without limitation) any prior shareholders' agreement). In this Clause 'this Agreement' includes the Articles, the Subscription Agreement, the Deed of Adherence and all documents entered into pursuant to this Agreement.

22.2   Survival of Rights, Duties and Obligations

Termination of this Agreement for any cause shall not release a party from any liability which at the time of termination has already accrued to another party or which thereafter may accrue in respect of any act or omission prior to such termination.

22.3   Conflict with the Articles

Except as otherwise provided herein, in the event of any ambiguity or discrepancy between the provisions of this Agreement and the Articles, it is intended that the provisions of this Agreement shall prevail and accordingly the Shareholders shall exercise all voting and other rights and powers available to them so as to give effect to the provisions of this Agreement and shall further if necessary procure any required amendment to the Articles. The Company is not bound by this Clause.

22.4   No Partnership

Nothing in this Agreement shall be deemed to constitute a partnership between the parties or constitute any party the agent of any other party for any purpose.

22.5   Invalidity

If any provision in this Agreement shall be held to be illegal, invalid or unenforceable, in whole or in part, under any enactment or rule of law, such provision or part shall to that extent be deemed not to form part of this Agreement but the legality, validity and enforceability of the remainder of this Agreement shall not be affected.

22.6   Assignment

Except as otherwise expressly provided in this Agreement, the benefit of the provisions of this Agreement may be assigned to any Associated Company provided that such assignment shall not be absolute but shall be expressed to have effect only for so long as the assignee remains an Associated Company.

22.7   Counterparts

This Agreement may be entered into in any number of counterparts, all of which taken together shall constitute one and the same instrument. Any party may enter into this Agreement by signing any such counterpart.

22.8   Costs

The Investor, the Founders and the Company, shall pay their own legal fees incurred in entering into this Agreement.

22.9   Contracts (Rights of Third Parties) Act 1999

This Agreement does not create any right under the Contracts (Rights of Third Parties) Act 1999 that is enforceable by any person who is not a party hereto.

23.   Governing Law and Submission to Jurisdiction

23.1   Governing Law

This Agreement and the documents to be entered into pursuant to it, save as expressly referred to therein, shall be governed by and construed in accordance with [English] law.

23.2   Jurisdiction

All the parties irrevocably agree that the courts of [England and Wales] are to have exclusive jurisdiction to settle any dispute which may arise out of or in connection with this Agreement and the documents to be entered into pursuant to it. All the parties irrevocably submit to the jurisdiction of such courts and waive any objection to proceedings in any such court on the ground of venue or on the ground that the proceedings have been brought in an inconvenient forum.

23.3   Appointment of Process Agent

23.3.1   The Investor irrevocably appoints [*company*] of [*address*] as its agent to accept service of process in England in any legal action or proceedings arising out of or in connection with this Agreement.
23.3.2   If such process agent ceases to be able to act as such or to have an address in England, the Investor irrevocably agrees to appoint a new process agent in England acceptable to the other parties and to deliver to the other parties within 14 Business Days a copy of a written acceptance of appointment by the process agent.
23.3.3   Nothing in this Agreement shall affect the right to serve process in any other manner permitted by law or the right to bring proceedings in any other jurisdiction for the purposes of the enforcement or execution of any judgement or other settlement in any other courts.

In witness whereof this Agreement has been duly executed by the parties or their duly authorized representatives.

SIGNED for and on behalf of

[   ]

SIGNED for and on behalf of

[   ]

SIGNED BY [   ]

SIGNED BY [   ]

SIGNED BY [   ]

Schedule 1

Shareholders of [   ] at Completion

Name	Address
[ ]	
	Phone:
	Fax:
	E-mail:
	Percentage of Shares: XX% of A-Shares
	XX% of B-Shares
[ ]	
	Phone:
	Fax:
	E-mail:
	Percentage of Shares: XX% of A-Shares
	XX% of B-Shares
[ ]	
	Phone:
	Fax:
	E-mail:
	Percentage of Shares: XX% of A-Shares
	XX% of B-Shares

Schedule 2

Particulars of the Company

Registered number:
Registered office:
Date and place of incorporation:
Director:
Secretary:
Accounting reference date:
Auditors:
Solicitors:
Authorized share capital:

Schedule 3

Deed of Adherence

THIS DEED OF ADHERENCE is made on [   ] by [   ]
of [   ] (the 'Covenanter')

SUPPLEMENTAL to a Subscription and Shareholders' Agreement dated
[*date*] and made between [A Co.], [B Co.] and [the Company] (the
'Agreement').

The Covenanter covenants as follows:

1.   The Covenanter confirms that it has been supplied with and has
read a copy of the Agreement and covenants with each of the persons
named in the Schedule to this Deed to observe, perform and be bound by
all the terms of the Agreement which are capable of applying to the
Covenanter as a [Manager/Investor] and which have not been performed
at the date of this Deed to the intent and effect that the Covenanter shall be
deemed with effect from the date on which the Covenanter is registered as
a member of [the Company] to be a party to the Agreement (as if named as
a party to that Agreement as a [Manager/Investor]).

2.   This Deed shall be governed by and construed in accordance with
English law and the Covenanter hereby submits irrevocably to the non-
exclusive jurisdiction of the English Courts (but accepts that this Deed may
be enforced in any court of competent jurisdiction) and hereby appoints [a
person resident in England and reasonably acceptable to the Board of
Directors of the continuing Shareholder] as its agent for service of all
process in any proceedings in respect of the Agreement.

EXECUTED as a deed on the date written above.

Schedule 4

Details of Business Plan

The key things to cover are: Market, Product Price, Resources and
Financials.

Table of Contents

Appendix 6

New developments

The law is constantly changing, and during the publication of this book, some changes have come to light that we have not been able to include in the main text of the book, yet which deserve mention here.

CONTENT AND COPYRIGHT – CURRENT LAW

There is a World Intellectual Property Organization Intellectual Property Treaty, or WCT, set to enter into force in 2002/03. The international treaty is designed to protect the rights of companies, artists, writers and others whose work is distributed over the Internet or other digital media. Thirty countries including Japan, Gabon (West Africa) and the US have signed up to it. However, Japan and the US are the only major industrialized nations to have ratified it so far. The EU is expected to do so, but the parliaments of all 15 member states must first separately pass the EU copyright directive 2001. This new treaty will set the standard for the protection of literary and artistic works which includes as wide a scope as film, e-books and computer programs. The WCT updates the treaty currently in effect – the Berne Convention For the Protection of Literary and Artistic Works. In parallel with the WCT is the related WIPO Performances and Phonograms Treaty (WPPT), specifically protects digital media rights of producers and performers of sound recordings. So far, 28 of the minimum 30 countries have signed it; the WIPO predicts WPPT will enter into force in the near future.

DATA PROTECTION – COOKIES

The European Parliament has recently decided that cookies should be prohibited unless the explicit and well informed and freely given consent of the user has been obtained. The Information Commissioner already advises that a visitor to a Web site must be informed whether a tracking system including cookies is being used to collect personal information. A comprehensive privacy statement has so far been sufficient to cover this requirement. However, the requirement for explicit consent involves the user being informed as to exactly what information is to be collected and how it is to be used. You will need to get an opt-in consent on each separate occasion that information is being processed. To my mind, if this added cost and inconvenience should become UK law it may be the end of the cookie.

INTERNET BUSINESS – SPECIFIC SECTORS

The consultations document on the e-commerce directive 2000/31/EC (ECD) in relation to financial services addresses the country of destination principle embodied in the FSMA, as the FSMA makes it a criminal offence for insurers, etc, based in other countries to provide services to UK investors, unless UK regulators have authorized them. Secondary legislation made under FSMA tries to narrow the scope to services directly targeting UK investors. These provisions imply that the UK can regulate services provided in other jurisdictions. This is contrary to the ECD, which is based on a 'country of origin' principle. That is, product providers are subject to regulation only by the country in which they are based. The government now plans to reconcile the 'country of origin' principle with the FSMA and is consulting on its proposals.

Index

NB: page numbers in italic indicate figures and tables